BEAUTIFUL ONE DAY, BROKE THE NEXT

Queensland's Public Finances since Sir Joh and Sir Leo

Gene Tunny

Published in 2018 by Connor Court Publishing

Copyright © Gene Tunny

Connor Court Publishing Pty Ltd.
PO Box 7257
Redland Bay QLD 4165
sales@connorcourt.com
www.connorcourt.com

Phone 0497 900 685

ISBN: 9781925826258

Cover design Maria Giordano

Printed in Australia

Front Cover Painting: Queensland Art Gallery - Joy of Museums - "Under the Jacaranda" by R Godfrey Rivers.jpg, Wikimedia Commons.

BEAUTIFUL ONE DAY
BROKE THE NEXT

Queensland's Public Finances since Sir Joh and Sir Leo

Gene Tunny

Connor Court Publishing

Contents

About the Author

Gene Tunny is an economist, with his own Brisbane-based consultancy practice, Adept Economics. He formerly worked as an official in the Commonwealth Treasury and in the Queensland public service in various departments. In 2016, Gene was co-course leader for the Australia Awards short-course *Strengthening Public Policy Processes for Emerging Leaders in the Indonesian Ministry of Finance*, delivered at the University of Queensland (UQ), Brisbane and in Bandung, West Java. He is a frequent media commentator on Queensland economic and budgetary issues and has his own blog, *Queensland Economy Watch*. Gene is the current Vice-President of the Queensland branch of the Economic Society of Australia. He is a graduate of UQ with a first class honours degree and university medal in economics.

Preface

I became particularly interested in Queensland's fiscal decline while working at the Australian Treasury in Canberra during the 2008-09 financial crisis. As a Queenslander, I was disturbed by what I was hearing about the state of Queensland's public finances from visiting Queensland Treasury officials who were pleading for Commonwealth intervention, such as the borrowing guarantee that was eventually implemented. The tranquil setting of the Treasury Executive Dining Room, with its superb view up to the Parliament House on Canberra's Capital Hill, did nothing to allay my anxiety.

After I returned to Brisbane, I would occasionally comment on state budget issues on 612 ABC Brisbane radio and in the *Courier-Mail*, which further increased my interest in Queensland's recent fiscal history. And when I read former Under Treasurer Sir Leo Hielscher's book *Queensland Made* last year, it occurred to me that the story of Queensland's fiscal decline and fall since Sir Leo's day would warrant a book length treatment.

This book is aimed at people interested in Queensland politics and history, but I hope its appeal is much broader and it will be of interest to public finance professionals and scholars all around Australia and indeed the world. The book raises important questions about the administration of government and the role of sub-national governments that are relevant in many jurisdictions. It is an important case study of a fiscal deterioration in a jurisdiction that for a while appeared at least to be doing things right, fiscally speaking.

Finally, I hope it is helpful to current Queensland Treasury officials and those from other jurisdictions, as well as to academics and other members of the public, in clearly explaining important government budgetary concepts. I also hope I will make it easier for future scholars of Queensland's public finances to understand the policy decisions and external factors that led to the outcomes observed, as well as the various changes in reporting and accounting standards that have occurred in recent decades. One of the great ironies is that the sophistication of our budgetary management and reporting has grown immensely, aided of course by the progressively greater use of information technology since the 1980s, but that our fiscal outcomes have got so much worse. Despite technological advancements, humans remain in charge, with all their talents, ambitions, fears and failings. I hope the story I tell illuminates the respective contributions of the economic, demographic, social, political and individual factors to Queensland's fiscal deterioration since the mid-2000s.

-- *Gene Tunny, Brisbane, April 2018*

Acknowledgments

I am deeply appreciative for the generosity of time and information that was provided to me by the following people, listed in alphabetical order, who have played important roles in the story I am telling in this book: Gerard Bradley, Keith De Lacy, Scott Emerson, Mark Gray, David Hamill, Sir Leo Hielscher, Paul McFadyen, Doug McTaggart, Joan Sheldon, Darryl Somerville, and Kenneth Wiltshire. I am also grateful to Steve Abson, Joe Branigan, Fabrizio Carmignani, Rachel Nolan, Gianna Shorney, Harriet Smith, Jon Stanford, Stephen Thornton, and Graham Young for helpful discussions and other assistance. Nick Behrens, Kerry Boulton, Keith De Lacy, Mark Gray, Helen Shorrocks and Jennifer Tunny all read through and provided me with extensive and valuable comments on the manuscript, and to them I am very grateful. I also need to acknowledge the assistance of Gregory Connolly at the Queensland Parliamentary Library for digitising past budget papers and forwarding them to me. Obviously, none of the views expressed in this book should necessarily be attributed to anyone named in these acknowledgements.

Abbreviations

AER	Australian Energy Regulator
ABS	Australian Bureau of Statistics
ALP	Australian Labor Party
CBRC	Cabinet Budget Review Committee
CGC	Commonwealth Grants Commission
CPI	Consumer Price Index
FTE	Full-time equivalent
GDP	Gross Domestic Product
GFCF	Gross fixed capital formation
GFS	Government Finance Statistics
GOC	Government-owned corporation
GSP	Gross State Product
GST	Goods and Services Tax
HFE	Horizontal fiscal equalisation
IGA	Intergovernmental agreement
KAP	Katter's Australian Party
LNG	Liquefied natural gas
LNP	Liberal National Party
MP	Member of Parliament
MYFER	Mid Year Fiscal and Economic Review
n.p.	Not published
PNFC	Public Non-financial Corporation
PPP	Public Private Partnership
PSMC	Public Sector Management Commission (Goss Government)
QAO	Queensland Audit Office
QCA	Queensland Competition Authority
QIC	Queensland Investment Corporation
QIDC	Queensland Industry Development Corporation
QR	Queensland Rail
QTC	Queensland Treasury Corporation
QUT	Queensland University of Technology
SA	South Australia
S&P	Standard and Poor's
SEQ	South East Queensland
SES	Senior Executive Service
SGIO	State Government Insurance Office
UQ	University of Queensland
VFI	Vertical fiscal imbalance

Glossary

Accrual accounting	A system of accounting in which transactions are recorded based on the period they relate to, not necessarily when cash is paid or received.
Asset recycling	Purportedly, selling or leasing out existing assets and using the proceeds to invest in new assets.
Basis point	Market jargon for one-one hundredth $(1/100^{th})$ of one percentage point. So that 0.2 percent is 20 basis points, for example.
Cash accounting	A system of accounting recording cash receipts and payments in the financial year in which they actually occur. Prior to the late 1990s, Queensland Budgets were prepared on a cash basis, making comparisons between recent government budgets prepared on an accruals basis and those prior to the Beattie government very challenging.
Dividends	In the context of this book, the part of the estimated net profits after tax of government-owned corporations that are paid to the general government sector, and which form part of the "Dividend and tax equivalent income" line item in the general government sector operating statement.
Fiscal balance	Revenue less all expenses, both recurrent and capital.
Forward estimates	The current budget year, such as 2017-18 for the 2017-18 Queensland State budget, and three years beyond it, i.e. 2018-19, 2019-20, and 2020-21. The forward estimates show Treasury's estimates of government spending and revenues in each of these years.
Golden rule of public finance	The government must balance the operating budget, but is allowed to borrow for capital spending.
Government Finance Statistics	The IMF-promoted international framework for public finance.
Gross State Product	The total value of final goods and services produced in the Queensland economy in a particular period, typically reported on either a quarterly or yearly basis. In 2015-16, Queensland's GSP was around $316 billion.
Horizontal fiscal equalisation (HFE)	Broadly speaking, the adjustment of revenues distributed to a lower level of government to provide them all with the same capabilities to provide the same level of services. In Australia, the Commonwealth Grants Commission applies HFE to the GST revenue pool, which it distributes to the states and territory governments.

Net acquisition of non-financial assets	Capital spending plus net asset revaluations less asset sales and depreciation.
Net debt	Debt minus assets that can be readily liquidated to pay off debt (e.g. cash, shares, bonds, etc.).
Net operating balance	Revenues less recurrent expenses, including an allowance for depreciation of capital assets.
Net lending	IMF GFS definition of surplus, as the government is then a net lender to other sectors. Negative net lending is a deficit.
Percentage point change	This means, for example, the difference between a 3 percent and a 4 percent growth rate (or interest rate, or unemployment rate). That is, it is 1 percentage point. This terminology is used in budget papers for precision. It is different from a percentage difference, such as revenue of $11 billion being 10 percent higher than revenue of $10 billion.
Primary balance	Fiscal balance excluding interest payments.
Public non-financial corporations	A government-owned corporation (GOC) that is not a financial business, which therefore excludes the Queensland Investment Corporation and Queensland Treasury Corporation.
Real gross state income	A measure of the real income generated within Queensland taking into account changes in the terms-of-trade (the ratio of export to import prices).
Tax equivalent payments	An amount paid to the state government in lieu of actual company income tax payments to the Commonwealth (via the Australian Taxation Office) by government-owned corporations (GOCs). This is a device to promote competitive neutrality between GOCs and private sector businesses, given state entities such as GOCs are exempt from Commonwealth company income tax.
Treasurer	The government minister overseeing the Treasury department who is responsible for delivering the state budget.
Under Treasurer	In Australia, the head of state Treasury departments, equivalent in level to the federal Secretary to the Treasury. The Under Treasurer is appointed by and reports to the Treasurer.
Vertical fiscal imbalance	The mismatch between state and territory government expenses and their own-source revenues, which leaves them reliant on grants from the Commonwealth.

1

INTRODUCTION

Good management was a long time coming for Queensland

In October 1867, near the town now known as Gympie in South East Queensland (SEQ), prospector James Nash found gold, and likely saved the fledgling Queensland colony, separated from New South Wales (NSW) only eight years earlier, from bankruptcy and economic ruin. The gold rush that the find created drove Queensland's economic development for the rest of the century, and a newly confident government was able to commit to the building of railways to facilitate that development.

The state of Queensland had started inauspiciously, and it seemed from the outset to rely on good luck rather than good management. For many decades, Queensland governments adopted an interventionist "colonial socialist" model.[1] Colonial socialism in Queensland featured some oddities such as government ownership of butcher shops among other businesses, and it was unable to sufficiently stimulate economic development to allow Queensland to catch up to its southern rivals, NSW and Victoria. Queensland would always remain at a lower level of economic development than the southern states, which had thriving manufacturing sectors to augment their agricultural production.

Arguably, Queensland had to wait until the 1970s for the sorely needed

---

[1]   We owe the term colonial socialism to the eminent late Australian economist Noel Butlin.

good management its economy and society deserved. It arrived in the form of an exceptional cadre of public servants, with the leading figure being Sir Leo Hielscher, Queensland Under Treasurer, i.e. the head of the department of Treasury, from late 1974 to 1988. This was a critical period in the state's economic development, which saw the opening up of major bulk commodity ports, the 1982 Commonwealth Games and World Expo '88 in Brisbane, among other achievements. Working on behalf of state governments with a strong commitment to economic development, particularly the government led by Sir Joh Bjelke-Petersen, Hielscher and his fellow Treasury officials established a model for Queensland's public financial management that made the state the exemplar of sound public finance in Australia and arguably one of the best among sub-national governments in the world.

Sir Joh and Sir Leo steer Queensland's economic development

The Queensland Premier for most of the seventies and eighties, and indeed Queensland's longest serving Premier (1968-1987), Sir Joh Bjelke-Petersen, had a strong commitment to Queensland's economic development. Sir Joh was born in New Zealand in 1911, but migrated to Queensland as an infant with his family, who established a farm, Bethany, at Kingaroy in SEQ. Before he entered the Queensland Parliament in 1950 as a Country Party member, he had worked as a peanut farmer and local councillor.[2] Prior to assuming the premiership in 1968, after the death in office of Premier Jack Pizzey, he had served as the ministers for housing and public works and police. Sir Joh is a towering and highly controversial figure in Queensland.

The full history of Sir Joh and Queensland's conservative governments from 1957 to 1989 is mostly outside the scope of this book. But Sir Joh cannot be mentioned without acknowledging the police corruption and

---

[2] The Country Party was the original name of the National Party, which in Queensland has merged with the Liberal Party to become the Liberal National Party.

suppression of civil liberties that occurred in Queensland during his reign, or his support for the controversial South African Springboks rugby tour in 1971. The tour saw violent clashes between police and demonstrators critical of South Africa's Apartheid regime and resulted in Sir Joh declaring a month-long state of emergency. That said, I will leave it to interested readers to pursue the full history of this period in other works. This book is focussed on Queensland's public financial management. Based on the state of Queensland's public finances at the end of the 1980s, the Bjelke-Petersen and other conservative governments since 1957 deserve high praise.

Sir Joh promoted Queensland as the "low tax state", with the lowest taxes and charges per capita in Australia. Queensland's low taxes and charges purportedly encouraged the migration to the state of both capital and people, particularly the so-called "white shoe brigade", the wealthy migrants to the Gold Coast. Folklore has it that they were attracted by Sir Joh's abolition of death duties in 1978. After Queensland had abolished death duties, other states and territories had to abolish their own, to staunch the flow of people and capital to Queensland.

Without wanting to diminish the contributions of ministers in the conservative governments of the time, in this book I emphasise the role played during this period of former Queensland Under Treasurer Sir Leo Hielscher, widely considered instrumental in the huge improvement in Queensland's public financial management during this period. Sir Leo was the last Under Treasurer to serve under the old Whitehall model of permanent departmental heads, a model which gave public servants considerable authority in their dealings with ministers and was hilariously satirised in the 1980's British television programs *Yes Minister* and *Yes Prime Minister*. Public servants had considerable scope to challenge the views expressed by ministers and to advance their own initiatives, confident they would outlast many ministers. One may ask whether ministers or public servants are more powerful? That depended on a range of factors, including the relative abilities of the minister, such as the Treasurer, and the public servant, such as the Under Treasurer. Up until at least the late 1980s in Queensland, it appears the public servants could stand their ground with ministers and play a huge role in decision making owing to their strengths vis-à-vis ministers.

As we shall see, the old Whitehall model has been replaced by a model with departmental heads on temporary contracts, and Premiers, Treasurers and ministers now exert far greater control over public servants. Also, the growing professionalism of government ministers and their advisers, and the proliferation of pundits and think tanks, has meant public servants have lost their near monopoly on the provision of information and advice to governments. But before this had occurred, Queensland was lucky to have had Sir Leo in the critical role of Under Treasurer.

It is indisputable the sound public finances that Queensland had up until the late 2000s were due in large part to the work of Sir Leo Hielscher, who served as Under Treasurer—the public servant heading up Queensland Treasury—from 1974 to 1988 and as foundation chairman of the Queensland Treasury Corporation (QTC), the government's cash and debt management office, from 1988 to 2010. Hielscher, a descendant of German immigrants to Queensland, was born in 1926 and grew up in Depression-era Brisbane and served during the Second World War. He worked as a public servant in various departments, including the Audit Office and the Department of Education where he noticeably increased the rigour of public administration, before entering the Queensland Treasury in the 1960s. He studied at night, and received a commerce degree from the University of Queensland (UQ), which meant that, unlike many public servants at the time, he had a firm grasp of accounting, economics and financial management, which would help him make an impression in the service.

The biography of Sir Leo, *Sir Leo Hielscher: Queensland made*, is aptly titled, and without much risk of exaggeration, the second title's words could be reversed, to say that Sir Leo made Queensland.[3] If Sir Leo had not been Under Treasurer, it is possible the Queensland Treasury would have been less committed to, or less competent at, directing economic development in the state, and the Queensland economy and society would be very different today. Sir Leo was instrumental in the development of Queensland's export coal industry and played an important role in Expo '88 and the development of the Cultural Centre. Both of these achievements played a large role in lifting Queensland out of its historical economic and social under-development relative to the southern states.

Prior to the strong economic growth that began in the 1970s, Queensland was well behind the rest of Australia and Queensland's public finances were in a parlous state. In his inaugural Parliamentary Oration in 2013, Sir Leo observed:

> Queensland's finances were desperate and the economy was at a standstill. In one year in the mid-sixties we were forced to apply to the Commonwealth for a short-term loan to pay for the wages and current running expenses—as we could do then under the Constitution. But as far as the economy was concerned, back then we had just one major company. That was MIM [Mount Isa Mines].[4]

As Under Treasurer from late 1974 to mid-1988, Sir Leo was the key economic adviser and a major influence on Premier Sir Joh Bjelke-Petersen, particularly after the Liberal-National Party Coalition split up in 1983. Sir Leo was given a high degree of autonomy by Sir Joh, who had taken on the Treasury portfolio after the Liberal's Treasurer Sir Llew Edwards vacated it. This period, from the mid-1970s to the late 1980s, was crucial in Queensland's economic development and the maturing of Queensland public financial management. But Sir Leo's influence on Queensland's

---

[3]   This chapter draws heavily on the information in Joanne Holliman, 2014, *Sir Leo Hielscher: Queensland Made*, University of Queensland Press.

[4]   Sir Leo Hielscher, 2013, *Inaugural Parliamentary Oration—Sir Leo Hielscher: Queensland's economic history and how the State's economy was transformed from the early 1960s onwards*, Queensland Parliament, Transcript of Proceedings, 18 October 2013, p. 2.

economic development had actually begun in the early 1960s, when he became the Deputy Under Treasurer responsible for commercial projects. In this role, he contributed to the development of Queensland's bauxite and coal industries, displaying innovative means to ensure projects were invested in with minimal cost to the state budget. These innovative means included arrangements such as requiring mining companies to provide security deposits that would help finance state government investments in infrastructure, with the cost ultimately recouped through freight charges paid to Queensland Rail (QR).[5] This was particularly clever, because additional royalty revenue may have affected Queensland's allocation of Commonwealth funding under its horizontal fiscal equalisation (HFE) methodology, while freight charges were not considered in the Commonwealth Grants Commission's (CGC's) HFE formula.[6] Given the disparity between Queensland's own-source revenue and its much greater expenditure responsibilities, alongside the reverse situation for the Commonwealth—the so-called vertical fiscal imbalance that afflicts the Australian federation—Queensland and other states and territories are highly dependent on Commonwealth grants, as discussed further below.

One of Sir Leo's great achievements, and one which made Queensland stand out from other states and territories, was the funding of Queensland's long-term liabilities, particularly the defined benefit superannuation for public servants.[7] The accumulation of a large pool of funds meant that the Queensland government became the largest player in Australia's short-term money market at one time.[8] The accumulation of these assets also helped reduce Queensland's reported net debt. Because they were liquid assets that could theoretically be used to meet debt repayments,

---

[5] David Lee, 2016, *The Second Rush: Mining and the Transformation of Australia*, Connor Court, p. 56.

[6] This point was made by Emeritus Professor Kenneth Wiltshire when interviewed for this book.

[7] Under a defined benefit superannuation scheme, benefits are determined by a formula rather than solely being based on amounts contributed and accumulated over time.

[8] Holliman, J., op. cit., p. 163.

they counted as an offset against the gross debt. Sir Leo's Treasury also set up best-practice cash management procedures, investing surplus funds held by agencies on the short-term money market.[9]

Sir Leo as budget maestro

Part of Sir Leo's conservative fiscal approach was to aim for what former Queensland Treasury officials sometimes describe as a "small but manageable surplus". This was achieved by setting aside money for long-term liabilities and by investing government money in trust funds. This kept surplus funds out of the hands of politicians who may have wanted to spend it on new roads or bridges, for example. Sir Leo preferred that new infrastructure assets paid for themselves, rather than requiring the government to run down other assets to pay for them. When the Queensland government wanted to build new infrastructure, such as the Gateway Bridge at the mouth of the Brisbane River in the 1980s, Sir Leo pushed for a toll so the bridge could pay for itself.[10]

An excellent illustration of Sir Leo's mastery of the budget is the 1986-87 state budget, handed down in August 1986. The 1986-87 budget papers estimated that, compared with $5.558 billion each of revenue and expenditure, both equal to three decimal places, the estimated surplus was $216,760. The surplus accounted for only around 0.004 percent, 1/250th of 1 percent, of revenues and expenditures.[11] Followers of recent budgets may wonder whether such a cigarette-paper-thin surplus could actually occur in practice. In Sir Leo's day, it more-or-less would, owing to the flexibility provided to the Treasury by cash accounting and the clever use of trust funds. The Treasury kept a close eye on cash inflows and outflows and tucked any surplus cash at the end of the year into one of

---

[9]   Ibid.
[10] Incidentally, when it was duplicated in the 2000s, both bridges were named in honour of Sir Leo Hielscher.
[11] Queensland Treasury, 1986, *1986-87 Estimates of the Probable Ways and Means and Expenditures of the Government of Queensland*, p. viii.

the government's trust funds. These numerous trust funds had been set up for various purposes, such as for capital works or disaster assistance. This was in the days of cash accounting, before accrual accounting was adopted in the late 1990s.

In actual fact, Sir Leo's surplus in 1986-87 turned out to be larger than estimated, but not much larger. It was still cigarette-paper-thin, based on estimates in the 1987-88 budget, the last one delivered while Sir Leo was Under Treasurer. The accumulated surplus at 1 July 1987 was $706,000, compared with the estimated accumulated surplus as at 30 June 1987 at the time of the 1986-87 budget of around $380,000, so there were a few extra hundred thousand dollar in the end, but in the context of a $6 billion budget, such amounts are trivial and reflect an extraordinary amount of control over Queensland's public finances by the Treasury under Hielscher's leadership.[12]

As noted above, the key to understanding the cigarette-paper thin surpluses were the trust funds, which were used to great effect by the Treasury in stashing away money. The 1986-87 budget papers revealed that the Treasury would invest around $572 million in 12 different trust and special funds, in addition to normal budgetary appropriations and contributions from the public. The recipient funds included the Workers' Compensation Fund ($221 million) and the State Service Superannuation Additional Benefits Fund ($157 million), among others.[13]

Sir Leo's clever budget manoeuvres were facilitated by the use of cash accounting, rather than accrual accounting, which has been used since the late 1990s in the interests of complying with widely used accounting standards.[14] The Treasury would record movements of cash in and out of

---

[12] Ibid., p. viii and Queensland Treasury, 1987, *1987-88 Estimates of Receipts and Expenditures*, p.4.
[13] Queensland Treasury, 1986, op. cit., p. 89.
[14] Appendix 2 discusses caveats regarding the analysis of historical Queensland budget data and contains information on accrual versus cash accounting.

different accounts of the government, rather than attempt to show the true economic nature of transactions. Some former Queensland Treasury officials interviewed for this book have suggested the change in accounting methods may have had real impacts on budget management. Under accrual accounting, the operating balance became the key metric, rather than the cash surplus or deficit. One former Queensland Treasury official commented that in the days of cash budgeting it was easier to hide money from the politicians. The Treasury could allocate excess funds to a special trust account, for example, and still deliver a "small and manageable" surplus, meaning politicians would not see large amounts of available funds that they could use for their own pet projects. While this sounds undemocratic, it may well have contributed to Queensland's sound public finances in the 1980s and 1990s. Whether it was good for the state, given some additional infrastructure projects or higher levels of health or education services may have been desirable at the time, is a question that is impossible to resolve.

While Hielscher engaged in some creative accounting, his underlying fiscal rectitude was never doubted. The Hielscher-led Treasury was also conservative in its budget forecasts, meaning it never faced the problem the Bligh government experienced in the 2000s when expected revenue did not eventuate. Stephen Rochester, who was a protégé of Sir Leo's and followed him as Chairman of QTC, observed in his foreword to *Queensland Made* that:

> Under his guidance, Treasury operated in the real, not the imagined. The economy always performed a bit better than forecast. Similarly, the fiscal position always achieved slightly better than planned, creating a series of 'financial kitties' that could be utilised for additional state developments or services.[15]

During the Hielscher-era, the strength of Queensland's budget management and public finances was widely recognised. For example, on

---

[15]   Stephen Rochester, S., 2014, quoted in Holliman, J., op. cit., p. 8.

14 October 1987, not long before he was forced to retire on 1 December 1987, Premier Sir Joh Bjelke-Petersen noted in the Queensland Parliament that:

> ...the respected Institute of Public Affairs States' Policy Unit based in Western Australia has this week announced that the Queensland State Budget for 1987-88 has been granted the IPA award for the most restrained and responsible budget presented by any State or Commonwealth Government in Australia.[16]

The essence of the Hielscher approach was prudent budgeting, while investing for the future in assets that would pay for themselves (e.g. the Gateway bridge which would be paid for by a toll), and setting aside money to meet long-term liabilities, particularly the state's defined benefit superannuation liability. The fiscal principles of the Hielscher-era were never codified, but were more-or-less adopted by the incoming Goss government in its "fiscal trilogy" discussed in the next chapter.

Sir Leo's contribution to the Treasury

One of Sir Leo's great contributions to Queensland was the fostering of a strong and effective state Treasury. One important contribution was boosting the Treasury's capability in Commonwealth-state financial relations, so Queensland could make the best case it could to the CGC in the HFE process. Sir Leo realised the importance of favourable estimates of Queensland's relative capacity to pay—or rather unfavourable estimates, which showed we had much less capacity to pay than other states—because this would mean a better HFE outcome and more money from the Commonwealth. Hielscher moved one of his protégés, John Hall, out the budget area to create a new Inter-Governmental Relations section.[17] John Hall later succeeded Sir Leo as Under Treasurer.

When interviewed for this book, a former member of the CGC during

---

[16] Sir Joh Bjelke-Petersen, 1987, *Ministerial Statement*, 14 October 1987.
[17] Holliman, J., op. cit., p. 92.

the Hielscher-era, UQ Emeritus Professor Kenneth Wiltshire recalls Sir Leo's prowess at extracting a better deal for Queensland in terms of the allocation of grants from the Commonwealth:

> Sir Leo knew the system well and would send us to places where Queensland suffered considerable disadvantage, particularly remote ones including police stations, jails, schools, and health centres, to convince us that Queensland needed the money. But the Treasury hospitality in Brisbane after the inspections was well handled and so we saw the worst and best of Queensland.

Hielscher was also instrumental in improving Queensland's profile among international financiers and investors in the 1970s and 1980s through international road shows regarding the Queensland economy. This was important because traditionally the Commonwealth government, via the Loan Council, had borrowed on behalf of state and territory governments, so they were not well recognised by international financiers and investors. Queensland's growing recognition internationally culminated in Queensland government bonds being rated by credit rating agencies for the first time in 1988. Standard & Poor's (S&P) and Moody's gave Queensland government bonds the second highest rating, AA+ and AA1 respectively.[18] As noted in the June 1987 cabinet submission seeking the state government's approval of the ratings, it was not at the time possible for Queensland to get the highest AAA rating, given Australia had lost its AAA rating earlier in the year. Even so, the government would have been pleased to accept the ratings. As the cabinet submission noted:

> The receipt of an international rating of AA+/AA1 is highly prestigious and places Queensland in a select group of borrowers

---

[18] Debt management offices, or central financing agencies, such as QTC typically borrow money on behalf of governments by selling, or issuing, to use the jargon, bonds, which are essentially IOUs. The government promises to pay the bond holder a regular coupon payment (i.e. interest), typically twice per year, and to return the money once the bond matures, typically after 3-10 years. Bonds are typically issued across a range of maturities to take advantage of market demand for bonds at different maturities.

who are sought out by international investors.[19]

The establishment of the Queensland Treasury Corporation (QTC), which Sir Leo did much to bring about, in the late 1980s facilitated easier and cheaper access to finance, for the state and also local governments. QTC was a dedicated central financing agency, and could build up expertise and profile in bond markets, through which it would borrow on behalf of the state. Arguably, easier access to debt turned out to be a mixed blessing, enabling the massive accumulation of debt since the late 2000s, but Sir Leo of course cannot be blamed for the deficits and debt-build up that occurred at that time, as it was long since he played an active role in government decision making.

Sir Leo's unconventional approach of "brending the rules"

Based on several stories recounted in Joanne Holliman's *Sir Leo Hielscher: Queensland Made*, Sir Leo undertook some rather unorthodox measures to promote economic development in Queensland. While not breaking the rules, Sir Leo was arguably doing a bit more than just bending them. Recognising this, Sir Leo himself coined the term "brending the rules."

In one instance of "brending the rules", Sir Leo essentially shamed the Commonwealth into providing financing for a major mining project via the Loan Council. He had approached the World Bank for financing, and the Bank subsequently rang the Commonwealth Treasury, asking why the Commonwealth itself was not financing the project. In another example of "brending the rules", in the mid-1970s, during the Queensland building societies' crisis, Sir Leo encouraged the State Government Insurance Office (SGIO), which later became Suncorp, to guarantee building societies that were at risk from a rush of withdrawals, after the Reserve Bank refused

---

[19]   Queensland Government, 1987, "Credit rating of Queensland", *Cabinet Minute*, no. 51715, p. 2.

to help.[20] He was a master at thinking laterally and finding non-traditional solutions.

It is clear that Sir Leo was not an economic rationalist. He had no hesitation in running an activist industry policy, by which the Treasury was actively trying to promote particular industries, which in Queensland's case was the resources sector. *Queensland Made* includes a quotation from a prominent businessman regarding Queensland:

> They have a government just slightly to the right of Genghis Khan, and a Treasury that's to the left of Karl Marx.

This brings into mind an important question regarding the Hielscher-approach, whether the heavy involvement of the state in economic development is desirable. This is not a debate that can be resolved in this volume. The state-led development approach has been historically popular in Queensland. Sir Joh Bjelke-Petersen was well known for his desire to develop the state, and he was following in a long tradition. After all, Queensland had been the exemplar of so-called colonial socialism, with the government-owned QR being instrumental in the opening up and development of the northern and western parts of the state.

Context is everything, and for much of Sir Leo's career, Queensland had a relatively under-developed economy compared with southern states. NSW and Victoria had larger manufacturing sectors (both in absolute terms and as a share of GSP), and they benefitted from the positive economic impacts of numerous corporate and Commonwealth head offices. To illustrate, in 1985, manufacturing employment was 16 percent of total employment in NSW, 21 percent in Victoria, but only 12 percent in Queensland.[21] When Sir Leo came to the Treasury, Queensland did not have export coal, bauxite, alumina and aluminium industries, and the state's main export was wool (at 33 percent of exports), followed by sugar (21 percent), and meat (18

---

[20] Holliman, J., op. cit., p. 84.
[21] Based on ABS Labour Force data. Thirty years later in 2015, those shares were much lower, at 7 percent for NSW, 9 percent for Victoria, and 7 percent for Queensland.

percent).[22] In contrast, in 2018, Queensland's largest export is coal, which accounts for 43 percent of Queensland's merchandise exports.[23]

Possibly it could be argued that a pro-development Queensland Treasury was necessary from the 1960s to 1980s to offset the adverse impact of Commonwealth tariffs on Queensland's industrial development. The tariff wall was beneficial to existing manufacturers in NSW and Victoria, and it reinforced their dominance of Australian industry. Any aspiring manufacturers in Queensland, and also farmers and other businesspeople, were disadvantaged by the tariffs applying to imported equipment. In a thought-provoking 1987 working paper for the Sir Robert Menzies Centre for Australian Studies in London, then UQ academic economist Jon Stanford argued that:

> ...the effect of the Australian Federation on the Queensland economy has been to distort the development of the Queensland economy by freezing the Queensland economy into an overdue dependence on primary production, into a "branch office" structure and generally into lower economic production than would otherwise have been possible.[24]

No doubt a desire to catch up with southern states would have been a motivating factor for the Queensland Treasury in Sir Leo's day, and indeed today we are still somewhat behind, with Queensland's GSP per capita in 2015-16 being at around 94 percent of the level of NSW's, although it was 5 percent higher than Victoria's. The catch up in living standards per capita that Queensland enjoyed in recent decades is no doubt partly attributable to economic development promoted by Sir Leo. Between 1989-90 and 2015-16, Queensland has gone from having a GSP per capita of around 11 percent below national GDP per capita to 5 percent below.

---

22 ABS, 2009, *Qld Stats*, cat. no. 1318.3, available via www.abs.gov.au.
23 Author calculation based on Queensland Government Statistician's Office, 2018, *Exports of Queensland goods overseas*, February 2018, p. 1.
24 Jon D. Stanford, 1987, "The long-term effect of federation on the Queensland economy", *Working Papers in Australian Studies*, working paper no. 37, Sir Robert Menzies Centre for Australian Studies, Institute of Commonwealth Studies, University of London, p. 2.

A professional public servant offering frank and fearless advice

Despite Sir Leo's sometimes unconventional approach, he was no doubt an outstanding public servant in the Northcote-Trevelyan tradition: a professional public servant who offers frank and fearless advice.[25] Interviewed for this book, UQ Emeritus Professor of Public Administration Kenneth Wiltshire said there were only three people who could say no to Premier Sir Joh Bjelke-Petersen, and Sir Leo was one of them. The two others were Coordinator-General of Public Works Sir Charles Barton and Chairman of the Queensland Public Service Board Sir David Muir.

An excellent example of Sir Leo's ability to exercise his own judgment was a multimillion-dollar investment that Premier Sir Joh Bjelke-Petersen wanted the Queensland Treasury to make in the Rothwells merchant bank as part of a bailout in 1987. When Premier Mike Ahern, Sir Joh's immediate successor, heard about the eventual collapse of the Rothwells Bank in 1988, he asked Sir Leo about the government's financial exposure to the collapse. Sir Leo then told the Premier he had not invested the money after all, a decision with which the Premier told him "You've made my day".[26] Of course, for a public servant to make a call to ignore an instruction from a Minister, let alone from a Premier, requires exceptional judgment and courage. Sir Leo had both of these. Developments since the 1980s have worked against the Northcote-Trevelyan tradition, which Sir Leo exemplified, as we shall discuss further in Chapter 10.

Toward the end of its life, the National Party government revamped the state government's financial accountability framework, which lessened the power of Queensland Treasury, following a report from Sir Ernest Savage's Public Sector Review Committee. The government amended the *Financial Administration and Audit Act* in 1988 to provide for greater

---

[25] Stafford H. Northcote and C.E. Trevelyan authored the 1854 report that provided the model for the UK civil service at least up until the time of the Thatcher government.

[26] Holliman, J. op. cit., p. 152.

autonomy by government agencies over their finances, ending the strict control by Treasury.[27]

Indisputably, Sir Leo made a monumental contribution to Queensland's economic history, and for good reason has been honoured with the naming of the Sir Leo Hielscher bridges spanning the Brisbane River after him. He was a tireless, apolitical worker for the state who served 15 Treasurers from both sides of politics. He transformed the Queensland economy by aiding the development of new commodity export industries, and he transformed the machinery of government, through promoting a merit-based public service and enhancing the Treasury's commercial and financial capabilities.

Sir Leo retired from the role of Under Treasurer on the day Expo '88 opened, 30 April 1988.[28] By that time, he had arguably done more than any other Queenslander to improve the state of the economy and the state's public finances. It was expected that he would leave an extraordinary legacy, and it would be up to others to carry on the good fight for fiscal rigour. But Sir Leo was soon given another job, the chairmanship of QTC, which he had advocated creating. This meant he had access to the corridors of power for another two decades. As we shall see in a later chapter, Sir Leo continued to provide advice to future Treasurers as QTC Chairman.

Upon Sir Leo's retirement from the Queensland public service on 11 February 2010, 68 years after he first joined it, the then Treasurer Andrew Fraser offered a fine tribute:

> Sir Leo has served both sides of politics with distinction. In fact, the politics never much mattered; it was the policy and the people of Queensland that mattered much more...
>
> ...His achievements are many and all deserve recognition today. The city of Gladstone largely owes its modern prosperity to the man, as

---

[27] Chris Ryan, 1993, "Financial and budgetary management", in Stevens, B. and Wanna, J. (eds.), *The Goss government: promise and performance of Labor in Queensland*, Macmillan Education, p. 135.

[28] Holliman, J., 2014, p. 155.

does the rapid development of the coal industry more generally. The preservation of the old Treasury and the concurrent development of a casino industry are also notable.

The massive—and unique—achievement of fully funding the state's long term superannuation and employee liabilities was a world first when first achieved, and remains to the best of our knowledge— unique today. And trust me, Leo has searched the world high and low and not yet found our peer on this front.[29]

Sir Leo's commitment to fiscal prudence did not please everyone, however. Low taxes and fiscal prudence resulted in a lower level of service provision in Queensland compared with levels in other states. As noted in Chapter 1, Queensland's reputation as the low tax state was solidified during the Hielscher-era, particularly due to the abolition of death duties. Queensland consistently ranked as having the lowest taxation per capita among Australian states, and this meant it could not afford the same levels of public services as the southern states. As we shall see, later governments would aim to lift the level of service provision. But for many in Hielscher's generation, low taxes and fiscal prudence were of the utmost importance.

The hallmarks of strong public financial management

By the late 1980s, Queensland had become an exemplar of public financial management. Consider that during the time of the Goss government in the early 1990s, Queensland had attained negative net debt and was the only state to have fully funded its defined benefit public service superannuation liability. That is, Queensland had built up assets to offset the liability estimated

---

29   Andrew Fraser, 2010a, *Ministerial Statement by the Treasurer on the retirement of Sir Leo Hielscher*, Media Release of the Treasurer and Minister for Employment and Economic Development The Honourable Andrew Fraser, p. 1.

by actuaries of future defined benefit superannuation payments.[30]

The standards of financial management set during Hielscher's reign as Under Treasurer (1974-1988) were more-or-less honoured by the Goss government, which won power in late 1989. After Sir Joh was forced to resign in December 1987, as a result of fallout from the Fitzgerald inquiry into police corruption, the conservative National Party government was in terminal decline. After Sir Joh, there were two more National Premiers, Mike Ahern and Russell Cooper, neither of whom could forestall the inevitable change of government, after more than three decades of conservative rule.

Queensland's sound public finances were an impressive achievement for a state that had historically failed to register with international investors and ratings agencies, as all borrowing was via the Commonwealth Loan Council.[31] And even though Sir Leo was no longer Under Treasurer, Queensland would continue to improve its fiscal position. In 1994, Treasurer De Lacy declared Queensland debt free. All this was achieved while maintaining Queensland as the low tax state, with the lowest level of tax per capita in Australia.

Another high point came in February 2003, when Queensland obtained a AAA credit rating when Australia finally regained its AAA credit rating after having lost it in December 1986.[32] Queensland would not have been

---

[30] In a defined benefit superannuation scheme, retirees receive a benefit defined according to a formula, typically relating to their final position and salary, rather than to an amount accumulated and saved in an accumulation fund with a super fund such as Q-Super. The Queensland Government closed down its defined benefit super scheme during the financial crisis in 2008-09.

[31] Holliman, J., op. cit., p. 167.

[32] When Queensland was first granted a credit rating in February 1988, the rating was AA+, equivalent to the rating for Australia at the time. But as the Australian rating was downgraded in late 1989, Queensland's rating was downgraded to AA in October 1989. Queensland's credit rating was upgraded from AA to AA+ in May 1999, when S&P upgraded Australia to AA+. And it was upgraded to AAA on 16 February 2003, when S&P restored Australia's AAA rating, following Moody's, which restored Australia's AAA rating in October 2002. I am grateful to QTC for providing the history of Queensland's credit rating. For the history of Australia's credit rating, see Paige Darby, 2013, *Australia's credit rating*, Australian Parliamentary Library.

in this position if it were not for the hard work of Sir Leo, his Treasury colleagues, and various Treasurers over the years.

Queensland in the 1990s and early 2000s was a completely different state, one with sound financial management, than the one that in 1867 was facing financial ruin. Hielscher's legacy would last into the 1990s and early 2000s. But something changed in the mid to late 2000s, and Queensland was no longer an exemplar of sound public financial management. Queensland's fiscal deterioration meant it was vulnerable during the financial crisis and had to lobby for Commonwealth support for its borrowing program, which eventually was forthcoming in the form of a borrowing guarantee.

The change in Queensland's fiscal circumstances meant that, in February 2009, during the Bligh government, the state budget was forecast to be in an operating deficit of $4 billion, a fiscal deficit incorporating capital spending of over $8 billion. Gross state debt was put on a path to around $70 billion today (in 2018) and a projected $83 billion in a few years' time (Figure 1.1).[33] Queensland's gross debt would become the highest among Australia's state and territories.

---

[33]   Queensland Treasury, 2012, *State Budget 2012-13: Budget Strategy and Outlook*, budget paper no. 2, Table 9.1, p. 174 and Queensland Treasury, 2018, *Queensland Budget* 2018-2019.

Figure 1.1 Queensland government borrowings

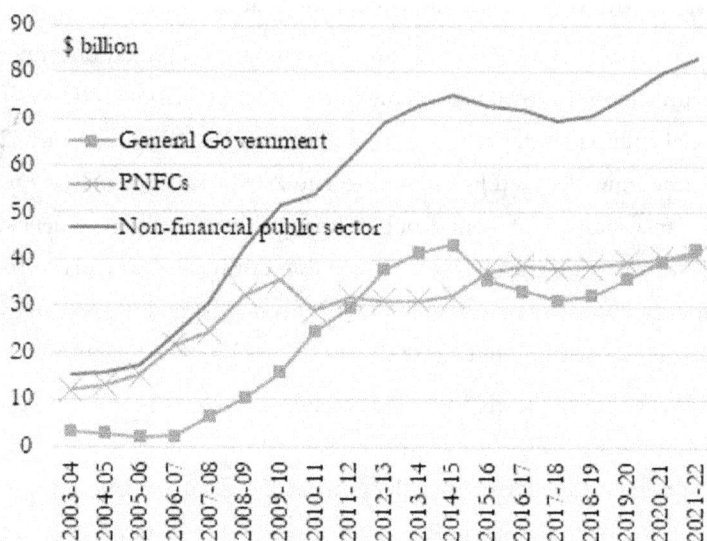

Source: Queensland Treasury, 2018-19 Budget Paper No. 2, Table D.1

Queensland's budget deterioration which became apparent in early 2009 spooked the ratings agency S&P, and Queensland's prized AAA credit rating was lost (Table 1.1). The other ratings agencies soon followed S&P and downgraded the state's credit rating.

Table 1.1 Credit ratings of Australian governments

Government	Standard & Poor's	Moody's
Queensland	AA+/stable outlook	Aa1/stable outlook
NSW	AAA/negative outlook	Aaa/stable outlook
Victoria	AAA/negative outlook	Aaa/stable outlook
SA	AA/positive outlook	Aa1/stable outlook
WA	AA+/negative outlook	Aa2/stable outlook
Tasmania	AA+/stable outlook	Aa2/stable outlook
Australia	AAA/negative outlook	Aaa/stable outlook

Source: Carling, 2017, p.11, updated to reflect change in Moody's outlook for Queensland in April 2017.

It was an extraordinary turnaround, made even more extraordinary by the circumstances of the time. For much of the 2000s, Queensland had experienced a resources boom, with exports earnings and royalty revenue for the government bolstered by higher coal prices, and with strong resources exploration and investment, particularly relating to the newfound coal seam gas sector.

Queensland's fiscal deterioration is even more extraordinary given that Queensland has increased its relative taxation effort through the 2000s compared with earlier decades when, regardless of the low taxation effort, the state's public finances were superior. Institute of Public Affairs Research Fellow Julie Novak, after noting that Queensland traditionally had relatively high taxation until the Bjelke-Petersen government, observed in 2011 that from the 1970s:

> Queensland progressively improved its tax competitiveness to eventually become the lowest taxing jurisdiction in Australia from 1978-79 until 2001-02. By the end of the last decade Queensland's status as the low tax state had been supplanted by Western Australia and Tasmania.[34]

And by 2017-18, South Australia (SA) would also have lower taxation per capita than Queensland (albeit marginally).[35]

Borrowing from the Queensland tourism slogan popular in the 1980s, it is tempting to say Queensland went from beautiful one day to broke the next. Of course, strictly speaking, the state is not broke, as it is running an operating surplus and can borrow money to fund its capital works, but there is no doubt its public finances are in much worse shape than they were when Queensland was the exemplar of sound fiscal management. As we shall see, successive Queensland governments have attempted to repair the

---

[34] Julie Novak, 2011, *Queensland the low tax state: The birth and death of an idea, and how to bring it back to life*, Institute of Public Affairs, pp. 6-7.

[35] Queensland Treasury, 2017a, *Queensland Budget 2017-18: Budget Strategy and Outlook*, budget paper no. 2, p. 85. Note that South Australia's state tax-to-GSP ratio is higher than Queensland's, though. WA has a lower tax-to-GSP ratio (but higher taxation per capita) than Queensland. Tasmania has both a lower state taxation per capita and tax-to-GSP ratio than Queensland.

budget, with varying degrees of success, but total debt is still on a path to be over $80 billion in 2020-21.

What is the point of this book?

This book asks how things went so wrong in Queensland. It considers the financial performance of Queensland governments beginning with Sir Joh Bjelke-Petersen's National Party government of the 1970s and 1980s, originally a coalition with the Liberals which dissolved in 1983, through to the current Palaszczuk government. It argues that a variety of factors, from generational change, the abandonment of strict fiscal principles, failures of public administration, and centralisation of power have all contributed to the poor state of Queensland's public finances. The book then asks how the state's public finances might be improved, and whether that eternal bogeyman of Queensland politics privatisation—now often euphemistically referred to as asset recycling—has a role.

The book tells a story full of grand achievements and errors, and is filled with colourful characters, all working in the volatile environment that is Queensland politics. For example, Queenslanders gave the Newman government a record majority in 2012, only to be voted out three years later in early 2015, after it had taken strong measures to improve Queensland's public finances. Perhaps understandably, as we shall see, the Palaszczuk government has been unwilling to undertake strong measures to repair the budget. It may be that in the current Queensland political environment it is politically impossible to undertake the strong actions needed to substantially repair our public finances. This is a critical question we shall return to throughout the book.

We continue the story in Chapter 2 with Goss government, which continued the strong public financial management, which started in the Hielscher era. The management of Queensland's public finances by successive state governments since Goss's are then discussed in Chapters

3 to 7. Chapter 8 asks the question: how worried should Queenslanders be about the level of state debt? By Chapters 9 and 10, we will be in a position to explore whether privatisation or other measures could help us restore Queensland's public finances. In Chapter 11, conclusions are presented, and we recap how Queensland went from beautiful one day to broke the next.

2

GOSS AND DE LACY INTRODUCE THE TRILOGY

Out of the wilderness

In November 1989, the ALP returned to power in Queensland after 32 years of conservative government. Wayne Goss, a 38-year-old lawyer who grew up in the working class outer Brisbane suburb of Inala, became Premier with an ambitious agenda of reform. The election of the Goss government was almost inevitable after the revelations of the Fitzgerald inquiry into police corruption. The inquiry began in late1987 following startling revelations of police corruption in the *Courier-Mail* and on ABC television. The political fallout was huge, as senior government figures were implicated in corruption. Indeed, several government ministers were convicted and served time in jail. Extraordinarily, former Premier Sir Joh Bjelke-Petersen narrowly avoided a conviction in controversial circumstances, later dramatised in the tele-movie *Joh's Jury.*

Goss was well served by his appointment of the 49-year old Keith De Lacy as Treasurer. Hailing from Cairns in Far North Queensland, De Lacy earned an Arts Degree from UQ and held a variety of occupations—including that of a miner, college principal and newsagent—prior to entering parliament in 1983, aged 43. De Lacy's broad experience, in life, work, and business would distinguish him from some future Treasurers who would have much less non-political life experience prior to attaining high office. As we shall see, the Goss government proved itself highly successful at managing the state's public finances, and for that much of the credit goes to Treasurer De Lacy.

Goss government finds it hard to fault the state of public finances

The newly-elected Government misstepped in trying to criticise the state of Queensland's public finances. While in opposition, Labor had criticised Queensland's public financial management and committed to improvements when it came into government. For example, in the Party's economic platform prior the election, it was argued:

...because Queensland's public sector finances have been in such disarray for so many years and the budget papers and annual reports of government departments have given so distorted a view of the true position, it is impossible and would be highly irresponsible to make binding commitments on taxation reform without first undertaking a thorough review once in government.[36]

The new Treasurer Keith De Lacy continued in this vein in his first speech to the Parliament, as Queensland Treasurer on 7 March 1990, a speech for which he sustained heavy criticism from the opposition and the *Courier-Mail*. De Lacy argued that:

For many years successive National Party governments have misrepresented the truth and perpetrated the following three great myths—the balanced budget myth; the low debt myth; and the strong investment myth.[37]

Budget documents in the 1980s were less transparent than those produced today, but the statements made by the Goss government in opposition and by Treasurer De Lacy were extraordinary, and ran counter to the high praise that was typically given to Queensland's public finances at the time. Indeed, the critical statements could not be supported, and the new government came to accept that it had inherited sound public finances from the previous government. Interviewed for this book, former Treasurer De Lacy noted:

Regardless of all the other criticisms we could make of the former

---

[36] Wayne Goss, 1989, quoted in Ryan, C., op. cit., p. 136.
[37] Queensland Parliament, 1990, *Record of Proceedings (Hansard)*, 7 March 1990, pp. 235-236.

government, deep down I knew that one we couldn't make was that of fiscal profligacy.

De Lacy had based his criticism of the previous government on a comment by Leader of the Opposition (and former Premier and Treasurer) Russell Cooper, who in the *Courier-Mail* on 20 February 1990 was quoted as saying:

> Successive National Party Governments deliberately under-estimated Stamp Duty receipts to provide a buffer in the Budget allowing flexibility on spending and reducing the chance of deficit Budgets.[38]

A criticism of the previous government based on this quote was certainly unwarranted, as taking a conservative approach to revenue forecasts and under-estimating stamp duty seems like prudent budget management. Stephen Rochester's comment regarding Hielscher's state budgets quoted in Chapter 1 are also relevant here. As we will see, the Bligh government, got itself into a fiscal mess partly by committing itself to high levels of spending based on budget revenue forecasts that later turned out to have been too optimistic.

Overall, the Goss government had inherited very sound public finances from the previous government, with a balanced budget and a fully funded public service superannuation scheme. However, Queensland's historically tight fiscal management had meant that teachers and nurses earned lower salaries than their counterparts in other states.[39] The Goss government soon came under pressure to loosen the purse strings from interest groups, including unions and non-government organisations. That the government was able to partly resist this pressure owed much to a codified set of fiscal principles, known as the "fiscal trilogy."

---

[38] Ibid., p. 236.
[39] Jamie Walker, 1995, *Goss: A political biography*, University of Queensland Press, p. 138.

The fiscal trilogy

In the formulation expressed in the Goss government's final state budget for 1995-96, its fiscal trilogy comprised:

- fully funding long-term liabilities such as superannuation and workers compensation; funding social capital assets such as schools and hospitals from recurrent revenues and only borrowing for assets which can generate an income stream sufficient to service the debt; and maintaining Queensland as the low-tax state.[40]

The trilogy was seen as essential to prudent budget management by the Treasurer Keith De Lacy. Interviewed for this book, he commented:

> The trilogy was a mantra known by all ministers. All ministers were conscious of it and it meant that all budget bids would be constrained by it and limited to what could fit in the fiscal envelope.

It was an outstanding achievement of Premier Goss and Treasurer De Lacy to hold the government to the trilogy, given there were large pressures from community groups and unions to spend money to lift Queensland's levels of service provision. Maintaining Queensland as the low-tax state meant that tax rates could not be lifted in an effort to fund expanded public services.

The rule against not borrowing for social infrastructure was arguably the most restrictive requirement, especially given that Queensland was fully funding its liabilities, according to actuarial estimates, and the state government balance sheet was very strong. The rule that assets should generate an income stream that would service their debts would also continue the preference for politically unpopular toll roads, such as the proposed South Coast Motorway that contributed to the Goss government's election loss.

As the Fitzgerald Commission of Audit for the Borbidge government later concluded, the rule against borrowing for social infrastructure is too strict from an economic perspective, which would allow public borrowing for projects yielding net benefits to the community.[41] But it may well have

---

[40] Quoted in Queensland Commission of Audit, 2012, *Interim Report*, p. 60.
[41] Vince Fitzgerald et. al., 1996, *Report of the Queensland Commission of Audit*.

provided much needed discipline on ministers with grand plans who may not have had a keen appreciation of the implications of their collective actions for long-term fiscal sustainability.

The Goss government's budgetary record

The Goss government had benefitted from a strong fiscal inheritance, and acquitted itself well in contributing to it. Indeed, it would be during the Goss government's term in office that Queensland registered negative net debt, with net debt of -$0.2 billion recorded as at 30 June 1994, and with the government's final budget (for 1995-96) projecting further falls.[42]

The Goss government continued with the Hielscher legacy in the running of budget surpluses (Table 2.1). This distinguished it from practically every other state and territory government during the period, which were all in deficit (except for the ACT) in 1990-91 and 1991-92.

Table 2.1. Goss government's budgetary record, underlying estimates as at the time of its last Budget

	1991-92 $ million	1992-93 $ million	1993-94 $ million	1994-95 $ million	1995-96 $ million
Current outlays	8,321	8,809	9,347	9,902	10,937
Capital outlays	2,535	2,584	2,724	3,200	3,499
Revenue & grants received	11,377	12,284	13,020	13,378	14,173
Financing transactions	-531	-891	-950	-276	263
Surplus	866	1,323	1,615	1,105	448
Net financing requirement*	-811	-1,269	-1,570	-979	-415

Source: Queensland Treasury, State Budget 1995-96, p. 102.
* a negative net financing requirement corresponds to a surplus according to the definition used by the ABS which is consistent with the National Accounts.

---

[42] Queensland Treasury, 1995, State Budget 1995-96, Budget Paper no. 2: Budget Overview and Statement of Receipts and Expenditure, p. 104.

Furthermore, Queensland had larger surpluses (as shares of GSP) than other states and territories for the remaining years of the Goss government (Figure 2.1). The Goss government was rightly proud of its fiscal record. Its final budget noted Queensland had "maintained surpluses in the ABS General Government sector for the past twelve years which is an achievement unparalleled by any other Government." [43]

Figure 2.1 State and territory surpluses during Goss government period, $million

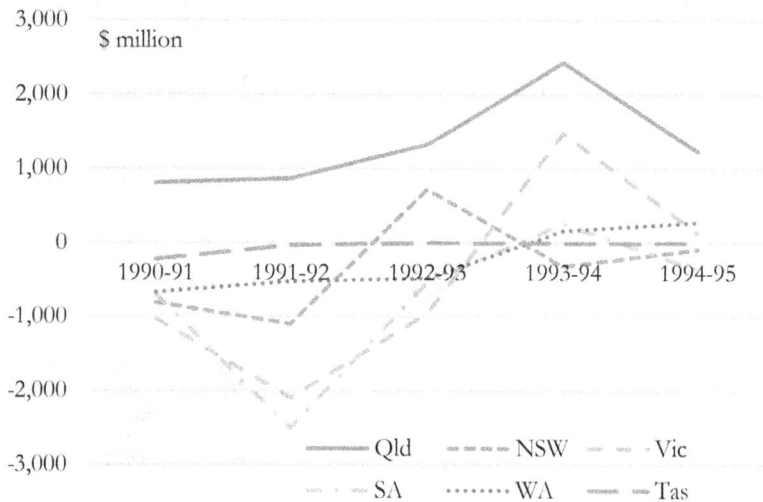

Source: *Queensland Treasury estimates based on ABS and State Budget data provided in 1995-96 State Budget Paper no. 2, p. 110.*

The Goss government managed to maintain its commitment to the fiscal trilogy while significantly increasing salaries for public servants. The 1991-92 budget noted "significant award increases granted to teachers, nurses and police during 1990-91", which combined with growth in public servant numbers, boosted salaries and related costs by a forecast 9.4 percent

---

[43]   Ibid., p. 102.

in 1991-92.[44] This was much higher than forecast growth in administrative and operating outlays at 4.2 percent.

It was a significant achievement that the Goss government managed to maintain budget surpluses while lifting expenditure on social services significantly. The government was concerned Queensland spent relatively less on social services than other states. For example, at the end of the 1980s, Queensland's state government spent only 82-83 percent of the national average on education, compared with NSW's at around 99 percent and Victoria's at around 112 percent.[45] The Goss government aimed to address this during its first term by bringing per capita funding up to the levels in other states. By 1991-92, Queensland was at 89 percent of national average education spending, a rapid increase on its previous levels of 82-83 percent.[46]

Leading Australian public finance expert John Wanna noted the fiscal trilogy constrained the ambitions of some big-spending Goss government ministers: "a commitment to match Victoria's level of educational spending was deflected by his Treasurer, Keith De Lacy, on the grounds that Victoria would eventually have to reduce its spending to the level of Queensland", owing to its fiscal problems.[47] By having a well-articulated fiscal strategy in the form of the trilogy, the Goss government was well positioned to restrain government spending. It was willing to allow some adjustment of social spending to address under-provision relative to other states, but it would be careful not to over-adjust.

---

[44] Queensland Treasury, 1991, *1991-92 State Budget, Budget Paper no. 4: Supplementary Budget Information*, p. 29.

[45] Clarrie Burke, 1993, "Education: Promise, Policy and Performance", in Stevens, B. and Wanna, J. (eds.), *The Goss government : promise and performance of Labor in Queensland*, Macmillan Education, p. 239.

[46] Ibid.

[47] John Wanna, 2003, "Wayne Keith Goss: The rise and fall of a meticulous controller", in Murphy, D., Joyce, R., Cribb, M. and Wear, R. (eds), *The Premiers of Queensland*, University of Queensland Press, p. 377.

Commonwealth cuts force austerity measures

The Goss government's commitment to fiscal discipline was well demonstrated in 1993 when it was forced to respond to funding cuts from the federal government, which incidentally was also an ALP government, led by Prime Minister Paul Keating. The Goss government was prompted to issue an *Interim Budget Statement* on 13 July 1993 as a result of the Premiers Conference on 5 July at which cuts to Commonwealth grants to Queensland in real terms were foreshadowed. Treasury estimated the shortfall to be worth $115 million in 1993-94 and $220 million in 1994-95. At a time when Queensland was experiencing very high population growth, due largely to high interstate migration from southern states, particularly Victoria which was badly affected economically by the early 1990s recession, the Commonwealth would not compensate the states for growing populations. As noted in the *Interim Budget Statement*:

> The Government must therefore commit any growth in State sourced revenue…to meet the infrastructure and service demand pressures arising from the State's increasing population. In the absence of tax increases, there is no capacity to absorb Commonwealth cut backs within the State's overall revenue base.[48]

The government would not recede from its fiscal trilogy, and it committed to achieving the necessary budget adjustment largely by expenditure cuts, although it acknowledged it would seek some additional revenue via higher fees and charges where they could be justified according to "user pays principles".[49] The government's fiscal adjustment plan featured cuts to non-teaching staff at schools, cutting overhead costs at QEII and Princess Alexandra Hospitals through organisational re-structuring, the closure of some lightly utilised uneconomic rail lines, and various efficiency (e.g. rationalisation of fringe benefits such as motor vehicles and housing) and cost recovery measures.[50] Government-owned corporations (GOCs),

---

[48] Queensland Treasury, 1993, *Interim Budget Statement: State Budget 1993-94*, p. 2.
[49] Ibid., p. 3.
[50] Ibid.

and ultimately their customers, would also have to contribute by paying a "QTC Performance Dividend", to reflect the benefits GOCs get from lower borrowing costs. This was justifiable as a competitive neutrality measure consistent with National Competition Policy.

The 1993 emergency measures were designed to save around $110 million in 1993-94 and $186 million per annum on an ongoing basis. There would be a small number of job losses, particularly of media and information services staff and of railway workers due to the closure of some rail lines. But the government committed to no forced redundancies, meaning the government would need to pay generous packages to prompt voluntary early retirements.

Arguably the rail line closures, which were a very sound decision economically, would mark a turning point in the Goss government's political fortunes. The negative reaction to announced budget cuts was swift, and particularly strident from the left. On 4 August 1993, in the *Green Left Weekly* columnist Dave Riley referred to "Goss the destroyer" and commented:

> After 44 months in office, the Goss government has turned vicious and nasty...The cuts provoked an explosion of popular anger. With unions and country townspeople rallying against him, Goss announced a rethink on some of the line closures but remains adamant that $40 million in savings will still have to be bled from the rail network. Announced cuts in health and education will proceed.[51]

In 2009, commenting on QR budget cuts that were then being proposed, the Rail, Tram and Bus Union President Bruce Mackie reminded Queenslanders that:

> The Goss Government lost support in regional Queensland when it closed down more than 2,800 kilometres of regional rail lines and

---

[51] Dave Riley, 1993, "Goss the destroyer", *Green Left Weekly*, 4 August 1993, available via www.greenleft.org.au.

shed 250 jobs to save $40 million.[52]

The government had a major opportunity to turn around its political fortunes with its final budget before the 1995 election.

A final election-focused budget

Perhaps learning from the political unpopularity of its 1993 austerity measures, and conscious that it would soon be fighting an election, in its final state budget handed down in May 1995, the Goss government budget committed to very large expenditure increases in some areas. IPA Fellow Julie Novak noted:

> In its 1995-96 Budget the government announced an expansion of recurrent funding for health and welfare, education, law and order and the environment by 10 per cent, as well as an $800 million program for the development of social infrastructure over a three year period.[53]

Novak points out that Treasurer De Lacy in his budget speech had defended what he admitted was a "big spending" budget on the basis of it being necessary to meet "the expanding needs of our rapidly growing community."[54] Over the second term of the Goss government, from 1992-93 to 1995-96, Novak noted that:

> Queensland experienced the largest increase in expenditure per capita of all the six states of 12.3 per cent over the period. By contrast, Victoria, Western Australia and SA [South Australia] had in fact reduced the amount of government spending on a per capita basis.[55]

The big spending budget was insufficient to restore the government's political fortunes, however. The Liberal-National coalition exploited community dissatisfaction with the Gold Coast motorway as well as rail line

[52] Quoted in Tony Moore, 2009, "Rail depot closures will be tip of the iceberg: union", *Brisbane Times*, 30 July 2009, available via www.brisbanetimes.com.au.
[53] Novak, J., 2011, op. cit., p. 18.
[54] Ibid.
[55] Ibid.

closures and came close to winning the 15 July 1995 election, leaving the government with only a one seat majority. It lost this majority when it lost a by-election in the Townsville seat of Mundingburra in February 1996, a by-election that was required after the Court of Disputed Returns over-turned the ALP victory in the seat at the election, owing to uncounted votes from overseas defence force personnel.

It is possible the Goss government lost office before it could tarnish its fiscal legacy, as the same forces that would eventually bring the Bligh government undone—a concerted push for big spending budgets from ministers—may have overtaken the Goss government in time. But it lost power in February 1996 before this could occur, and prima facie its fiscal record is exceptional. Certainly, the Goss government was viewed at the time as being fiscally conservative. Indeed, it may have even been too conservative in its early years, maintaining surpluses during the early 1990s recession. Professor Fabrizio Carmignani of Griffith University has estimated that Queensland government fiscal policy was contractionary over the first half of 1991, a period in which Australia was in recession.[56]

The Goss government's record on GOCs and privatisation

Another major achievement of the Goss government, in addition to its strong budget management, was the reform of GOCs in the early 1990s, with the Queensland government producing a white paper on corporatisation in 1992. Queensland's GOC reforms were contemporaneous with the nationwide program of microeconomic reform that was occurring at the time. The federal, state and territory governments had agreed to develop a National Competition Policy in 1992, and established an Independent Committee of Inquiry led by Professor Fred Hilmer, which reported in 1993.

In 1993, the *Government Owned Corporations Act 1993* was passed by

---

[56] Fabrizio Carmignani, 2015a, "Can public expenditure stabilise output? Multipliers and policy interdependence in Queensland and Australia", *Economic Analysis and Policy*, vol. 47, p. 78.

the Queensland Parliament. This was also known as the corporatisation legislation, as the intention was that government-owned businesses would start to act as corporations. Prior to corporatisation, GOCs had tended to be parts of government departments or independent boards without clear commercial objectives—e.g. the South East Queensland Electricity Board (SEQEB). The Act brought into effect commitments in the government's corporatisation white paper of 1992. In the second reading speech introducing the bill on 12 May 1993, Treasurer Keith De Lacy noted:

> ...corporatisation is a structural reform process for GOEs [government-owned enterprises] which changes the conditions under which they operate, so that they are placed, as far as practicable, on a commercial basis in a competitive environment. Corporatisation is a major component of the Goss Government's program to improve the efficiency of the public sector in the delivery of its commercial and non-commercial objectives. Under the Government's corporatisation model, public ownership of GOEs will remain, but the strategic focus, structure and operating practices of these entities will be aligned with the best commercial practice to provide an operating environment for improved commercial performance and increased efficiency in the delivery of community service obligations— CSOs—undertaken by GOEs.[57]

The goal was to improve efficiency, profitability and responsiveness to customers. These were important reforms, and ultimately would pave the way for privatisations of some of the businesses such as Suncorp and QR's freight operations, but the reforms required discipline by the government, which was still the owner of the businesses. Ideally, the government would not interfere in the management of the businesses, and management would be free to make its own operational decisions, including around hiring, firing and remuneration, so long as it was achieving the objectives set by the shareholding ministers. As we will see in later chapters, over the last few decades, various ministers have revealed themselves as being unable to resist the temptation to interfere with GOCs for political reasons.

---

[57] Queensland Parliament, 1993, *Record of Proceedings (Hansard)*, May 12 1993, p. 2705.

Regarding the Goss government's GOC reforms, De Lacy concluded in 2001 that:

> Eight years after the grand strategy was implemented, my observation is that it has not been as successful as we hoped at the time. I say this because I don't think it has brought about the commercial independence that was envisaged in the legislation and unsurprisingly therefore neither has it brought the efficiencies.[58]

It may be that a framework reliant on corporatisation of government businesses is insufficient to guarantee efficiency improvements because there is always the temptation provided to ministers to interfere in the affairs of the businesses. Privatisation may well be the only way to protect GOCs from political interference.

The Goss government undertook some significant and controversial privatisations during its term, including the sale of the Greenslopes Repatriation Hospital, which was part-owned by the Commonwealth, and the Gladstone power station. The sale of the Gladstone power station to Comalco for $750 million was arguably a blot on the Goss government's otherwise excellent record. Australian shareholder activist Stephen Mayne wrote on the *Crikey* website in 2000:

> There is no bigger disaster than the PPA [power purchase agreement] with Comalco's giant Gladstone power station which this soon-to-be 100 per cent foreign company bought from the Goss government for a song in 1993-94. Not only did Comalco get the security of supply they demanded for their nearby Boyne Island aluminium smelter, but they struck a long term contract to sell all the surplus capacity back to the state at inflated prices.[59]

As the example demonstrates, the net benefits of privatisation depend on its implementation and the post-privatisation arrangements including

---

[58] Keith De Lacy, 2001, *Corporate Governance—GOCs*, speech delivered on 11 July 2001, copy provided to author.

[59] Stephen Mayne, 2000, "Queensland's $800 Million Power Disaster", *Crikey*, 27 February 2000, available via www.crikey.com.au.

contractual arrangements and economic regulation of local monopolies. That said, it is a credit to the Goss government that it was willing to privatise government GOCs and was not ideologically opposed to privatisation as the current Palaszczuk government appears to be.

The Goss government's approach to public administration—Rudd and Coaldrake shake up the bureaucracy

Soon after it was elected in late 1989, the newly installed Goss government prioritised tackling corruption and reforming electoral boundaries, ending the "gerrymander" that favoured the National Party through over-representation of regional Queensland (i.e. more seats in regional Queensland than justified by population levels) in the parliament. The new government committed itself to integrity in public administration and set up, among other bodies:

- the Criminal Justice Commission, now called the Crime and Corruption Commission;

- the Electoral and Administrative Review Commission, which was wound up in 1993 after having completed its review of the electoral system and public administration;

- the Public Sector Management Commission (PSMC), which was intended to oversee reform of the Queensland public service and which has been superseded by various bodies with a less ambitious mandate, including the current Public Service Commission; and an Expenditure Review Committee, now the Cabinet Budget Review Committee (CBRC).

The Goss government was characterised by a high degree of policy coordination, led by an Office of Cabinet established in 1991. The Office was headed by Premier Goss's former Chief of Staff: a highly ambitious former diplomat in his early thirties, later to be Australia's 26th Prime Minister, Kevin Rudd. During his time at the Office of Cabinet, Rudd earned the nickname "Dr Death."[60] As reported in the *Sydney Morning Herald* in 2007:

> There are varying accounts of how the title [of Dr Death] came about. Ministers used to complain that Rudd would kill off submissions before they got to cabinet; others say it was because it was often Rudd who delivered bad news to key public servants. "The nickname arose because if you got called in to see him it wasn't a good look," says a former minister. "And that's when people would say with some dread: 'I've got an appointment with Dr Death.'"[61]

Another important behind-the-scenes figure in the Goss government was the Chair of the PSMC Peter Coaldrake, who later became Vice-Chancellor of QUT. The PSMC was designed to oversee the reform of the public service, and it began by undertaking reviews of the activities of government agencies. Given PSMC was headed by Coaldrake, an academic who had previously been external to the public service, PSMC reviews were resented by many senior public servants, and some public servants allegedly leaked news of their dissatisfaction to the media.[62] Nonetheless, the PSMC appears to have had some notable successes, including the opening up of all Queensland public service positions to external recruitment.[63] A major aim of the PSMC was to end the "closed shop" of public service employment, which favoured insiders with adverse implications for culture and efficiency.[64]

As would be expected from a new government, there were some initial

---

[60] Walker, J., op. cit., p. 135.

[61] Sydney Morning Herald, 2007, "The making of Kevin Rudd", *Sydney Morning Herald*, 21 February 2007, available via www.smh.com.au.

[62] Helen McMonagle, 2012, "Queensland's Public Sector Management Commission: Goss's Governmental "Reformation"?", *Centre for the Government of Queensland Summer Scholar Journal*, 2, p. 5.

[63] Linda Colley, 2005, "Reworking merit: Changes in approaches to merit in Queensland public service employment 1988 to 2000", in Baird, M., Cooper, R. and Westcott, W. (eds.) *Reworking work: proceedings of the 19th conference of the Association of Industrial Relations Academics of Australia and New Zealand*, p. 143.

[64] Linda Colley, 2009, "The politics of an apolitical public service", in Bowden, B., Blackwood, S., Raferty, C. and Allen, C., *Work and Strife in Paradise*, Federation Press, p. 10.

missteps in its relationship with the public service. In addition to the PSMC, these included the creation of the so-called "gulags" to which public servants out of favour with the new government would be sent, relieved of their normal duties and given practically nothing worthwhile to do.

Despite several missteps, the Goss government deserves credit for major reforms to Queensland's public administration and the electoral system, and it also deserves credit for improvements to public financial management. The Goss government built on improvements to financial accountability under the National Party government that were discussed in the previous chapter, and it introduced its own. These included the introduction of a forward estimates process, whereby the budget would be estimated for the current budget year and three years out, the development of financial management guidelines, improvements in budget reporting, and the simplification of the public accounts.[65] These were all undeniably positive developments.

Notwithstanding some concerns about politicisation, especially regarding the Office of Cabinet, the Goss government strove for high standards in public policy advice and development. One example, that of Treasury-led internal reviews is interesting in hindsight given the large failures in public administration in Queensland we have seen in recent years—e.g. the water crisis, the Queensland Health payroll debacle, and the "rail fail"—failures which may have been identified early and averted if the system of internal reviews had been continued.

The internal reviews of Queensland government agencies and programs were led by a dedicated program strategic review area within Queensland Treasury. The Treasury-led internal reviews had the advantage of being able to use sensitive and confidential information internal to government and could identify and confidentially resolve issues at an early stage before they became problems in the public arena for the government. The

---

[65]   Ryan, C., op. cit., p. 141.

involvement of Treasury was critical in these reviews given the detailed financial information held by Treasury and Treasury's influence on the ongoing budgetary relationship between Treasury and the line agencies— i.e. the departments delivering services, as opposed to the central agencies of Premier and Cabinet and Treasury.

The reviews were endorsed by a steering committee comprising the Treasurer, then Keith De Lacy, and the relevant Minister and the Under Treasurer and Director General of the relevant department. Combining the political and administrative heads of Treasury and the line agency in the steering committee meant that the steering committee had the authority to endorse the policy, fiscal and administrative recommendations of the review.

Former Treasury official Paul McFadyen recalled an internal review of fire and emergency services that he conducted during the Goss government. This review identified over-resourcing in some established suburbs but under-resourcing in newly established suburbs, and was important in re-directing future service delivery.

The Treasury-led reviews were arguably more effective than external reviews commissioned by the PSMC. This is because agencies were less resistant to a Treasury-led review in which they had a close involvement than PSMC reviews, which were resisted by many in the public service, as noted above.[66]

Assessment of the Goss government

The Goss government's fiscal record speaks for itself, although it appeared to retreat somewhat from its highly disciplined approach in its final budget (1995-96) due to political necessity. That said, with its string of budget surpluses recorded in the official ABS data and its attainment of negative net debt, it did well to uphold the Hielscher legacy of sound public finances.

---

[66]   McNonagle, H., op. cit., p. 1.

And it lost office in part due to a public policy decision that hindsight suggests was a wise one, planning to build a second highway to the Gold Coast.

The Goss government did well to reform GOCs by introducing a *Government Owned Corporations Act*, but its principles were not respected by future governments. Also, a notable achievement of the government's was the system of internal reviews it established, which allowed it to identify and head off future service delivery issues.

The fiscal conservatism of the Goss government can be understood as the result of a government aiming for very high standards in budget management, to render ineffective the criticism that Labor governments were spendthrift and poor economic managers. Treasurer De Lacy was especially conscious that former Premier Sir Joh Bjelke-Petersen had previously warned Queenslanders that a future Labor government would be similar to the crisis-prone Whitlam government at the federal level (1972-75).

Arguably, by showing that a Labor government can successfully manage public finances, the Goss government made it easier for future Labor governments, which were under less suspicion of fiscal mischief. Possibly this allowed them to eventually deviate from principles of sound public finance, as we shall see in future chapters.

3

BORBIDGE AND SHELDON'S BRIEF AND PRECARIOUS REIGN

An uncertain hold on power

The Borbidge government assumed office in February 1996, after the Goss government lost power as result of the by-election loss in the seat of Mundingburra in suburban Townsville. With the support of Liz Cunningham, independent MP for Gladstone, the National-Liberal coalition assumed power, led by 41-year-old Nationals MP Rob Borbidge. With such a slim majority, the new government always knew its position was precarious. One sign of this recognition was placing its senior bureaucrats on short-term contracts, so it would not have to suffer the opprobrium associated with any large contract payouts when the government changed. Professor Richard Mulgan, a consultant to the Australian Parliamentary Library commented:

> Such a course of action, while fiscally responsible, underlines the assumption that agency heads can expect to serve only the government of the day.[67]

The new Premier Rob Borbidge was born in regional Victoria in 1955, but his family relocated to the Gold Coast when he was young, purportedly due to the abolition of death duties by the Bjelke-Petersen government. He attended the Southport School and worked in the family motel business before becoming the National Party MP for Surfers Paradise in 1980. Upon becoming Premier, he was able to draw on only a relatively brief period of

---

[67] Richard Mulgan, 1998, *Politicising the Australian Public Service*, Parliamentary Library Research Paper, no. 3, 1998-99, p. 7.

ministerial experience in the Ahern and Cooper cabinets after the fall of Sir Joh in late 1987. It may have been insufficient experience to prepare him for the turbulence he would experience as Premier.

The incoming Treasurer Joan Sheldon was a 52-year old former physiotherapist from Queensland's Sunshine Coast. She had operated her own physiotherapy practice for several years in Brisbane, and hence had some familiarity with business issues and budgeting. But it was her first ministry, and in one of the toughest portfolios, Treasury. Sheldon wisely sought out trusted counsel and expert and independent advice on fiscal matters. Treasurer Sheldon was not prepared to go along with the commonly accepted view of the Goss government as sound economic managers with strict control on the budget. In opposition, Sheldon and Borbidge had claimed Labor's fiscal management was not as good as they had proclaimed, and now they had their chance to turn the resources of government toward investigating the Goss government's record.

Borbidge and Sheldon call on outside help

Two early decisions of the Borbidge government relating to the Treasury portfolio are noteworthy.

First, the government replaced highly-regarded Under Treasurer Gerard Bradley with Dr Doug McTaggart. McTaggart had served as an informal adviser to Sheldon while in opposition, and she trusted him and valued his counsel. McTaggart was, at the time, an academic at Bond University who had distinguished himself with rigorous analytical thinking and his strong work ethic. He had earned a PhD in economics from the University of Chicago, so he was expected to offer sound conservative advice on managing the state's public finances.

Although Gerard Bradley's replacement by McTaggart was controversial, McTaggart was clearly very talented and suited to the role. The new government informally said it would consider Bradley for a position as Director-General of a Queensland government line department—e.g. health or education and not a central agency such as Treasury or Premier and Cabinet—but this was of no interest to him. Instead, he accepted a job as Under Treasurer of SA. As we shall see, it turned out that Bradley's absence from Queensland Treasury was a short one, as Bradley was returned to the position of Under Treasurer by the Beattie government.

Bradley's replacement raised the issue of the politicisation of the public service. Interviewed for this book, Joan Sheldon rejected the proposition that McTaggart's appointment was political. She noted she had very high regard for Queensland Treasury and that Queensland needs a strong non-political Treasury. As an example of how she tried to promote this, Sheldon provided the example of former Treasury official Tony Bellas, who went on to chair several prominent private sector companies and GOCs. She noted:

> Tony Bellas had been in Treasury. Sir Leo had shifted him to either QIC [Queensland Investment Corporation] or QTC as he was concerned that with the election of our government he might be sacked or demoted. His father had run as a Labor candidate in South Brisbane.
>
> After the election and when I became Treasurer Sir Leo came to see me. He told me what had happened and said he thought Tony wanted to come back to Treasury. Sir Leo said he was very good at his job. I told Sir Leo I would like to see Tony. He came to see me and said he would like to return. I told him I didn't care how he voted. I was more interested in good competent people who dealt with their employers, in this case me, honestly. I also told him that if he betrayed me I would cut him off at the knees.
>
> Tony Bellas was an extremely good, efficient and loyal public servant to me. We became friends and still occasionally see each other. He left public service not long after I left government and is now chair of a number of energy companies.

As a result, Bellas came back into the Treasury, where he stayed until he was appointed CEO of the government-owned CS Energy. While in

Sheldon's Treasury, Bellas worked on the highly-successful Suncorp Metway merger and privatisation, which is discussed below.

Second, early in its term, the Borbidge government established a Commission of Audit, to be headed by the Queensland-born Dr Vince Fitzgerald, a highly respected economist, co-founder of the Allen Consulting Group and former Commonwealth Treasury official who had served time at postings in the OECD in Paris and the International Monetary Fund (IMF) in Washington, DC. The Fitzgerald Commission of Audit had a broad terms of reference and delved into the service delivery performance of different agencies and also explored the scope for privatisation.

Early in the Borbidge government's term, Treasurer Sheldon claimed to have uncovered some issues with the Goss government's budgeting. For example, on 2 April 1996, the Treasurer claimed the then forecast 1995-96 cash surplus of $2-3 million would be achieved partly by running down the opening Consolidated Fund balance of $51 million, meaning expenditure was actually greater than revenue by around $48 million, on the policy settings inherited from the Goss government. Also, there were one-off transfers from trust funds of $50 million and a one-off $87 million corporatisation payment, which appeared to be an equity withdrawal from the electricity GOCs, although the Treasurer was not explicit.[68] The Treasurer argued that, adjusted for these alleged budget fiddles, there was actually an underling deficit of $185 million.[69]

When it reported in July 1996, the Commission of Audit delivered to Treasurer Sheldon some additional ammunition, allowing her to back up her claims of a pre-election spending spree in the Goss government's last budget. Tabling the Commission's report in the Queensland Parliament on 9 July 1996, Treasurer Sheldon advised the House:

---

[68] Joan Sheldon, 1996, *Budget Position and Outlook for 1996-97*, ministerial statement, 2 April 1996 and also Queensland Treasury, 1996a, *State Budget 1996-97: Budget Overview*, budget paper no. 2, p. 49.

[69] Sheldon, J., 1996, op. cit.

> ...the Commission noted that the Operating Statement, the first prepared on a full accrual basis, shows a recent sharp deterioration in the Government's operating position from a surplus operating result of $325 million in 1994-95 to an estimated deficit of $337 million in 1995-96.

> The report supports the Coalition's claims of an underlying deficit and proves that the Opposition's claims that such a deficit did not exist were nothing but ludicrous excess.

> The major factor in this deterioration was a set of significant increases in spending approved in the 1995-96.

Undeniably there was strong expenditure growth approved in the Goss government's final budget, as discussed in the last chapter. Expenditure growth for 1995-96 was estimated by the Fitzgerald Commission of Audit at nearly 12 percent, in a year in which Brisbane CPI inflation was only 3 percent (Table 3.1). The Commission's accrual accounting estimates were produced with assistance from accountants Arthur Andersen and the Treasury. Regarding accrual accounting, the Commission noted it:

> ...accounts for the full resource costs to the State in providing public services and which brings all accruing liabilities to account, and not merely cash costs.[70]

For example, this means that, to the extent future liabilities such as superannuation or long-service service were inadequately provisioned for, expenses estimated on an accrual basis would be higher than those estimated on a cash basis. At the time, in June 1996, the state government was provisioning for its superannuation liability, but not for its long service leave liability ($767 million) or recreation leave liability ($294 million).[71]

---

[70] Fitzgerald, V. et al., op. cit., p. xiv.
[71] Ibid., p. 95.

Table 3.1 Fitzgerald Commission of Audit's estimates of Queensland's operating budget

Budget item	1994-95	1995-96	Percentage change
	$ million	$ million	
Revenue			
Commonwealth payments	4,537	4,847	6.8%
Taxes, fees and fines	3,930	4,115	4.7%
Other revenue	2,203	2,262	2.7%
Total revenue	10,670	11,224	5.2%
Expenses			
Service delivery costs	10,345	11,561	11.8%
Operating balance (+ is surplus, - is deficit)	*325*	*-337*	

Source: Fitzgerald et al., 1996, p. xiv and author's calculations.

The Commission was scathing of the cash surplus measure reported in budget papers—the figure Joan Sheldon was critical of in her 2nd April 1996 statement mentioned above—because it did not cover trust funds (e.g. Ambulance Services Trust Fund, Gaming Machine Community Benefit Fund, among many others) and state-owned entities outside of the official public accounts (e.g. South Bank Corporation, State Library of Queensland), nor did it include depreciation.[72] It also treated privatisation proceeds as revenue, did not distinguish between current and capital expenses, and was subject to manipulation, "through shifting items 'off budget' to or from other funds."[73] The Commission found that depreciation, particularly of the road network, had a major influence on the Queensland government's operating balance, and different assumptions regarding the effective life of roads could substantially affect the result.[74]

Given the Queensland Treasury has not produced consistent historical

---

[72] Ibid., p. 87. Incidentally, the Commission of Audit was also critical, but to a lesser extent, of the ABS's GFS estimates. While the ABS estimates covered the whole general government sector, and were hence not as susceptible to having items shifted off-budget, they were deficient in that they were also prepared on a cash basis. This meant they did not include depreciation nor did they consider accruing liabilities.

[73] Ibid.

[74] Ibid., p. 97.

budget data for Queensland prior to the early 2000s, it is difficult to assess the Commission of Audit's claim that the Goss government's last budget was in deficit in accrual terms, although given the highly reputable Commissioners it is appropriate to accept it. The Commission's finding of a deficit run in the Goss government's final fiscal year appears to have been forgotten, however. The Newman government's Commission of Audit in its Interim Report in June 2012 charted ABS Government Finance Statistics (GFS) data showing Queensland's fiscal balance remained in surplus until 1998-99. It should have identified the pre-1999-00 estimates were not on a comparable accrual basis, but on a cash basis, as done in Figure 3.1.

Figure 3.1. Queensland general government budget balances as a percentage of GSP

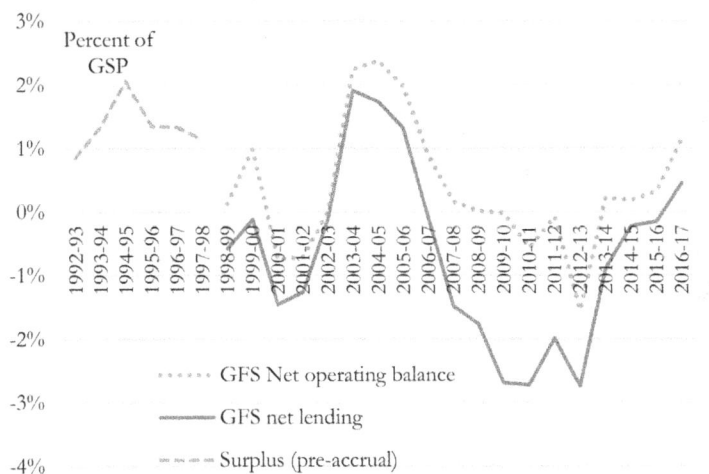

Source: ABS Government Finance Statistics, cat. no. 5512.0 and ABS State Accounts, cat. no. 5220.0.

The Fitzgerald Commission of Audit had identified trends that would lead to a deterioration of Queensland's public finances over time. In a statement on Queensland's long-term budgetary outlook made on 20 March 1997, Treasurer Sheldon told the Parliament:

> The Commission found that, based on the policies, practices and
> planning assumptions current at the time, there is an in-built trend
> to a progressive deterioration of the general government operating
> result, which if, unchecked, could reach a deficit of $2.7 billion by
> 2005-06.[75]

While she could point to recent policy settings that could promote a
future deterioration, particularly expenses growth in excess of revenue
growth, Treasurer Sheldon could not point to gross fiscal mismanagement
on the part of previous governments, including the Goss government.
Indeed, she was implicitly complimentary of previous governments. As she
noted in the same ministerial statement:

> In Queensland, we should all be proud of the fact that, over the
> long-term, over many years, Queensland Governments have built
> up a strong balance sheet. Our State's net worth as estimate by the
> Commission of Audit, is over $51 billion. This equates to $15,600 per
> Queenslander.

As the Treasurer observed, this was far in excess of other states at
the time, such as NSW at $11,400, WA at $10,700 and Victoria at only
$1,400 public sector net worth per capita.[76] In contrast with Queensland's
relatively sound public financial management, Victoria had experienced a
fiscal blowout under the Cain Labor government in the 1980s, and had also
suffered from the failure of the publicly owned State Bank of Victoria,
due to imprudent lending by its merchant banking arm Tricontinental.
That said, there were problems with current budget policy settings that
needed correcting. Interviewed for this book, Joan Sheldon noted that "the
Commission of Audit had found Queensland asset rich, but cash poor."

[75] Joan Sheldon, 1997, *Ministerial Statement: Queensland's Long Term Budgetary Outlook*, 20 March 1997.
[76] Ibid.

Fiscal principles

The Borbidge government more-or-less adopted the Goss government's fiscal trilogy, although it created a new principle which made it clear the rule against borrowing for social infrastructure also implied governments would not borrow to fund for recurrent expenditure either. The principles were:

- keep taxes low;
- fully fund contingent liabilities, such as superannuation and workers' compensation;
- not borrow for recurrent expenditure; and
  restrict borrowings to infrastructure projects able to service the debt.[77]

The Commission of Audit had proposed a new charter of fiscal responsibility, which the Borbidge government referenced in its first budget, but did not explicitly adopt. Instead, the 1996-97 state budget noted the government's fiscal principles were "fundamentally consistent" with the proposed charter.[78]

The new fiscal objectives recommended by the Commission, and which were to be enshrined in the charter were:

1. maintaining the State's net worth,
2. maintaining a competitive tax system,
3. establishing an efficient regulatory system, and
4. establishing structures and processes designed to ensure efficient service delivery.[79]

Notice how in the Commission's recommended charter there was no explicit principle relating to the budget balance or to borrowings, but rather there is a focus on the government's net worth. By focussing on the state government's net worth, the charter of fiscal responsibility would have

---

[77] Queensland Treasury, 1996a, op. cit., p. 4.
[78] Ibid.
[79] Queensland Commission of Audit, 2012, op. cit., p. 60. Also see Fitzgerald, V., et al., op. cit., pp. xxv-xxvi.

effectively done away with the fiscal trilogy principle of not borrowing for social infrastructure. It would be possible to justify some borrowing for social infrastructure if it improved net worth, or at least did not detract from it, by sitting on the state's balance sheet as an asset. Indeed, the Fitzgerald Commission of Audit did not see the need for the strict rule against borrowing for social infrastructure. Instead, it could see a role for borrowing in certain circumstances, which it expressed in careful language, as if to say it was a last resort where you could not obtain the finance by other means such as selling assets:

> To the extent that the Government cannot free up additional capital from its balance sheet for infrastructure which has an attractive benefit cost ratio in total economic and social terms, but which cannot be self-financed from user charges, the Government should make greater use of borrowing—within the fiscal responsibility guidelines articulated in Part A of this Volume.[80]

We will see that the Commission's economically correct assessment, of the circumstances in which borrowing for social infrastructure would be allowed, later provided the intellectual backing for future departures from the strict rule against such borrowing, with regrettable consequences for Queensland's public finances. It was wise that the Borbidge government did not fully embrace the charter recommended by its Commission of Audit.

Budgeting for greater capital spending

The first Borbidge-Sheldon budget reported that, on the Goss government's policy settings, the deficit for 1996-97 would have been $240 million. That said, the forecast ignored the fact that, were it to have remained in office, the Goss government may well have taken measures to reduce the 1996-97 deficit. In addition to the underlying fiscal deficit it claimed it inherited from the Goss government, the Borbidge government also pointed to reductions in Commonwealth funding of $250 million and unfunded

---

[80] Fitzgerald, V. et al., op. cit., p. 180.

workers' compensation liabilities of around $400 million. Importantly from the balance sheet perspective emphasised by the Fitzgerald Commission of Audit, the Borbidge government enacted reforms to workers' compensation—including the establishment of WorkCover Queensland which had some degree of independence from government as a statutory authority—with a view to closing the funding gap, following an inquiry by businessman Jim Kennedy.

In its first budget, for the 1996-97 financial year, the Borbidge government announced measures to ensure the budget remained in balance, both revenue and expense measures, and the budget forecast a small closing surplus for 1996-97 of $7.6 million.[81] It appears the government slightly exceeded this targeted closing surplus, with the 1996-97 closing surplus estimated in the 1997-98 budget in May 1997 at $10.9 million.[82]

Revenue measures included an increase in the rate of tobacco franchise fees, from 75 percent of the average of other state's fees to 100 percent, and an increase in the bank accounts debits tax to the levels in NSW, Victoria and SA. Incidentally, both these revenue items would end up being taken off the states as result of an unfavourable High Court decision, to be discussed later in this chapter.

In its first budget, the Borbidge government claimed it had found savings of around $500 million in 1996-97, which comprised savings in administration costs, cuts to some "low value adding non-core services" and additional user charges.[83] It also announced it would not proceed with $140 million of commitments made by the Goss government.[84]

A theme of Treasurer Sheldon's first budget, and also her second, was "a shift in emphasis towards capital spending."[85] Recurrent outlays were

---

[81]   Queensland Treasury, 1996a, op. cit., p. 8.
[82]   Queensland Treasury, 1997a, *State Budget 1997-98: Budget Overview*, budget paper no. 2, p. 7.
[83]   Queensland Treasury, 1996a, op. cit., p. 5.
[84]   Ibid.
[85]   Queensland Treasury, 1996b, *State Budget 1996-97: Budget in Brief*, budget paper no. 4, p. 8.

budgeted to increase 5.0 percent, while capital expenditure was budgeted to increase by 17.8 percent.[86] Higher infrastructure spending was seen as necessary given the "rapid population and economic growth in the State". Queensland's population growth was correctly forecast to exceed the national growth rate for the entire 1990s (Figure 3.2), as was economic growth for the majority of the decade.

Figure 3.2 Economic growth in Queensland compared with the national average over the 1990s, annual GSP and GSP growth

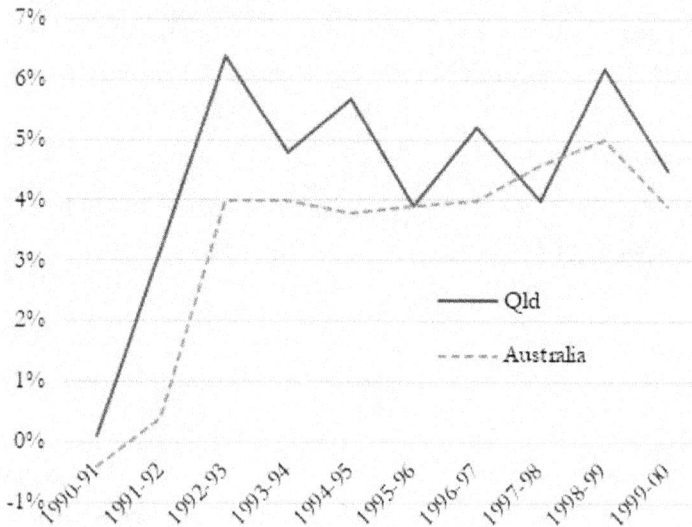

Source: ABS, Australian National Accounts: State Accounts, cat. no. 5220.0.

By the time of Sheldon's second budget, for 1997-98, tabled in the Parliament on 27 May 1997, economic conditions had continued to improve, with GSP growth forecast at 4.5 percent, compared with 3.75 percent nationwide. The budget featured a large boost to capital spending, up 24.2 percent, and restraint in recurrent spending, forecast to grow at 3.6 percent, broadly in line with the sum of forecast population growth (2

---

[86] Queensland Treasury, 1996a, op. cit., p. 5.

percent) and inflation (1.5 percent). Total outlays were budgeted to increase 5.6 percent, and included new spending on job-creation initiatives, among other measures in education, health and justice, for example. Revenues were forecast to grow relatively strongly at 5 percent, even though Commonwealth payments were expected to decline 0.8 percent.

The 1997-98 budget was another responsible budget from Treasurer Sheldon, who was budgeting for a surplus of $848 million in the general government sector in 1997-98, on a cash accounting basis (Table 3.2). Adjusting for changes in the scope of what was considered the general government and GOC sectors, the 1997-98 revealed Treasurer Sheldon was actually targeting a surplus of $203 million. These changes of scope include reclassification of the government's Forestry Fund from the general government sector to the GOC sector, the reclassification of QTC as a public financial enterprise and not part of the general government sector, and the exclusion of Grainco (a grain handling company acquired by NSW-based Graincorp in 2003) from the Queensland government as it was effectively a private sector company, among other changes. The 1997-98 surplus reported in the 1998-99 budget was around $1.1 billion, a substantial improvement over what Treasurer Sheldon was effectively targeting. This was largely due to a surge in revenue classified as interest received. Earnings from the money the state government had invested to meet its super liabilities were high due to the buoyant market in 1996-97, and these earnings entered the budget in the 1997-98 financial year.[87] So Treasurer Sheldon's final surplus was a strong one, at 7.8 percent of revenue and 1.1 percent of GSP.[88]

---

[87]   Queensland Treasury, 1998, *State Budget 1998-99: Budget Overview*, budget paper no. 2, p. 88.

[88]   Incidentally, the Uniform Presentation Framework figures, which were designed to be consistent with ABS GFS estimates and were first presented in the 1998-99 state budget for the 1997-98 budget year, closely corresponded to the figures later reported by the ABS.

Table 3.2 Final Sheldon budget results based on Uniform Presentation Framework adopted in 1998-99

	1997-98 Budget estimates $ million	1997-98 Actual figures $ million
Outlays	12,867	12,957
Current outlays	10,268	10,635
Capital outlays	2,599	2,322
Revenue	13,069	14,058
Taxes, fees and fines	4,640*	4,663
Interest received	1,103	1,833
Grants received	5,813	5,913
Dividends from GOCs	1,060*	808
Other revenues (incl. royalties)	453	841
Surplus	**203**	**1,102**

Source: Queensland Treasury, 1998, 1998-99 State Budget, Budget Paper no. 2, p. 37.
*I have amended these figures slightly to fix apparent typographical errors in the Budget documents which meant that items did not add up to the total revenue figure.

The 1997-98 budget also featured tax cuts, particularly an increase in the payroll tax threshold, so fewer businesses would have to pay it, and increased land tax concessions. The Borbidge government was very proud that Queensland would remain as the low tax state, and the 1997-98 budget papers estimated Queensland state taxes were $732 per capita lower than in NSW.[89] The budget noted Queensland had lower payroll tax and stamp duty rates, and did not have a financial institutions duty or state petrol tax.

---

[89]   Queensland Treasury, 1997b, State Budget 1997-98: Budget in Brief, budget paper no. 4, p. 9.

Turbulence in Commonwealth-state financial relations

The 1997-98 budget was an impressive achievement, given it had to manage reductions in real per capita funding from the Commonwealth. This had followed from a bitter Premiers Conference in March 1997, which revealed the Commonwealth's expectation that the states and territories would contribute to Commonwealth deficit reduction through lower grants relative to what was expected. Indeed, the Borbidge government would experience significant turbulence in Commonwealth-state financial relations.

In federal financial relations, Treasurer Joan Sheldon faced similar difficulties as many of her predecessors and successors. At many times, Queensland Treasurers have found little interest in cooperative federalism from the Commonwealth, which has viewed state and territory governments merely as supplicants. Unfortunately for state and territory treasurers, the vertical fiscal imbalance (VFI) discussed later in Chapter 8 places the Commonwealth in a dominant position. This dominance led to severe turbulence in early 1997. On 25 March 1997, four days after the financial Premiers' Conference had failed to resolve the level and distribution of financial assistance to the states and territories, Treasurer Sheldon stated to the Parliament that:

> ...following the collapse of last week's financial Premiers Conference, the days ·of consultation over Commonwealth-state financial relations may well be over. The Commonwealth has adopted the stance that what they say goes, and there will be no consultation...
>
> ...this is the first time that this [i.e. a failure to make a resolution] has happened in the history of the Premiers' Conference and represents a significant deterioration in Commonwealth-state financial relations, arising directly as a result of the intransigence of the Commonwealth Government.[90]

Owing to the Commonwealth's dominant position, the states and territories really had no choice but to accept the Commonwealth's terms. The collapsed Premiers Conference would serve as another milestone in the

---

[90]   Sheldon, J., 1997, op. cit.

increasingly fraught financial relationship between the Commonwealth and states and territories that continues to cause tension and blur accountabilities, encouraging the "blame game", to the detriment of the nation.

The 1997-98 Queensland budget papers contain very strong criticism of the Commonwealth—that is, the Howard government, which incidentally was also a Liberal-National Coalition government. For example, the budget papers noted:

> In recent years, the Commonwealth has exercised its fiscal dominance…
> to further disadvantage the States and Territories. In particular, the
> Commonwealth has significantly reduced its payments to the States in
> the interests of national fiscal restraint, but at the same time generally
> has failed to apply the same discipline to its spending…
>
> …While Commonwealth own-purpose outlays have increased by a
> cumulative 17% in real per capita terms over this period, grants to the
> States have actually declined by a cumulative 9%.[91]

Additional turbulence came a few months after the handing down of the 1997-98 state budget. On 5 August 1997, the High Court, in the case *Ha v New South Wales*, ruled that state franchise fees were unconstitutional. This was because they were effectively excise taxes—that is, taxes on production—and hence the sole prerogative of the Commonwealth under section 90 of the Constitution. Franchise fees on service stations or tobacco sellers, for example, were effectively excise taxes because they were calibrated to the volume of sales and hence production, to which excise taxes apply. As a result the Commonwealth had to impose temporary arrangements, whereby the Commonwealth collected excise on behalf of the states. Incidentally, the High Court decision on franchise fees and the uncertainty it created for state revenue was a primary motivation for state and territory governments accepting the need for a Goods and Services Tax (GST) in the late 1990s, during the first term of the Beattie government, as discussed in the next chapter.

---

[91] Queensland Treasury, 1997a, op. cit., p. 110.

The High Court decision also had implications for Queensland government expenses. Queensland's lack of a petrol tax meant that, when the Commonwealth imposed fuel excise across Australia, petrol prices would increase in Queensland. So, in 1997, the Queensland government introduced a fuel subsidy, technically a rebate of federal excise, set at 8.354 c/litre. This subsidy came at a high cost and was considered dubious by many observers, considering the environmental impact of greenhouse gas emissions. Unsurprisingly, this subsidy was later discontinued, by the Bligh government in 2009, when it was facing immense budgetary pressures, as we shall see in Chapter 6.

The government wisely gets out of insurance and banking

Despite its short reign, the Borbidge government did manage to earn a major achievement: the privatisation of Suncorp after its merger with the Metway Bank and the Queensland Industry Development Corporation (QIDC). It was a courageous act because it subjected the government to intense criticism, particularly from the *Australian Financial Review*. Critics labelled the newly merged Suncorp Metway as Banana Bank and Queensland Inc, a reference to the so-called WA Inc, the dubious network of politicians and business people in freewheeling 1980s WA. The *Financial Review* went so far as to have caricatures of Sheldon and Borbidge dressed as B1 and B2 from the Bananas in Pyjamas from the ABC children's show *Play School*, and opposition members mocked the Premier and Treasurer in the Parliament with these labels.[92]

In the mid-1990s Queensland was out of step with other states in still owning financial businesses such as Suncorp Insurance and Finance and QIDC, a state development bank. Suncorp was the dominant insurance business in Queensland, but with only a small presence in other states. It had started its life as the SGIO in 1917, before being corporatised and becoming Suncorp in the mid-eighties.

---

[92] Queensland Parliament, 1996, *Record of Proceedings (Hansard)*, 11 July 1996, p. 1576.

Interviewed for this book, Joan Sheldon recalled that she had two significant visits very early in her term as Treasurer. One visit was from Sir Leo Hielscher, in his capacity as QTC Chair. In opposition, Treasurer Sheldon had signalled she was interested in selling Suncorp and QIDC. Sir Leo, who was supportive of selling Suncorp and QIDC, wanted to know whether she would now do so as Treasurer. Another important visit, in her first week as Treasurer, was from the then Chairman of Suncorp, who requested an equity injection from the government in the range of $250-300 million. Sheldon could not see a need for government involvement in insurance, and she was concerned about diverting budget money from other uses. Also, according to her *Queensland Speaks* interview, she had been advised that competition in the insurance industry was getting more intense, and so Suncorp would likely need future equity injections from the state government.

Regarding QIDC, Sheldon considered that it was clearly in a position where it could be sold and its original rationale no longer applied. While it had a regional development focus, QIDC performed account keeping and lending services that other banks could readily provide. It was relatively small, with the Commission of Audit noting it was only "two percent of the size of the average major bank."[93]

The Fitzgerald Commission of Audit supported Sheldon's plan to sell off Suncorp and QIDC and observed in August 1996:

> Government owned financial institutions, both Commonwealth and State, have long been a feature of the Australian financial system. Overall, experience with these institutions has been less than positive, with most jurisdictions either privatising or winding up their institutions over the past decade, often in distressed circumstances. In this respect, Queensland stands against the national trend with a significant and continuing involvement in this sector.[94]

93   Fitzgerald, V. et al., op. cit., p. 402.
94   Ibid., p. 399.

A major benefit of privatisation would be to take risky financial businesses off the state government's balance sheet, avoiding the risk of failures akin to the Victorian and SA state banks. There were also issues of competitive neutrality and the efficiency, or rather lack of efficiency, of government-owned financial institutions that were relevant. The businesses were "high cost producers of financial services relative to market standards."[95] Also, Treasurer Sheldon was conscious of the need to recapitalise Suncorp and QIDC—that is, investing money into them to increase assets and the level of equity relative to debt on the balance sheet. Sheldon could not see a justification for using the state government's balance sheet to recapitalise financial institutions.

Given the complexity of the privatisation, Queensland Treasury and Treasurer Sheldon deserve credit for arranging it. The Reserve Bank of Australia in a 1997 *RBA Bulletin* article outlined the transactions:

> Suncorp and the Queensland Industry Development Corporation were wholly owned by the Queensland Government. These businesses were merged with Metway Bank Limited on 1 December 1996. Consideration received by the Queensland Government for contributing these businesses to the merger comprised $698 million and 142.8 million shares in Metway Bank Limited. Subsequently the Government sold down part of its shareholding for $610 million, to be received in two instalments in 1997/98 and 1998/99.[96]

In September 1997, the Borbidge government engineered a highly successful float of the merged company by selling notes that could be exchanged for shares, which were over-subscribed and which gave preferential treatment to Queenslanders. Overall, the privatisation returned proceeds of around $1.3 billion.

The purchase of Metway and its merger with Suncorp was seen by the government as important, not just because it added to and strengthened

---

[95] Ibid.
[96] Reserve Bank of Australia, 1997, "Privatisation in Australia", *RBA Bulletin*, p. 16.

Suncorp, but because it prevented the bank from leaving Queensland. The Chairman of Metway, Frank Haly, had met with Sheldon early in her term as Treasurer, and he had alerted her to the possibility of Metway being bought by another bank and its headquarters leaving Queensland. Sheldon thought it was important to have as many corporate headquarters in Queensland as possible, as she considered head offices helped to maintain a network of capable business people in the state.

There were some dramatic moments in the privatisation process, particularly the competition with St George for the purchase of Metway toward the end of 1996. At one time during the auction, which was held at the Brisbane Convention Centre, Under Treasurer McTaggart urgently phoned Treasurer Sheldon. St George Bank had matched the Queensland government's bid price for Metway and McTaggart was requesting authority to bid higher. After conferring with the Premier by phone, Sheldon called McTaggart back and said he could go just one cent per share higher, but that was the limit. Fortunately, that proved sufficient, as St George would not match it.

Another moment of high drama came when the government was seeking authority to pursue the sale of Suncorp Metway in the Parliament, by introducing a bill which also allowed for the sale of the Queensland government's shares in Bank of Queensland. Treasurer Sheldon was giving the second reading speech for the bill when independent MP Liz Cunningham, whose support the government needed to get the bill passed, came up to Treasurer Sheldon on the floor of the Parliament. Cunningham dropped the bill on the floor, and said she could not support it. She was concerned that, if the government sold its share of the Bank, the Bank would close its Calliope branch, Calliope being Liz Cunningham's hometown in the Wide Bay-Gladstone region of Queensland. The speaker called an adjournment and the government had an emergency meeting in the cabinet room, where McTaggart and other Treasury officials were waiting. To get the bill passed, the authority for the sale of the Bank of Queensland shares had to be removed from the bill. Suncorp, QIDC and Metway were finally merged on 1 December 1996.

Regarding the float, Professor John Wanna, formerly of Griffith University and now at ANZSOG, commented at the time that:

> The fact that Queenslanders received favoured treatment which allowed them to purchase larger portions of notes was locally popular but damaged the pro-business reputation of the government in southern markets.[97]

It is unclear whether this mattered or had any material impact, particularly given the government only had less than a year in office after the privatisation. Broadly speaking, the strong criticism of the Borbidge government for the Suncorp privatisation appears misplaced in hindsight. For example, consider the criticism from Labor opposition member for Sandgate Gordon Nuttall in July 1996, who incidentally was later convicted for corruption:

> If they think they have a big bank, they are kidding themselves. If they read all the economic advice and commentary on that issue, they will find that the experts are saying that that new institution could be swallowed up tomorrow. The big banks such as the National Australia Bank, the Commonwealth, ANZ and Westpac will sit back and wait. When the new bank gets into trouble and the shares fall through the floor, those big banks will come in over the top and take it. Where will the head office be then?[98]

By successfully purchasing Metway and merging it with Suncorp, Sheldon had created a financial institution that was viable on its own. And its headquarters have remained in Brisbane to this day, although many senior positions are based in Sydney.

---

[97] John Wanna, 1998 "Queensland: July to December 1997", *Political Chronicles*, p. 269
[98] Queensland Parliament, 1996, op. cit., p. 1576.

Assessment of the Borbidge government

Given it lasted only around two-and-a-half years, the Borbidge government typically does not receive favourable reviews from commentators. It was a government that seemed ill fated from the start. In its first year, the government had to refer to the Criminal Justice Commission a Memorandum of Understanding it had made with the Queensland Police Union while in opposition. Following this, a series of events occurred that eventually led to a no confidence motion in Attorney-General Denver Beanland being passed by the Parliament. And, in early 2008, Borbidge dismissed one minister and two others resigned on the same day, reportedly over matters relating to an extra-marital affair. In an essay in the UQ Press book *Premiers of Queensland*, political scientist Rae Wear was critical of the government's regard for the Westminster system. In addition to suggesting that, in not dismissing Attorney-General Beanland after a no-confidence vote, Premier Borbidge had gone against the Westminster tradition, Wear noted:

> The Westminster system was also a casualty of increasing politicisation of the public service, despite early assurances to the contrary by Borbidge. One of the first tasks embarked upon by the Borbidge Government was to replace Labor appointees in the public service and statutory authorities with Coalition supporters.[99]

In addition to replacing Gerard Bradley with Doug McTaggart as Under Treasurer, the Borbidge government also replaced the PSMC with an Office of the Public Service headed by Kevin Wolff, who was viewed by some observers as a "political appointee".[100] Also, it has been alleged that several public servants, including Jo-Ann Miller, later Labor member for Bundamba, and Jan Williams were on a Borbidge government "hit list" and were forced out.[101] As discussed elsewhere in this book, such politicisation is regrettable,

---

[99] Rae Wear, 2003, "Robert Edward Borbidge; In the Shadow of Bjelke-Petersen", in Murphy, D., Joyce, R., Cribb, M. and Wear, R. (eds), *The Premiers of Queensland*, University of Queensland Press, p. 396.

[100] Colley, L., 2009, op. cit., p. 12.

[101] Mike Fishpool, 1997, "Departure of senior PS women sparks row", *Courier-Mail*, 7 March 1997.

and actually works against the long-term interests of governments.

Also, any assessment of the Borbidge government should keep in mind that one of its election commitments has possibly had long-term adverse implications for the state. By rejecting the second motorway to the Gold Coast in favour of an upgrade of the current highway, it arguably only temporarily forestalled the inevitable capacity constraints that would eventually emerge, and which Goss government Transport Minister David Hamill had warned about. Interviewed for this book, David Hamill noted he had seen a transport model forecast that a widened existing motorway would reach full capacity by 2012. This appears to have been a reasonably accurate forecast. In early 2016, the Gold Coast Mayor Tom Tate said there was merit in considering a second motorway to the Gold Coast.[102] And, somewhat ironically, in the 2017 election campaign the Liberal National Party supported an alternative route to the M1.

Whatever judgments are made of the Borbidge government for its political missteps and its transport policy, it deserves credit for maintaining Queensland's traditionally sound public finances, running budget surpluses (Table 3.2), and for making hard decisions, including the Suncorp-QIDC privatisation that were in the best interests of the state. In the assessment of the Borbidge government's Under Treasurer Doug McTaggart:

> Rob and Joan were courageous, and I mean that in the right sense.

Certainly, they appeared willing to make tough decisions on revenue and spending in the interests of fiscal sustainability. The Borbidge government did very well to cut back on current outlays and return total outlays to sustainable rates of growth, after the 15 percent blow out in 1995-96 that was largely attributable to budget decisions made by the previous Goss government in its final budget (Table 3.3).

---

[102] Tony Moore, 2016, "Second route to Gold Coast should be considered: Tom Tate", *Brisbane Times*, 2 February 2016, available via www.brisbanetimes.com.au.

Table 3.3 Borbidge government's budgetary record compared with final two years of Goss government's

	1994-95 (Goss) $ million	1995-96 (Goss) $ million	1996-97 (Borbidge) $ million	1997-98 (Borbidge) $ million
Current outlays	9,012	10,230	10,003	10,413
Capital outlays	1,479	1,835	2,171	2,323
Total outlays	10,492	12,065	12,174	12,735
Revenue	12,164	13,091	13,390	13,827
Current surplus	2,604	2,315	2,946	3,009
Total surplus	**1,672**	**1,153**	**1,216**	**1,092**
Revenue growth	3.2%	7.6%	2.3%	3.3%
Expenses growth	0.0%	15.0%	0.9%	4.6%

Source: ABS GFS, cat. no. 5512.0, various issues.

At the June 1998 election, the Borbidge government fell victim to several factors, including a popular Labor leader Peter Beattie who was a master showman and media performer, and the rise of the One Nation party since Pauline Hanson's emergence on the national scene, following her shock win in the federal seat of Oxley in the 1996 federal election. One Nation was able to capitalise on dissatisfaction, which was particularly strong in regional areas, with the gun buyback initiated by the Howard government and supported by the states and territories following the Port Arthur massacre in April 1996. The buyback was implemented on the ground by state and territory governments, and several state, territory and federal politicians received threats of harm. At one stage, Treasurer Sheldon was under police protection. One Nation ended up winning nine seats at the 1998 election, mainly gained in regional seats taken from the Borbidge government, costing the government power. Labor, led by Peter Beattie, formed government with the support of independent Peter Wellington, who also later played an important role in the Palaszczuk Labor government's path to power in 2015.

4

BEATTIE PRESIDES OVER THE START OF THE DEBT BUILD UP

The showman and the scholar

In June 1998, the ill-fated Borbidge government was replaced by a Labor government led by Peter Beattie, formerly a Health Minister in the dying months of the Goss government following the shock July 1995 election result. Beattie was of the same generation as Wayne Goss, being born one year later in 1952, and was likewise a lawyer before he entered politics. However, he was a much better politician than Goss ever was, and went on to decisively win three more elections in 2001, 2004 and 2006, serving as Premier for over nine years compared with Goss's six years. By the end of his nine years, Beattie had earned a reputation for media management, particularly during times of crises, of which there were several during his premiership. These included an electricity crisis, when the state experienced brown outs in 2004, and a water crisis, during which Brisbane was less than twelve months away from running out of drinking water.

Premier Beattie initially appointed David Hamill, member for Ipswich, as Treasurer. Hamill was a 40-year old Rhodes Scholar who was a protégé of former national ALP leader and Governor-General Bill Hayden. Hamill had previously served as Minister of Transport in the Goss government, and was instrumental in the advancement of the new Gold Coast motorway project that was a factor in costing the Goss government power—even though the huge levels of congestion we now see on the M1 suggest Hamill put forward the correct policy at the time.

Hamill was trained in political science and, prior to entering the Queensland Parliament in 1983, had experience as an adviser to Bill Hayden, then federal Leader of the Opposition. Hamill appeared to be a very good choice for Treasurer, but he lasted only one term as Treasurer and he did not recontest his seat at the 2001 election. His term was eventful and controversial. For instance, he had to stand aside for the 1999-00 budget, which Premier Beattie had to deliver instead. This was due to a political controversy over the granting of an internet gaming licence, for which he was later cleared of any wrongdoing by the Auditor-General. While only serving one term as Treasurer, Hamill participated in at least two fateful decisions that ultimately had profound effects on Queensland's future public finances.

The Commonwealth flexes its muscles over the Intergovernmental Agreement and GST

In the late 1990s, the Commonwealth was planning a revamp of Australia's tax system and federal financial relations, and this culminated in the Inter-governmental Agreement (IGA) that brought in the GST on 1 July 2000. The Howard government had developed the *A New Tax System* (ANTS) package that it took to the 1998 election, which was largely fought on the issue of the GST. While the Howard government received a large swing against it in the 1998 election, it was nonetheless returned to power.

Arguably, ANTS and the IGA would never have come to fruition if the *Ha v NSW* High Court case, discussed in the previous chapter, had not put state and territory revenues at risk by invalidating franchise fees levied by state and territory governments. The Commonwealth had imposed temporary arrangements, whereby it stepped in to levy excise taxes on a range of products across Australia, but at uniform rates nationwide.

Money was then be remitted to state and territory governments as revenue replacement payments.

The Borbidge government had created a problem for the future when it introduced an expensive fuel subsidy of 8.354 cents per litre, lest Queensland motorists experience an increase in fuel payments. At the time, it was able to pay for the subsidy out of the revenue replacement payments—for petrol franchise fees it never levied in the first place—effectively just restoring the pre-*Ha* case situation for Queensland motorists. This was appropriate at the time, but with respect to the fuel subsidy, Queensland was then placed in a difficult position by the IGA that was signed between the Commonwealth and the states and territories in 1999, which brought in the GST but ended the revenue replacement payments in July 2000. It had lost revenue replacement payments but was still committed to offsetting the federal fuel excise. That said, the underlying uncertainty to state revenues caused by the *Ha* case meant that the state government really had no alternative but to sign the IGA and receive a share of revenue from a GST.

State and territory governments were largely motivated to sign this by the prospect of the GST revenue being exclusively for their use, with the allocation to be determined by the CGC. The IGA was attractive because GST, being linked to consumption expenditure, was a source of revenue that would grow in line with the economy, and initially the states and territories believed the GST revenue would provide them greater autonomy. They effectively had to sign the IGA to lock in what appeared to be a growing and secure revenue source, conscious as they were that a previously substantial source of revenue, the franchise fees, was lost, and they would have to otherwise rely on the goodwill of the Commonwealth to provide them with revenue replacement payments.

Peter Beattie, the other state premiers and territory chief ministers, and Prime Minister John Howard signed the IGA on 24 June 1999. The state and territory leaders agreed to their states and territories accepting shares of

GST revenue subject to a number of conditions, including among others:

- abolishing bed taxes from 1 July 2000, financial institutions duty and stamp duties on market securities from 1 July 2001, and the bank accounts debit tax by 1 July 2005;

- reviewing a range of other stamp duties by 2005; and

- introducing a First Home Owners Scheme to offset the impact of the GST on the cost of new houses.[103]

So the Intergovernmental agreement did not give the states and territory governments as much freedom as they may have hoped for, as they were directed to abolish particular revenue sources and to spend money on a First Home Owners Scheme. As noted above, the states and territories really had no choice but to sign the IGA and accept the conditions. In a 2007 conference paper, David Hamill, who as Queensland Treasurer was a key player in the negotiations of the IGA, noted:

> The Commonwealth presented the final form of the IGA to the States and Territories as a *fait accompli*. Despite claiming the new arrangements as a significant reform of federal-State financial relations, the IGA's terms were steeped in the way Australian fiscal federalism had been conducted since the passage of the uniform tax legislation in 1942. Indeed, the Commonwealth's plan was virtually identical to that of 1942. That is, in return for their relinquishing the ability to raise certain of their own-source taxes, compliant States would be rewarded through their participation in the pool of revenue generated by uniform Commonwealth taxation. With the States again ceding a measure of their fiscal autonomy, and hence their fiscal capability, in return for a share of a growing revenue stream, albeit liable to conditions imposed by the Commonwealth, the ANTS package and its implementation should be seen as the Australian federation taking yet another step along the path of centralism.[104]

---

[103] Commonwealth of Australia et al., 1999, *Intergovernmental Agreement on the Reform of Commonwealth-State Financial Relations*, available via www.coag.gov.au.

[104] David Hamill, 2007, "W(h)ither Federalism?", *Proceedings of the Nineteenth Conference of the Sir Samuel Griffith Society*, Chapter 5, p. 46.

Finally, the two-year transitional arrangements under the IGA arguably disadvantaged Queensland because they required that states and territories would be placed in at least the same budgetary position as before, and would not be better or worse off. This meant that states which had taxes that Queensland did not have, such as NSW and Victoria with a fuel excise, would be compensated by a larger GST share than they would otherwise deserve. Hence, for these two years, Queensland had a temporarily lower share of GST revenue than it would have had otherwise.

A Charter of Social and Fiscal Responsibility for a "Smart State"

Queensland's fiscal performance during Treasurer Hamill's term was sound, with two operating surpluses, and a net operating deficit in 2000-01 largely due to special factors, such as the collapse of HIH Insurance and lower than anticipated investment earnings (Table 4.1).[105] Taking into account net capital expenditure, Treasure Hamill recorded three fiscal deficits. It appears the surge in capital spending, labelled gross fixed capital formation (GFCF) in the GFS statistics, in 1999-00, which meant there was a sharp drop in 2001-02, was related to road infrastructure investment.[106]

---

[105] Queensland Treasury, 2001, *State Budget 2001-02: Budget Statement*, budget paper no. 2, p. 17.
[106] Queensland Treasury, 2000, *State Budget 2000-01: Budget Overview*, budget paper no. 2, p. 22.

Table 4.1 Budget outcomes under Treasurer David Hamill in the Beattie government

	1998-99 $ million	1999-00 $ million	2000-01 $ million
A. Revenue	16,487	18,598	18,259
B. Total expenses	16,356	17,537	19,120
C. Net operating balance (A-B)	**131**	**1,061**	**-861**
D. Gross fixed capital formation	2,029	2,674	2,248
E. Depreciation (& other adjustments)	1,306	1,489	1,436
F. Net acquisition of non-financial assets (D-E)	723	1,185	812
G. Net lending (C-F)	**-592**	**-124**	**-1,673**
Indicators			
Net lending as percentage of GSP	-0.6%	-0.1%	-1.4%
Revenue growth	n.a.	12.8%	-1.8%
Expenses growth	n.a.	7.2%	9.0%
GFCF growth	n.a.	31.8%	-15.9%
Revenue growth - real per capita	n.a.	8.2%	-9.1%
Expenses growth - real per capita	n.a.	2.9%	1.0%
GFCF growth - real per capita	n.a.	26.4%	-22.1%

Source: ABS GFS, cat. no. 5512.0, various issues. Note: prepared on new GFS accrual accounting basis. Also the CPI spike in 2000-01 is due to the introduction of the GST and hence real growth figures in this year should be interpreted with this in mind, noting GST payments will be refunded.

Hamill described himself as a "pretty conservative Treasurer" and he was happy to follow the Goss government's approach with one major exception. Hamill noted:

> Whilst I broadly kept in line with the Goss government approach, I was happy to take a recommendation from the Borbidge Government's Commission of Audit report. The Commission of Audit considered it to be a narrow view that government should only borrow money for infrastructure where that infrastructure generated income that

could service the debt.

I argued that it was permissible for governments to borrow money for capital assets providing the debt was repaid over the economic life of the asset. This was important in the context of budget management at the time: the operating budget was very tight, but there was significant capacity to borrow if the government chose to do so. There was no way that we would ever borrow for recurrent spending, however the revised policy around borrowing for capital assets recognised that there are may intangible returns from assets in addition to strictly commercial returns.

Hamill certainly was on sound economic ground following the Fitzgerald Commission of Audit's recommendation, and adopting essentially the same fiscal principles as the Borbidge government. The Goss government fiscal principle on borrowing was very strict and would rule out funding many infrastructure investments that would pass the cost-benefit analysis. However, it may have been the case that a strict rule was necessary to keep Queensland's public finances under control, given the temptations to spend money and buy votes that face politicians. It may be argued that the deterioration in Queensland's finances was partly related to the abandonment of the strict rule in the mid to late 1990s by both the Borbidge and Beattie governments.

In the 1999-00 budget, the Beattie government introduced a *Charter of Social and Fiscal Responsibility*. Note the insertion of "social" and its placement before "fiscal" in the charter's title, suggesting a less strict approach to public finances (see Box 4.1 for full text of the charter).

The new Charter adopted the so-called golden rule of public finance, prohibiting borrowing for recurrent expenses, but allowing borrowing for infrastructure investment:

Box 4.1 The Beattie government's 1999 Charter of Social and Fiscal Responsibility

1. Competitive tax environment: The Government will ensure that State taxes and charges remain competitive with the other States and Territories.

2. Affordable service provision: The Government will ensure that its level of service provision is sustainable by maintaining an overall General Government operating surplus, as measured in Government Finance Statistics terms.

3. Capital funding: Borrowings or other financial arrangements will only be undertaken for capital investments and only where these can be serviced within the operating surplus, consistent with maintain a AAA credit rating.

4. Managing financial risk: The Government will ensure that the State's financial assets cover all accruing and expected future liabilities of the General Government Sector.

5. Building the State's net worth: The Government will at least maintain and seek to increase Total State Net Worth.

Borrowings or other financial arrangements will only be undertaken for capital investments and only where these can be serviced within the operating surplus, consistent with maintaining a AAA credit rating.[107]

It fell upon Premier Beattie to formally announce the Charter of Social and Fiscal Responsibility as he had to temporarily assume the role of Treasurer and deliver the 1999-2000 state budget after Treasurer Hamill had to temporarily step aside due to investigations into the so-called Net Bet affair. This was a pivotal budget, as it also marked the introduction of Beattie's "Smart State" agenda, the first of his big spending plans. Beattie clearly distinguished his government from previous Queensland governments, including that of Goss's, with a budget speech eschewing economic rationalism:

---

[107] Queensland Treasury, 1999a, *State Budget 1999-2000: Budget Overview*, budget paper 2, p. 3.

> The Charter is a unique document because, for the first time, it commits a Government not only to adhere to strict fiscal principles, but also to deliver on social policy objectives.
>
> In other words, a strong financial position is not an end in itself, but a means to achieving a broader range of objectives necessary to advance the prosperity, welfare and quality of life of all Queenslanders.[108]

These were fine words, and from a public policy perspective, the consideration of social policy objectives is sound, and it would obviously be wrong to see a strong financial position as an end in itself. But in this fateful budget, the Beattie government laid the groundwork for the fiscal deterioration that Queensland saw in the later 2000s. This was because truly living up to the new Charter's goals would require ongoing fiscal management and public administration of a high standard that would prevent poor investment projects being funded. Arguably, Queensland had something close to that in the first half of the Beattie government. It had a relatively conservative first Treasurer in David Hamill. And Hamill was succeeded as Treasurer by a man Peter Beattie later described as Queensland's best ever Treasurer, the Labor stalwart known as the Fox, Terry Mackenroth, who presided over very strong fiscal outcomes. [109] But as we shall see, the high standard of fiscal management did not last beyond the mid-2000s, and Queensland suffered from the discretion provided by the new fiscal principles. That said, there were worrying signs even during Mackenroth's time as Treasurer, as discussed in the next section.

Three record surpluses under Mackenroth

Premier Beattie appointed 51-year old Terry Mackenroth as Treasurer following David Hamill's retirement at the 17 February 2001 election. Mackenroth had been serving as Deputy Premier since November the

---

[108] Queensland Treasury, 1999b, State Budget 1999-2000: Budget Speech, budget paper 1, p. 20.
[109] Peter Beattie, 2016, "Peter Beattie book extract: Reform of the federation", *Sydney Morning Herald*, 20 February 2016, available via www.smh.com.au.

previous year, and would now serve as Treasurer as well. Unlike many others who had served in Labor ministries since Goss, Mackenroth had a traditional blue-collar Labor background. He had a welding qualification and had worked in a steel fabrication business.

Mackenroth presided over three record budget surpluses in dollar terms (Table 4.2)—and as a percentage of GSP for the comparable budgetary data since the late 1990s—driven to a large extent by strong economic growth and a strong property market, which drove up tax revenue, especially stamp duty on property transactions, surging coal exports (due to volume and price increases) which drove up royalty revenue, and strong investment returns worldwide which the state government benefited from due to its large investment portfolio. To illustrate, in the 2004-05 budget, the Queensland government estimated a net operating balance for 2003-04 of nearly $2.4 billion compared with the budgeted $153 million. For that financial year, although estimated expenses of $22.1 billion exceeded the budget forecast by around $900 million, revenue came in $3.1 billion higher than expected.[110] So favourable economic circumstances played a large part in the three record surpluses recorded during Mackenroth's term as Treasurer.

Furthermore, while the strong budget balances recorded during Mackenroth's time were highly commendable, expenses growth accelerated towards the end of his term as Treasurer. Also, it should be acknowledged that he was Beattie's Deputy Premier at the time commitments were made to the SEQ Infrastructure Plan, which foreshadowed large amounts of spending over ten years. So his record needs to be qualified somewhat. Also, while Mackenroth was Treasurer, the Beattie government undertook some fairly dubious transactions with its GOCs, as discussed below. This failure to adhere to best practice in the oversight of GOCs should be taken into account in any assessment of Treasurer Mackenroth.

---

[110] Queensland Treasury, 2004, *State Budget 2004-05: Budget Strategy and Outlook*, budget paper no. 2, p. 5.

Table 4.2 Budget outcomes under Treasurer Terry Mackenroth in the Beattie government

	2001-02 $ million	2002-03 $ million	2003-04 $ million	2004-05 $ million	2005-06 $ million
A. Revenue	18,857	20,255	25,211	27,632	30,149
B. Total expenses	19,759	20,243	21,876	23,724	26,453
C. Net operating balance (A-B)	-902	12	3,335	3,908	3,696
D. Gross fixed capital formation	2,248	1,596	1,909	2,465	2,723
E. Depreciation (& other adjustments)	1,540	1,440	1,409	1,412	1,487
F. Net acquisition of non-financial assets (D-E)	708	156	500	1,053	1,236
G. Net lending (C-F)	-1,609	-144	2,835	2,854	2,460
Indicators					
Net lending as percentage of GSP	-1.2%	-0.1%	1.9%	1.7%	1.3%
Revenue growth	3.3%	7.4%	24.5%	9.6%	9.1%
Expenses growth	3.3%	2.4%	8.1%	8.4%	11.5%
GFCF growth	0.0%	-29.0%	19.6%	29.1%	10.5%
Revenue growth - real per capita	-2.0%	2.1%	18.0%	4.5%	2.4%
Expenses growth - real per capita	-1.9%	-2.6%	2.4%	3.4%	4.6%
GFCF growth - real per capita	-5.1%	-32.5%	13.4%	23.1%	3.6%

Source: ABS GFS, cat. no. 5512.0, various issues.

From the 2003-04 state budget, Mackenroth's second as Treasurer, the Beattie government started setting out its vision for Queensland's economy in specific economic strategy chapters of the budget. These emphasised the importance of government investments in human capital, innovation and infrastructure as drivers of growth. These economic strategy chapters were presented as justifying policy measures such as the broader Smart State agenda and a new preparatory year of schooling (aligning Queensland with the other states).

The generosity that crept into the Beattie government budgets over time has to be seen in the context of an economy that was undergoing a resources boom, with a surge in commodity prices and exploration and construction activity, including the development of the coal seam gas industry. These were years in which Queensland's GSP and gross state income were growing at a very high rate (Figure 4.1). It may well have been thought by ministers at the time that the good times would last forever, even though history warns us that they usually do not.

Figure 4.1 Historical real GSP and real gross state income growth, Queensland

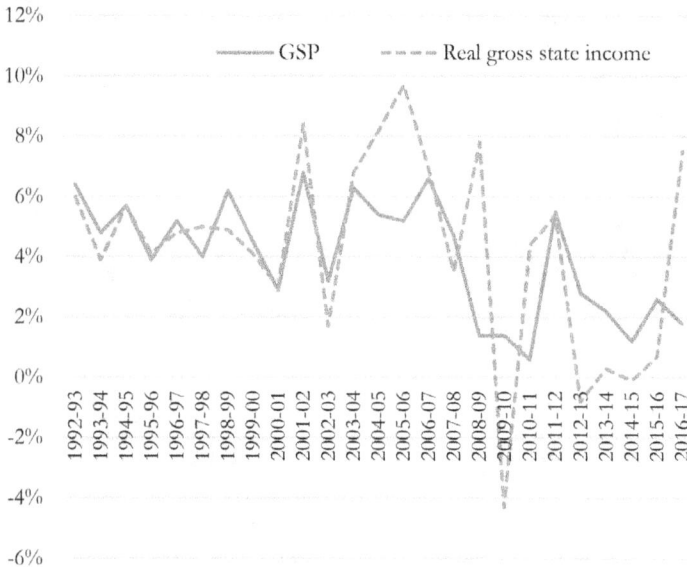

Source: ABS, Australian National Accounts: State Accounts, cat. no. 5220.0.

Mackenroth was very much aligned with Beattie in his desire to improve public services and his willingness to undertake grand policy schemes, such as the SEQ Infrastructure Plan and the Smart State agenda. In his last budget speech delivered on 7 June 2005, Treasurer Mackenroth announced:

> This Budget represents a landmark in the delivery of our vision for Queensland by providing for:
>
> - a first ever long-term plan for infrastructure development for South East Queensland including an additional investment of approximately $2 billion over four years for the first phase of the plan;
> - more than $470 million over four years to support a 10 year Smart State Strategy; and
> - comprehensive measures to assist the most disadvantaged people in our communities, including an additional $180 million over four years for disability services, further funding to support our child safety reforms, initiatives to improve indigenous health and a package of initiatives to address homelessness.
>
> In addition, this Budget provides an unprecedented commitment to the progressive abolition of six stamp duties together with a significant land tax relief and simplification package.[111]

Treasurer Mackenroth considered the state could afford such a generous budget based on the good work the Beattie government had done to date in budget management. But what Mackenroth did not foresee was that his successors would add to this additional spending with new programs and projects, and that the Beattie government's legacy of strong budget management up to that point would be squandered after Mackenroth was no longer Treasurer.

Overall, owing to his record surpluses and the fact that he left government in mid-2005 before the massive increases in debt, Mackenroth should be favourably regarded as Treasurer, if not as the best ever, arguably an honour which, for the last few decades of Queensland's history, should be given to Goss government Treasurer Keith De Lacy.

---

[111] Queensland Treasury, 2005, *2005-06 State Budget: Budget Speech*, budget paper no. 1, pp. 1-2.

Electricity crisis

Peter Beattie's first political near-death experience came with the 2004 electricity crisis. The crisis began with severe storms in SEQ in the last week of January 2004. This resulted in tens of thousands of customers of Energex (the government-owned electricity distribution business servicing SEQ, now part of Energy Queensland) being without power for several hours longer than usual. At its peak, around 120,000 households were without power.[112]

As a result of the blackouts associated with the late January storms, and wider concerns that had been around for some time around network reliability, on 1 March 2004 the Beattie government announced an independent inquiry into the electricity distribution system. The review was required to assess the reliability of the network, evaluate the adequacy of capital and operational expenditures of Energex and Ergon (the government-owned distribution business servicing regional Queensland, now also part of Energy Queensland) and to evaluate internal systems and communications to the public.

Beattie appointed highly regarded PwC partner Darryl Somerville as chairperson of the Independent Panel for Electricity Distribution and Service Delivery for the 21st Century, which also included Electrical Safety Commissioner Jack Camp and electricity industry expert Steve Blanch as panel members. The Independent Panel reported to the government in July 2004. It identified deficiencies in network infrastructure, parts of which were many decades old and needed urgent replacement. In 2016, comments to *The Australian* regarding the parallels between Queensland's electricity crisis and that gripping South Australia at the time, Peter Beattie noted:

> The Queensland problem was that my government inherited an antiquated power infrastructure that had not been modernised

---

[112] Darryl Somerville et al., 2004, *Summary Report of the Independent Panel for Electricity Distribution and Service Delivery for the 21st Century*, Queensland Government Department of Natural Resources, Mines and Energy, p. 24.

for decades to keep tune with the revitalisation of the CBD and surrounding suburbs.[113]

A large part of the problem, according to the Somerville inquiry report, was that Energex had cut back its maintenance program. As a result, power outages due to failures of cross-arms on power poles nearly doubled from 53 in 1997 to 99 in 2003 in SEQ.[114] The independent panel considered this "inappropriately high."[115] It found that Energex "some years ago" had discontinued its low-voltage cross arm inspection program for "financial reasons".[116] While the independent panel was undertaking its review, Energex decided to reinstate the program, from 1 July 2004.

Some critics alleged the Beattie government bore part of the responsibility for the failure to modernise the electricity system, as it had already been in government for 5½ years when the electricity crisis began, and it had been extracting substantial dividends, including special dividends, from the electricity businesses. In his final report to the Queensland Parliament, retiring Auditor-General Len Scanlan observed:

> In recent years, I have reported on the payment of special dividends by GOCs. In particular, I outlined my concerns over these dividends being sourced from Asset Revaluation Reserves. The payment of special dividends was discontinued by the Shareholding Ministers in 2003-04.[117]

For example, in a 2002-03 report to the Parliament, the Auditor-General noted that in 2001-02, in addition to paying an ordinary dividend of around $94 million, Energex, the SEQ electricity distribution GOC, paid a special dividend of $150 million. This was based on an unrealised capital gain and was sourced from the Asset Revaluation Reserve. The Auditor-General commented:

---

[113] Graham Lloyd, 2016, "Energy security: Peter Beattie, like Jay Weatherill, learned the hard way", *The Australian*, available via www.theaustralian.com.au.

[114] Somerville, D. et al., op. cit., p. 123.

[115] Ibid.

[116] Ibid.

[117] Queensland Audit Office, 2005, *Auditor-General's Report No. 7 2004-05*, p. 60.

The sourcing of a special dividend payment from the Asset Revaluation Reserve is an unusual transaction in terms of generally accepted accounting principles.[118]

The transaction did however comply with the relevant legislation and Energex's constitution.

However, the Independent Panel did not support the view that special dividend payments were responsible for under-investment in the network, considering that the businesses did have sufficient resources to invest in the network.[119] The Independent Panel's analysis of the issue is rather thin, however, at less than half a page; arguably it should have done more to refute the claimed impact of special dividends on Energex's capacity to maintain and invest in the network.[120] Instead of special dividends having an adverse impact on network investment, the Panel found instead that an intense focus on the bottom line, unrelated to the need to pay special dividends—a view which may be considered debatable—was responsible:

> In the case of ENERGEX, it is the Panel's view that this position has been reached because there has been too much focus over a considerable period on producing an improved financial result. While expenditure has certainly been reduced, the Panel believes that this has been at the expense of the condition of the network. It is now operating at a utilisation of about 76% whereas the prudent industry level is around 60% to 65%. The assets are stressed and this impacts on reliability.[121]

As a result, the Independent Panel concluded that:

> In short, there is a need for greater accountability and some catch up expenditure on both networks to bring them back to an acceptable condition.[122]

---

[118] Queensland Audit Office, 2003, *Auditor-General's Report No. 7 2002-03*, p. 9.
[119] Somerville, D. et al., op. cit., p. 6.
[120] Ibid., p. 202.
[121] Ibid., p. 8.
[122] Ibid.

Ultimately the level of investment that the businesses would need to make would be determined by the government's decision regarding the desired reliability of the system, a core concept in regulatory economics known as the level of service. The Independent Panel recommended the adoption of the so called N-1 reliability standard for Energex and Ergon that was used in other states. N-1 is a very strict standard for reliability. It means that there is sufficient redundancy in the system that load shedding is only required if two or more extreme events occur. The government announced that it would adopt this recommendation. The huge investment in the electricity network that followed by Energex and Ergon was necessitated by meeting this requirement. It ultimately resulted in large power price increases as the businesses, being regulated utilities, could recover for these expenditures, provided they were prudent and necessary, through electricity charges.

The impacts on the GOCs were felt immediately. For example, Energex proposed a 37 percent increase in its capital expenditure within the 2004-05 financial year, and a 20 percent increase in operational and maintenance expenditure.[123] There were consequently substantial impacts on state public finances. The crisis response required an increase in borrowings by the electricity businesses. These borrowings would have to be repaid by the distribution businesses, which would then charge the retail electricity businesses higher prices, which would then be passed on to households and businesses.

The government was quick to adopt the recommendations of the Independent Panel in full, demonstrating a strong commitment to resolving the crises. Arguably the government should have undertaken further analysis of the implications of the N-1 requirement. Subsequently, criticism emerged that the N-1 requirement was too stringent, and resulted in "gold plating" of the system.

---

[123] Peter Beattie, 2004, the Honourable Peter Beattie, 2004, *Electricity Fact Sheet Available for All Queenslanders*, media release of the Queensland Premier and Minister for Trade, 18 August 2004, available via www.statements.qld.gov.au.

In 2012, the Newman government's Independent Review Panel on Network Costs, led by former Ergon Energy CEO and Queensland Treasury official Tony Bellas, found that, regarding N-1 reliability standards:

> These standards were originally introduced to improve the reliability of the network but have driven excessive costs and resulted in a degree of over-engineering of the networks. The entrenching of the standards within State licences and through government direction have also limited the ability of the economic regulator, the Australian Energy Regulator (AER), to adequately assess the prudence of these investments.[124]

Responding to criticism of the N-1 requirement, the Newman government changed the requirement to a less prescriptive approach. Instead of requiring in-built redundancy to guarantee supply under the N-1 standard, the government would set service performance targets. A March 2014 Newman government Cabinet paper noted the change would involve:

> Moving from a requirement to plan transmission system augmentation to maintain all supply for any failure of a system element, to an approach which accepts there may be some loss of supply if there is a problem at times of peak demand, but limits the allowable extent of such outage exposures.[125]

It was expected this regulatory change would mean savings in network capital expenditure of $2 billion over fifteen years, and would result in lower electricity prices than otherwise.

Health crisis

The Beattie government's second crisis was in health. The health crisis began with allegations against Bundaberg Base Hospital doctor and Director of Surgery Jayant Patel about medical malpractice over the deaths of numerous

---

[124] Independent Review Panel on Network Costs, 2012, *Electricity Network Costs Review Final Report*, p. iv.
[125] Queensland Government, 2014a, *Reforming Queensland's electricity network reliability standards*, Cabinet Paper lodged by the Minister for Energy and Water Supply.

patients. A report in *The Age* newspaper later referred to an investigation over the deaths of 87 patients.[126] The story broke in March 2005, and Patel left Australia for the US in early April 2005, flying on a business class fare that was paid for by Queensland Health.

Two inquiries followed. The first inquiry was undertaken by Tony Morris QC, who recommended charging Patel with murder when he reported in mid-2005. However, the inquiry had to prematurely conclude, and its findings and recommendations were disallowed, after the Supreme Court found there was an apprehension of bias against two Queensland Health officials.[127]

The second inquiry, led by Geoffrey Davies QC, was a broader Queensland Public Hospitals Commission of Inquiry, commencing in September 2005. The findings of the Commission of Inquiry were wide-ranging and touched on many issues, including the administrative failure to check Patel's background and credentials, but also the issue of stressed public hospital budgets. The Commission's Final Report found that budget stress contributed to the Patel scandal:

> The Hospital budget contributed in two ways. The first was that, although a Director of Surgery is ordinarily, and should be, a registered specialist surgeon, a surgeon who had Australian specialist qualifications would have probably required an offer of salary and conditions more generous than Queensland Health would have permitted the Hospital to offer; and so also would an overseas trained specialist surgeon who would have been able to satisfy the Royal Australasian College of Surgeons that his qualifications and experience were sufficient for them to recommend that he be granted deemed specialist registration. It is unlikely that the Hospital would ever have obtained the money to pay this. The second aspect was the focus, dictated by the budget, upon elective surgery throughput. Dr Patel made himself so valuable in that respect that the administrators

---

[126] Jo Chandler, 2005, "The scandal of 'Dr Death'", *The Age*, May 28 2005, available at www. theage.com.au.

[127] Mark Todd, 2005, "Court edict kills inquiry into Patel", *Sydney Morning Herald*, 3 September 2005, available via www.smh.com.au.

were plainly reluctant to offend him, let alone investigate him.[128]

In October 2005, the Beattie government announced an ambitious Health Action Plan, committing it to "a major transformation and renewal of Queensland's public health system", which involved very large expenditure increases.[129] The plan included, among other initiatives:

- additional funding of $1.3 billion for four years to boost health system remuneration,

- additional recurrent funding of $157 million over four years for the Mater Hospital,

- additional funding of $134 million to Disabilities Services Queensland, which saw its budget for 2006-07 increase by over 22 percent (adding to the $180 million over four years committed in the 2005-06 budget); and

- additional funding of $54 million to treat spinal cord injuries.

The Health Action Plan was of such a scale that it required a budget update to accompany it. In its *Special Fiscal and Economic Statement* (SFES) mini-budget on 25 October 2005, the government committed to higher expenditures out to 2010-11, well beyond the then existing published budget forward estimates to 2008-09. Future commitments of spending beyond the forward estimates are risky given it is never clear what future expenditure priorities will emerge or whether revenues will continue to grow as expected.

The funding increase in the health portfolio announced in October 2005 was extraordinary, and there was more to come. The following year, in 2006, the Beattie government announced the building of three new hospitals: a new children's hospital in Brisbane and new university hospitals on the Gold and Sunshine Coasts. The planning for these new hospitals fell far short of best practice. As was pointed out by the

---

[128]   Geoffrey Davies QC, 2005, *Queensland Public Hospitals Commission of Inquiry Report*, p. 6.
[129]   Queensland Treasury, 2006, *State Budget 2006-07: Budget Strategy and Outlook*, budget paper no. 2, p. 62.

Auditor-General in 2014 regarding the three new hospitals announced by the Beattie government in August 2006:

> None of these projects can objectively demonstrate how the new hospitals will improve health outcomes in their communities compared to defined targets, because they did not identify and set a baseline for the benefits.[130]

The three hospitals were subject to large cost blowouts beyond forecasts in August 2006. In 2014, the Queensland Auditor-General found the costs of the Beattie government's three new hospitals were under-estimated by over $2 billion, and the final bill at over $5 billion was 77 percent higher than expected.[131] This was partly because the hospitals were built during the resources boom, which was elevating construction costs. But the larger problem was poor planning by Queensland Health. The Auditor-General found "the original [cost] estimates were unrealistic and not informed by business cases or detailed planning".[132] The three hospitals were subject to large cost blowouts.

With several billion dollars of additional spending committed to, the government was not going to be accused of not spending enough money to fix the health crisis. As the 2006-07 budget papers noted:

> ...Queensland Health's Budget in 2006-07 is estimated at $6.6 billion, which is a 24% increase on the 2005-06 Budget of $5.4 billion. Queensland Health's Budget is estimated to grow to $7.8 billion in 2009-10. This represents an increase of 45% on the 2005-06 Budget.[133]

The Beattie government was establishing a pattern of behaviour in spending big to resolve political crises. It confirmed this pattern with its reactions to its third crisis regarding the SEQ water supply.

---

[130] Queensland Audit Office, 2014, *Hospital Infrastructure Projects*, Report 2: 2014-15, p. 13.
[131] John Taylor, 2014, "Three new Queensland hospitals cost $2.2 billion more than promised, auditor-general says", *ABC News*, available via www.abc.net.au.
[132] Ibid.
[133] Queensland Treasury, 2006, op. cit., p. 62.

Water crisis

The water crisis began after the worst SEQ drought on record. Dam levels in SEQ fell to reach worrying low levels and were projected to fall further. The water crisis was a genuine crisis, and one that arguably was inherited from previous state governments, which had not invested in dams. For example, the Goss government in 1989 had scrapped the planned Wolffdene dam on the Albert River on the Gold Coast. Former Queensland Treasury official Paul McFadyen, who was a key Treasury adviser on water policy during the water crisis, described the crisis in these terms when interviewed for this book:

> Brisbane was within 12 months of running out of water which meant no electricity, no petrol, and no jobs for over 2 million people. People don't realise how close we came to catastrophe. It was due to opposition to dams by the earlier Goss and Beattie governments. It was due to the greenies.

Clearly successive governments have failed to plan adequately for Queensland's population growth.

The government began responding to the water crisis in August 2005, with announcements that it would bring forward the construction of dams that were foreshadowed in its SEQ Infrastructure Plan, particularly the Cedar Grove Weir on the Logan River and the Mary River Weir on the Mary River near Gympie. The latter was also known as the Traveston Crossing Dam. It would have involved hundreds of millions of dollars of capital expenditure and it was not apparent that the Beattie government had yet properly examined the economic feasibility of the project. The government also announced it would further investigate and progress the proposed Wyaralong Dam near Boonah and provide several million dollars to Councils for their own water conservation measures, and it would investigate the feasibility of desalination and recycling waste water to use as drinking water.[134] Out of these studies came the Tugun desalination plant

---

[134] Peter Beattie, 2005, *Queensland Government takes lead on urban drought*, media release of the Queensland Premier and Treasurer, 23 August 2005, available via www.statements.qld.gov.au.

and the Western Corridor Recycled Water scheme.

The government was prompted to further action in 2006. Premier Beattie announced an early election for 9 September 2006, partly to seek a mandate for the government's plans so far, which included the construction of the two new dams and a water recycling scheme, with recycled water controversially intended for use as drinking water. The government faced a challenge convincing the electorate of the merits of water recycling. Recycling water for reuse as drinking water had previously been rejected by the people of Toowoomba when it was put to a local plebiscite on 29 July that year.

The Beattie government declared a water supply state of emergency, and established a Queensland Water Commission to coordinate the development of water supply policy in SEQ. Its Commissioner Elizabeth Nosworthy became a minor celebrity when she implored SEQ residents to have four-minute showers.

The parameters of the Queensland government's response to the water crisis were set in the Beattie government, but it largely ended up the responsibility of the Bligh government to implement it. It was the Bligh government that faced large cost blowouts on the infrastructure projects and had to suffer the embarrassment of one of the major elements of the response, the Traveston Crossing Dam, being blocked by the Federal Environment Minister, former Midnight Oil lead singer Peter Garrett. The dam was blocked due to the risk it created to a local lungfish, a protected endangered species.

The new water infrastructure was largely be delivered by GOCs such as:

- the newly created Queensland Water Infrastructure which managed the construction of the dams;

- LinkWater which delivered the water grid, a series of pipes connecting storages and reservoirs across SEQ; and

- Water Secure, which would own the recycled water scheme and desalination plant.

Under later machinery of government changes these water infrastructure assets were transferred to Seqwater. QWI and Water Secure were merged into Seqwater in 2011 by the Bligh Government and LinkWater was merged into Seqwater by the Newman Government in 2012.

Given the infrastructure investments were being made by GOCs they did not directly impact the general government sector and the budget bottom line. But they increased total government borrowing which the ratings agencies such as Moody's, S&P and Fitch Ratings consider in their ratings decisions. Queensland kept its AAA credit rating in the final years of the Beattie government's term, but decisions made during Beattie's premiership contributed to its eventual loss during the Bligh years.

The water crisis revealed even more policy fiascos, pointing to a failure of governance. For the Traveston dam, which was never built, the government spent $500 million on land resumptions in the Mary Valley, at arguably very generous prices. This land was later sold at a loss by the Queensland government over 2012 to 2015, with a shortfall of $250 million.[135] Also, the hugely expensive drought resistant water infrastructure turned out to be largely unnecessary after the rains returned at the end of 2010. The $2.7 billion Western Corridor recycled water scheme, begun during the Beattie government, was eventually mothballed. And the $1.2 billion on a desalination plant at Tugun on the Gold Coast, on which construction also commenced during the Beattie government, has been rarely used. It now operates in "hot standby mode," meaning it can be brought online to desalinate seawater and supply water to the grid at short notice. This costs tens of millions of dollars per year in operational expenditure, even though it is not contributing meaningfully to the water supply. The electricity bill for the desalination plant runs

---

[135] Pip Courtney, 2015, "Mary Valley revival: Last of properties sold during Traveston dam project back in private hands", *ABC News*, 19 April 2015, available via www.abc.net.au.

at around $13 million per annum.[136] This is a good example of the operational expenditure consequences of capital expenditure decisions. Unfortunately, these impacts on future operational expenses are not often appreciated by decision makers or adequately forecast by Treasuries.

Ultimately, Peter Beattie blamed the Bligh government for the botched response to the water crisis. In 2013 he said the Bligh government had made a "tragic error of judgment" in its response, noting he "was disappointed with a number of decisions the Bligh government made in relation to water."[137] These included not appointing former Coordinator General Ross Rolfe to oversee the construction of the drought resilient infrastructure. But there appears little doubt it was the decision to proceed with the construction of unnecessary infrastructure made during the Beattie government that as largely to blame, not just deficient implementation. And by spending up big in knee jerk responses to political crises, Peter Beattie established a pattern of behaviour it was only natural his successor would follow. Beattie deserves a large part of the blame for the errors of judgment he has attributed to the Bligh government.

Bligh as Treasurer

Anna Bligh was Peter Beattie's last Treasurer. She served as Queensland Treasurer for two Budgets: 2006-07 and 2007-08. Prior to becoming the MP for South Brisbane at the age of 35 in 1995, Bligh had worked for community organisations and the public service. With Anna Bligh appointed as Treasurer, and also serving in other important ministries, there was a massive centralisation of power that arguably led to poorer outcomes. SMART Infrastructure Facility Senior Research Fellow Joe Branigan commented in a 2013 opinion piece in *The Australian* that:

---

[136] Kathleen Skene, 2017, "'Rustbucket' perception dogs Tugun Desalination Plant a decade after its conception", *Gold Coast Bulletin*, 27 April 2017, available via www. goldcoastbulletin.com.au.

[137] Des Houghton, 2013, "Beattie-era Western Corridor Recycling Scheme a $2.7b white elephant", *Courier-Mail*, 13 September 2013, available via www.couriermail.com.au.

Beattie centralised power and sidelined naysayers. He achieved this objective on September 13, 2006, when he claimed he had "reshaped the government so that it is ideally positioned". What that meant was reducing the number of decision-makers to just two, himself and Anna Bligh, who became deputy premier, treasurer and minister for infrastructure.[138]

Delivering the budget speech for 2007-08 on 5 June 2007, a few months before she became Queensland Premier, Anna Bligh expressed pride in the state government's huge infrastructure program. She commented:

> Mr Speaker, our Government is investing in the economic infrastructure of the State at an unprecedented rate. Ten years ago, total capital spending was $5 billion. Today we will commit to a capital program of more than $5 billion in roads and transport alone and our total program will exceed $14 billion. This Government invests in infrastructure at levels far in excess of other states. Per capita we are investing almost 50%, or $1,000 per person, more than our nearest rival, Western Australia. In this Budget the Queensland Government will spend 6% of its GSP on capital, compared with just 1% of GDP by the Australian Government.[139]

Other than the usual motherhood statements, Treasurer Bligh did little to justify this massive level of capital expenditure (Figure 4.2). Nor did it appear she was conscious of the risks to Queensland's long-term fiscal position and its financial reputation. The Treasury at the time must have cautioned against the massive capital program, but clearly the government was not listening too closely to the Treasury.

Overall, Bligh's tenure as Treasurer was very concerning. She appeared largely unconcerned about fiscal sustainability issues. Indeed, the rates of expenditure growth and the final budget outcomes during her tenure foreshadowed worse to come (Table 4.3).

---

[138] Joe Owen, 2013, "Big spending Beattie and Rudd perfect partners", *The Australian*, 26 August 2013, available via www.theaustralian.com.au. Note Joe Branigan's former surname was Owen.

[139] Queensland Treasury, 2007, *State Budget 2007-08: Budget Speech*, budget paper no. 1, p. 2.

Figure 4.2 Queensland general government capital spending as a percentage of GSP during Beattie government

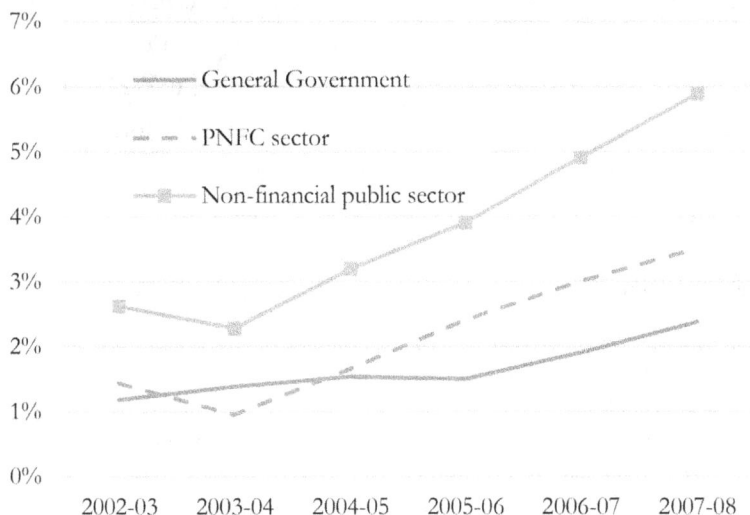

Source: Queensland state budget papers.

Table 4.3 Budget outcomes under Treasurer Anna Bligh in the Beattie government

	2006-07 $ million	2007-08 $ million
A. Revenue	32,052	31,493
B. Total expenses	30,201	33,052
C. Net operating balance (A-B)	1,852	-1,559
D. Gross fixed capital formation	3,691	5,090
E. Depreciation (& other adjustments)	1,624	1,423
F. Net acquisition of non-financial assets (D-E)	2,067	3,667
G. Net lending (C-F)	-215	-5,226
Indicators		
Net lending as percentage of GSP	-0.1%	-2.3%
Revenue growth	6.3%	-1.7%
Expenses growth	14.2%	9.4%
GFCF growth	35.5%	37.9%
Revenue growth - real per capita	1.0%	-8.9%
Expenses growth - real per capita	8.5%	1.5%
GFCF growth - real per capita	28.8%	27.8%

Source: ABS GFS, cat. no. 5512.0, various issues.

The balance sheet under the Beattie government

General government and GOC debt increased relatively modestly in the first two phases of the Beattie government, under Treasurers Hamill and Mackenroth (Table 4.4). The increase in GOC debt seen under Mackenroth was due to investments in assets that were most likely economically viable and justifiable, such as the Kogan power station and the RG Tanna coal terminal expansion project at the Port of Gladstone.

Table 4.4 Selected Queensland government balance sheet items under Beattie

	Borrowings – general government $ billion	Borrowings – GOCs $ billion	Borrowings – public non-financial sector $ billion	Net debt – general government $ billion	Net worth – general government $ billion
1998-99	2.56	8.92	11.43	-11.07	58.46
1999-00	3.07	10.31	12.98	-10.12	57.77
2000-01	2.58	11.19	13.66	-10.67	57.62
2001-02	2.93	12.21	15.07	-11.61	58.09
2002-03	3.19	13.37	16.47	-11.84	64.90
2003-04	3.21	12.04	15.25	-14.81	77.72
2004-05	2.79	13.03	15.82	-19.35	92.15
2005-06	2.08	15.23	17.31	-23.20	104.45
2006-07	2.27	21.70	23.97	-26.62	118.53
2007-08	6.33	24.53	30.86	-22.59	193.84

Source: 2016-17 State Budget paper no. 2, p. 191, 2008-09 State Budget Paper no. 2, p. 168 and ABS GFS Statistics, various issues.

Toward the end of the Beattie government, under Treasurer Anna Bligh, state debt started to take off, setting itself on the trajectory to the much higher level of debt Queensland has today. At the end of the Beattie government, total Queensland government borrowings were almost three times larger in dollar terms and key metrics had substantially increased relative to GSP (Figure 4.3). This increase in debt was largely related to increased GOC borrowings for the purposes of building new infrastructure. Some of this additional indebtedness, but not all, was likely defensible as it financed economically viable assets. But a surge in general government indebtedness in 2007-08—the financial year corresponding to Bligh's last budget before she became Premier—heralded worse to come. As we will see, GOC debt also continued to climb during Bligh's years as Premier, as GOCs invested in a wide variety of assets, some dubious, to fulfil the government's commitments forged in the various crises that marked the Beattie government.

Figure 4.3 Queensland government borrowings and net debt to GSP ratios during the Beattie government

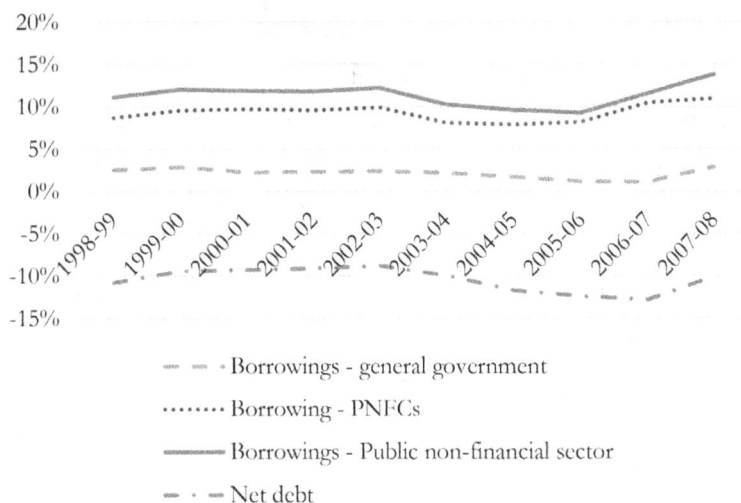

Source: *Queensland State Budget papers, ABS GFS data, and ABS National Accounts: State Accounts data.*

Assessment of the Beattie government

Premier Peter Beattie won four elections and presided over a period of strong economic and population growth and increases in government services levels and infrastructure. And, to its credit, the Beattie government was not so constrained by ideology and its union affiliations that it would not countenance privatisation. Indeed, the government privatised a range of businesses, including, in its first term, TAB Queensland, and, in the Beattie government's fourth and final term, Sun Retail, Allgas and Powerdirect, with the $3 billion of proceeds of these later sales injected into a Queensland Future Growth Fund.

The Beattie government certainly had some important successes, including pushing through politically unpopular amalgamations of small economically unviable local councils throughout regional Queensland and the development of Queensland's coal seam gas industry. There was also the abolition of the bank debits tax, as required by the IGA associated with the GST, and reductions in land tax and abolition of stamp duty in some cases.[140]

Despite many positive achievements, the Beattie government nonetheless set in motion a deterioration of the state's public finances through poor decision making. Without a doubt, Queensland's fiscal deterioration began during the Beattie government. To an extent, the Beattie government had inherited the problems it faced. Recall that critics had long pointed out that Queensland's status as a low tax state implied lower levels of public services and public infrastructure. Arguably previous governments should have spent more to lift service levels and build new infrastructure.

But the Beattie government had several years in government and indeed nearly two terms before these problems became apparent—i.e. the electricity and health crises which emerged in 2004 and the water crisis which emerged in 2006—so the extent to which it could blame previous governments is limited. It over-reacted to what it perceived as crises, and it made decisions that were incautious and imprudent. The government spent big in response to crises while at the same time increasing expenditure in favoured areas such as education and innovation, with major policy packages

---

[140] Queensland Treasury, 2006, *State Budget 2006-07: Budget Strategy and Outlook*, budget paper no. 2, p. 2.

such as Education and Training Reforms for the Future and the Smart State. The Beattie government set up a pattern of responding to a crisis by throwing money at the problem. It was a government that committed to major capital works programs that would substantially impact the budget, such as the three new hospitals, in the absence of business cases. Also, the Beattie government arguably contributed to a breakdown in accountability of GOC leadership, which in turn may have contributed to various crises.

Beattie's first two Treasurers David Hamill and Terry Mackenroth appeared to keep a tight rein on expenditure, but in the mid-2000s, when Mackenroth was no longer Treasurer, budget discipline declined. Bligh was a regrettable choice as Treasurer, given that her words and actions as Treasurer, and later as Premier, revealed she lacked an appreciation of the need to consider the long-term budget implications of decisions. Of course, Beattie may not have had much choice but to appoint Bligh as Treasurer, given the Bligh's Socialist Left faction was strong within the government's caucus of MPs.

Another contributing factor to the decline of fiscal discipline at the end of the Beattie government may have been the passage of time. As time moved on, peoples' memories faded of financially dubious Labor governments at the federal level (i.e. Whitlam) and in other states (i.e. Bannon in SA, Cain in Victoria). So the usual warnings about big spending Labor governments from conservatives became less effective politically. Recall that Goss and De Lacy were afraid of comparisons to the Whitlam government of 1972-75. The Labor government prior to Beattie's was the Goss government, which in comparison to most governments had an enviable record. Arguably the previous Queensland Labor government's reputation for financial management protected the Beattie government for some time against doubts around its abilities as economic manager of the state.

Generational change may also have been a factor. In part, the strong

111

fiscal compass possessed by Sir Leo Hielscher and his contemporaries may have reflected his Depression-era upbringing. Reflecting on what distinguished the governments which Hielscher served as Under Treasurer from subsequent governments, former Queensland Treasury official Paul McFadyen, observed when interviewed for this book:

> There are broad generational and demographic changes at work between the Joh Bjelke-Petersen governments and the Goss and subsequent Labor governments, which are not just because of different political views. The Joh government period was dominated politically and in the Public Service by the war generation, who had grown up during the depression and World War II. Many had served. Labor after 1990 was very much the baby boomer generation of the cultural revolution of the sixties in politics and in the public service. There was a real generation gap in attitudes. The 1980s was the handover period between the generations.

Arguably, in the absence of strong personal convictions in favour of fiscal rectitude, fiscal rules are highly desirable. An important lesson that emerged from the Beattie government was that, if you abandon the rule against borrowing for social infrastructure—one of the elements of the Goss government's fiscal trilogy—you need rigorous cost-benefit analysis of projects. Governments should only borrow for projects with positive net benefits to the community, which can encompass economic, social and environmental benefits. But if governments do not prepare business cases, including rigorous cost-benefit analysis, they cannot be confident that they have borrowed money for assets that were worth the burden on present and future taxpayers.

In conclusion, the policy failures of the Beattie government were inherited by the Bligh government, which went on to compound those failures. The trajectory to higher debt was set in the Beattie government, particularly during Anna Bligh's time as Treasurer, but it was the decisions of the Bligh government that locked in the blow out in debt and the loss of the AAA credit rating, as we shall see in the next chapter.

5

BLIGH AND FRASER
LOSE THE AAA RATING

Beattie hands over premiership to Bligh

Peter Beattie handed over the Queensland premiership to Anna Bligh in September 2007, around one year after the 2006 state election. Bligh was Queensland's first female Premier. She is a descendent of legendary British sailor Captain William Bligh, who was infamously subject to a mutiny on his ship the Bounty, and later lost the Governorship of colonial NSW during the Rum Rebellion.

For several years she was seen as the logical successor to Beattie, despite hailing from the ALP's Socialist Left faction. As noted in earlier chapters, it was during Bligh's premiership that Queensland lost its AAA credit rating due to the large debt build up. To some extent, Premier Bligh was a victim of circumstances inherited from the Beattie government, but she was also the victim of her own choices, and she suffered badly at the March 2012 election, which saw the largest swing against a government in Queensland history.

Fraser harks back to past Labor Treasurers

Bligh's Treasurer Andrew Fraser was relatively young when appointed to the position as a 30 year old, but he was a gifted parliamentary performer. In his first budget, delivered in June 2008—in the first phase of the financial crisis but before the collapse of leading Wall St investment bank Lehman

Brothers in September which shattered global financial markets—Treasurer Fraser described the challenges facing him as follows:

> Mr Speaker, "the duty of placing before the [House] the annual review of the finances of the state and the Estimates for the current year imposes, on this occasion, a more difficult task than usual." So began the Budget Speech in 1915. It serves also to introduce the Budget of 2008-09.[141]

Treasurer Fraser was quoting from the wartime 1915 budget speech delivered by E.G. Theodore, also known as "Red Ted", Queensland Treasurer from 1915 to 1920, and who remains a Labor icon. Theodore also served as Queensland Premier from 1919 to 1925 and Federal Treasurer for around nine months in 1929-30, but he was subject to a large scandal, the Mungana affair, and forced to resign. Theodore was a proto-Keynesian, and famously rejected the austerity recommended for the Australian government by the Bank of England's Otto Niemeyer during the Great Depression, instead favouring an expansion of credit to farmers and small businesses. It is possible that Fraser modelled himself on Theodore and saw parallels between the challenges he faced and those faced by Theodore, although arguably Theodore's 1915 budget was delivered in graver circumstances than Fraser's 2008 speech. At the time of the 2008-09 budget, the challenge Treasurer Fraser faced was not really comparable to war or depression. While the national economy was slowing, Queensland was still expected to grow at a strong rate of 4¼ percent and royalties were expected to more than double in 2008-09 compared with 2007-08. Instead, the challenge Treasurer Fraser faced was that Queensland's share of GST revenue was to be much lower than previously expected, owing to Queensland's good fortune with resources royalty revenue in previous years, which was now penalising Queensland in the CGC's revenue redistribution methodology. Treasurer Fraser noted:

> ...the demand for further infrastructure investment comes at

---

[141] Queensland Treasury, 2008a, *State Budget 2008-09: Budget Speech*, budget paper no. 1, p. 1.

a challenging time. In 2008-09, for the first time, Queensland will receive less than a per capita share of GST revenue. We will be a donor State. At the end of the Budget's forward estimates in 2011-12, Queensland will have had a cumulative loss in GST funding of more than $1.8 billion since the 2004 Review of the Methodology by the Commonwealth Grants Commission. In addition, by 2011-12, the revenue foregone from the abolition of State taxes will be over $1.3 billion. Together this curtails our capacity to meet the funding challenges before us. [142]

The Bligh government had inherited a huge program of capital works from the Beattie government, particularly for health and water infrastructure, and added its own new capital works, and it did not want to be constrained by the cuts to its GST funding. So despite the reduction in GST revenue flowing to Queensland, Treasurer Fraser announced an extraordinary increase in the capital budget of 21 percent for 2008-09.[143] Consider that Queensland's average economic growth rate over the last three decades is 7 percent (in nominal terms, unadjusted for inflation), and the huge magnitude of the increase is even more apparent.

A conscious decision and the AAA rating is lost

By the time of Fraser's second budget in June 2009, Lehman Brothers had collapsed and there were grave fears for the global economy, as well as for the Australian and Queensland economies. Between the first and second Fraser budgets, Queensland's economic and fiscal outlook changed profoundly. In December 2008, Fraser announced a substantially weaker budget outlook, due to the expected deterioration in fiscal conditions. Then, just two months later, on 20 February 2009, Treasurer Fraser revealed an even worse fiscal situation than announced at the mid-year update at the end of 2008, at which time a small surplus was still forecast for 2008-09.

[142]   Ibid., p. 3.
[143]   Ibid., p. 12.

The Bligh government's 20 February *Economic and Fiscal Update* followed just over two weeks after the Australian governments *Updated Economic and Fiscal Outlook* released on 3 February.

Given the Commonwealth had substantially downgraded its own economic and fiscal forecasts, the state government was essentially forced to provide its own update. On 20 February 2009, Treasurer Fraser announced that the "Global Financial Crisis wipes out $12 billion of revenue". The revenue write down was largely the result of lower stamp duty receipts, owing to a lack of confidence and decline in property market transactions, and lower resource royalty revenues over the forward estimates.

The revenue write down was forecast to lead to a blow out in state debt that would concern the ratings agencies, and it prompted them to downgrade Queensland's credit rating. Consider what the ratings agencies would have seen in the new information released 20 February 2009, by comparing the outlook for borrowings at the time of the mid-year outlook in December 2008, with the revised estimates published on 20 February 2008 (Table 5.1).

Table 5.1 Fiscal deterioration between December 2008 and February 2009

Budget items	2008-09	2009-10	2010-11	2011-12
General government net operating balance ($ billion)				
Major Economic Statement (Dec-08)	0.054	-0.124	-0.085	0.092
Economic and Fiscal Update (Feb-09)	-1.573	-3.166	-3.204	-2.910
Variation	-1.627	-3.042	-3.119	-3.002
Non-financial public sector borrowing ($ billion)				
Major Economic Statement (Dec-08)	42.473	52.203	58.694	63.242
Economic and Fiscal Update (Feb-09)	43.901	56.650	66.452	74.032
Non-financial public sector revenues ($ billion)				
Major Economic Statement (Dec-08)	44.659	45.464	47.342	50.238
Economic and Fiscal Update (Feb-09) - implied	43.032	42.422	44.223	47.236
Borrowings/Revenue				
Major Economic Statement (Dec-08)	95.1%	114.8%	124.0%	125.9%
Economic and Fiscal Update (Feb-09) - implied	102.0%	133.5%	150.3%	156.7%

Source: Queensland Treasury, 2008-09 Major Economic Statement and Economic and Fiscal Update.

The blow out in the ratio of total borrowings to total revenues in the non-financial public sector to around 150 percent over the forward estimates was beyond the apparently previously tolerable figure of 125 percent (Figure 5.1).

The budget update was of concern to ratings agencies, and S&P was the first to move, downgrading Queensland's credit rating from AAA to AA+ on 21 February 2009. S&P was concerned about the state's "projected deteriorating budgetary performance, which is a result of both declining revenues and structural operating expenditure."[144] The AAA rating that was the culmination of Queensland's past budget discipline—due in large part to the influence of Sir Leo Hielscher—was lost.

Figure 5.1 Ratio of borrowings to revenue for Queensland non-financial public sector, as projected at the time of the financial crisis

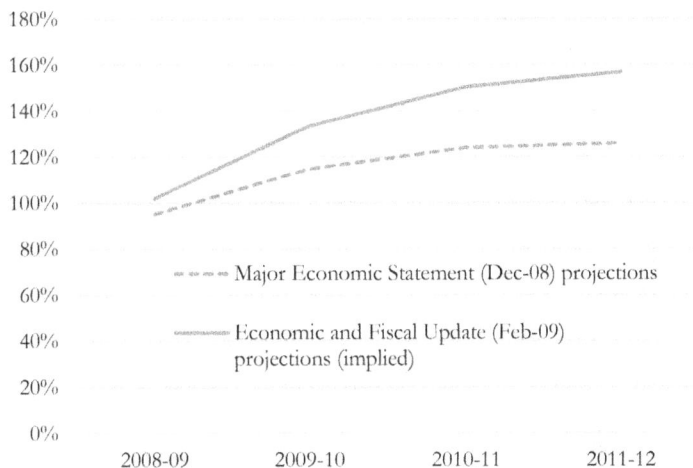

Source: Queensland Treasury, 2008-09 Major Economic Statement and Economic and Fiscal Update.

The loss of the AAA rating was a blow to the state's prestige and once

---

144 Quoted in David Barbeler, 2009, "Qld loses AAA credit rating after budget blow-out", *Brisbane Times*, 21 February 2009, available via www.brisbanetimes.com.au.

sterling fiscal reputation. It meant higher borrowing costs for the state government than otherwise. The rates at which the Queensland government could borrow from the market, reflected in the yields on QTC bonds, would be higher than the rates faced by governments that had maintained a AAA credit rating, such as NSW and Victoria. The Commission of Audit for the Newman government found that, in mid-2012, when Queensland interest rates on bonds were 30 to 40 basis points (i.e. 0.3 to 0.4 percentage points) higher than for the AAA States NSW, Victoria and WA:

> The additional borrowing costs faced by Queensland, relative to the other large states, are estimated to be more than $100 million in 2012-13 and continue to rise each year as Queensland's debt increases and existing debt is refinanced.[145]

The Newman government's Commission of Audit projected that the additional annual cost would be around $140 million by 2013-14.

Extraordinarily, Treasurer Fraser more-or-less acknowledged that the Bligh government did not try to avert the loss of the credit rating. Maintaining the credit rating was subordinate to other priorities. In a statement at the time Queensland's AAA credit rating was lost, 21 February 2009, Treasurer Fraser noted:

> In handing down the Economic and Fiscal Update I said we would put all policy levers at our disposal to full forward in order to sustain growth in the Queensland economy. We took the conscious decision to put the need to preserve the capital program and the 119,000 jobs it supports at the forefront of our decision-making. The update states future state budgets will need to address the state's medium and long-term budget outlook.[146]

The government did not want anything preventing it from fulfilling its

---

[145] Costello et al, 2012, p. 24. Note that the interest rates Queensland can borrow at are now slightly lower than those faced by WA, given WA has had its credit rating downgraded to below Queensland's by Moody's in recent years.

[146] Andrew Fraser, 2009, *Statement—Treasurer*, media statement by the Queensland Treasurer, 21 February 2009, available via www.statements.qld.gov.au.

ambitious capital program, which for the entire Queensland government, GOCs included, was estimated at over $17 billion in 2008-09. Incidentally, Treasurer Fraser's estimate of the jobs supported by the capital works program, some 119,000 jobs, appears too high—one job per $144,000 of capital expenditure—and obviously assumes a large multiplier effect.

Partly, the Bligh government's capital program was locked in by the Beattie government, although as Queensland Treasurer in that government's last few years, Premier Bligh had some responsibility for that. Consider the examples of substantial spending plans that were already underway when the 2008-09 budget was prepared in mid-2008 in Table 6.2. Capital works already underway included the Western Corridor Recycled Water Scheme, the Tugun desalination plant, the three hospitals announced by Premier Beattie in 2006, and Airport Link, among others.

Table 5.2 Capital works estimates at the time of the 2008-09 Budget, selected examples

Project	Total estimated cost, $ million	Expenditure to 30 June 2008, $ million	Budget 2008-09 $ million	Post 2008-09, $ million
Gold Coast University Hospital	1,549.0	21.9	103.7	1,423.3
Queensland Children's Hospital	1,044.0	21.9	97.5	924.5
Sunshine Coast Hospital	1,210.0	53.6	29.5	1,126.9
Western Corridor Recycled Water Project	2,493.0	1,698.0	795.0	-
Traveston Crossing Dam	1,592.0	431.8	442.3	717.9
SEQ Desalination Plant	1,209.0	760.9	448.1	-
Wyaralong Dam	333.0	28.0	89.5	215.5
SEQ Water Grid pipeline interconnectors	887.0	704.9	234.1	375.0
Southern Regional Water Pipeline	901.0	683.6	217.3	-
Airport Link	258.7	115.3	80.5	63.0
Abbot Point expansion	1,107.3+	134.9	367.2	613.9

Source: Queensland Treasury, 2008-09 State Budget Paper no. 3, Capital Statement.

Despite the credit rating downgrade, the Bligh government was returned at the March 2009 election, although it did experience a 4.1 percent swing against it. This election was the first at which Labor was up against the combined LNP, which was created by the merger of the state National and Liberal parties the previous year. The government ran with the slogan "Keep Queensland Strong", and it emphasised its infrastructure program and focus on job creation, with Bligh promising 100,000 new jobs over three years. The opposition, led by 41 year old Lawrence Springborg—who had previously led the coalition parties to defeat in the 2004 and 2006 elections—was highly critical of the Bligh government's economic management. The opposition highlighted the large increase in debt and cost blowouts on major infrastructure projects, such as the desalination plant, northern water pipeline (part of the SEQ Water Grid), and Airport Link, which together were over budget by almost $1 billion.[147]

To distinguish itself from the Bligh government, the opposition campaigned on a platform of fiscal restraint, which included the application of a much larger efficiency dividend—3 percent—than what the government had introduced. This provided the opportunity for the government to criticise the opposition on the basis that its efficiency target could only be met by cuts to so-called frontline services, such as teaching and nursing jobs, and it had a commissioned report from ANU Professor John Wanna to support its claim.

By winning the 2009 state election, Anna Bligh made history by becoming the first woman to win an Australian state (or federal) election. It appeared Queenslanders were largely willing to overlook the government's fiscal failures, but it should be acknowledged the LNP needed a massive swing of over 8 percent (i.e. an extra 20 seats) to win the election, and that the adverse economic climate meant the public was receptive to the government's message regarding the need for stability and to reject the LNP's proposed public service job cuts.

[147] Mark Rodrigues, 2009, "Queensland Election 2009", *Parliamentary Library Research Papers 2008-09*, no. 34, p. 8.

The Commonwealth helps out with a guarantee of state borrowings

The need to borrow large sums of money to fund the government's capital investment program was of concern to Queensland Treasury and QTC even before the credit rating downgrade. In the second half of 2008, Treasury and QTC had started exploring ways that QTC's borrowing task could be made easier. Among other measures, they advocated greater purchases of state government bonds, also known as semi-government bonds, by the federal government's debt management office, the Australian Office of Financial Management (AOFM). Also, the Queensland and Victorian governments advocated a government guarantee of state government borrowings. The desire for federal government assistance stemmed from the dislocation in world financial markets that occurred during the financial crisis. State governments were very concerned about the marketability of their bonds among international investors who were a large source of their funding. As the QTC notes on its website:

> The Global Financial Crisis had a very adverse effect on the state government bond market threatening the capacity of state governments to deliver critical infrastructure projects.
>
> In response to this, on 25 March 2009, the Australian government announced that it would provide a time limited, voluntary guarantee over Australian state and territory government borrowing. The guarantee was available for both existing and new issuances of securities over a range of maturities, but did not extend to issuances denominated in foreign currencies.
>
> The Queensland Government, on 16 June 2009, announced that it would take up the Australian Government's offer of the guarantee on all existing AUD denominated benchmark bond lines (global and domestic) issued by QTC with a maturity date of between 12 months and 180 months (1-15 years).[148]

The guarantee was provided by the Australian government for a

---

[148] Available via www.qtc.com.au.

small fee, expressed in terms of basis points (i.e. each one hundredth of a percentage point). States with a AAA credit rating such as NSW and Victoria would pay 30 basis points for additional borrowings and 15 basis points for existing borrowings, while states with AA+, such as Queensland, would pay 35 basis points for additional borrowings and 20 basis points for existing borrowings.[149] The scheme was closed to new borrowings at the end of 2010 and only Queensland and NSW, which were the largest borrowers, had taken advantage of it by then.[150]

The guarantee of state borrowings provided the QTC with comfort and allowed it to borrow relatively smoothly and without experiencing a spike in borrowing costs. Also, it meant Queensland would not have to resort to drastic measures. For example, if Queensland had been unable to borrow to fund the government's capital program, the government may well have had to draw down on its investments managed by its own Queensland Investment Corporation (QIC), which are intended to fund the government's defined benefit superannuation liability.

Stimulation for the nation

Introducing his second budget, Fraser referred to another former Queensland Labor Treasurer (and later Premier) Forgan Smith, after whom the main building at UQ is named. Smith was responsible for large infrastructure investments during the Depression, including Brisbane's Story Bridge. Similar to his first budget speech, Fraser's second budget speech also featured an emphasis on infrastructure, but he had to also acknowledge the deterioration in the fiscal situation and the loss of the AAA rating. Regarding the 2009-10 budget, Treasurer Fraser noted:

> It is delivered at a time of immediate upheaval and uncertainty, but delivered with a focus on sustainability in the decades ahead. It is a Budget

---

[149] Australian Government, 2009, *Guarantee of State and Territory Borrowing Scheme Rules*, p. 17.
[150] David Lancaster and Sarah Dowling, 2011, "The Australian Semi-government Bond Market", *RBA Bulletin*, September quarter 2011.

that has a dual task—to support the economy during this time of need, and to chart a course for a new future beyond these dark hours.[151]

A deficit on the operating budget was estimated for 2008-09 and large net operating deficits were forecast over the budget forward estimates (Table 5.3). However, the major downward revenue revisions the Treasury had made turned out to be excessive, and the actual budget outcomes turned out much better than expected. An important reason for this was that, consistent with the Australian Treasury, Queensland Treasury had over-estimated the adverse impact of the global financial crisis on the Queensland economy. Economic growth certainly slowed, but the Queensland economy managed to grow 1.4 percent in 2009-10, compared with the Queensland Treasury forecast of a contraction of ¼ percent. In the 2010-11 budget, Queensland Treasury noted the role of "resilient demand from China boosting coal exports, and public stimulus helping to offset a decline in business investment."[152] But in June 2009, the Bligh government was expecting a major economic downturn, and this meant it would maintain its large capital program despite the forecast budget deterioration.

Table 5.3 Queensland general government net operating balance estimates

	2008-09 $ million	2009-10 $ million	2010-11 $ million	2011-12 $ million	2012-13 $ million
2008-09 Budget	809	540	215	265	-
2008-09 Major Economic Statement	54	-124	-85	92	-
2008-09 Economic and Fiscal Update	-1,573	-3,166	-3,204	-2,910	-
2009-10 Budget	-574	-1,954	-3,459	-4,090	-3,290
Actual outcomes	-21	128	-1,466	-226	-4,558

Source: Queensland Treasury, various budget statements.

---

151 Queensland Treasury, 2009a, *State Budget 2009-10: Budget Speech 2009-10*, budget paper no. 1, p. 1.
152 Queensland Treasury, 2010, *State Budget 2010:11 Budget Strategy and Outlook*, budget paper no. 2, p. 21.

At the time, Fraser's actions in supporting a big spending capital works program were supported by the Rudd government at the federal level, which was engaging in its own massive fiscal stimulus. The 2009-10 budget saw a massive increase in forecast capital expenditures relative to what had been forecast previously (Table 5.4). This was largely due to the state government undertaking capital works funded by the Australian government under the Nation Building and Jobs Plan, the Rudd government's second stimulus package announced in February 2009. These capital works included spending on new school facilities such as multipurpose halls under the Building the Education Revolution program, a key part of the stimulus package. Ultimately, capital expenditures typically fell short of what was initially expected owing to delays in the rollout of projects. This was an issue experienced by later governments, including the Palaszczuk government.

Table 5.4 Queensland government non-financial public sector capital purchases

	2008-09 $ million	2009-10 $ million	2010-11 $ million	2011-12 $ million	2012-13 $ million
2008-09 Budget	16,637	14,132	13,641	10,757	
2008-09 Major Economic Statement	17,095	14,681	11,848	10,576	
2008-09 Economic and Fiscal Update	n.p.	n.p.	n.p.	n.p.	
2009-10 Budget	16,195	17,272	14,632	11,427	9,081
Actual	15,101	15,007	13,306	11,980	10,774

Source: Queensland Treasury, various budget statements.

Was the stimulus necessary?

Much of the massive ramp up in expenditure at the time was justified in terms of necessary stimulus to offset the adverse impacts of the financial crisis. The expected impacts on the Australian economy—a decline in business investment, a reduction in hiring and an increase in unemployment, and lower government revenues—prompted both the Commonwealth and Queensland governments to announce special fiscal stimulus measures.

But, as noted above, the Queensland economy performed much better during the financial crisis than was forecast by the Queensland Treasury, and the Australian economy performed much better than forecast by the Australian Treasury. The Updated Economic and Fiscal Outlook which announced the Nation Building and Jobs Plan presented Treasury forecasts of GDP growth of 1 percent in 2008-09 and ¾ percent in 2009-10, and an unemployment rate of 7 percent in 2009-10, even taking account of the stimulus package. But GDP growth turned out to be 1.9 percent in 2008-09 and 2.1 percent in 2009-10. The economy had slowed from its growth rate of 3-4 percent in the preceding two financial years, but not to the large extent the Treasury had forecast. Furthermore, the national unemployment rate peaked at 5.9 percent in June 2009, before declining.

Arguably, both the Federal and state governments ended up spending much more money than was justifiable on stimulus, but the decision makers involved argue that the economic outlook at the time justified it. Certainly the Australian Treasury and international agencies such as the OECD and IMF were supportive of stimulus, as were many academic economists, although there was an extensive divergence of views in academia. In 2012, the then Australian Treasury Secretary Ken Henry reflected that during the financial crisis:

> It did look like we were not going to be able to avoid recession. It did look that way...As Secretary of the Treasury, I was not going to stand on the sidelines.[153]

The critical empirical question is whether the multiplier for government expenditure is positive or negative. If it is positive, then a fiscal stimulus increases GDP relative to what it would have been otherwise, known as the baseline. In a 2015 study of government spending by the Australian and Queensland governments, Griffith University Professor Fabrizio Carmignani found positive fiscal multipliers, and multipliers greater than

---

[153] Herald Sun, 2012, "Use fiscal stimulus again: Henry", *Herald Sun*, 16 May 2012, available via www.heraldsun.com.au.

one, meaning the economy expands more than the increase in government spending.[154] Carmignani is careful in his interpretation of this finding. There are well-known risks with discretionary fiscal policy, relating to action, implementation and impact lags, and it has the potential to destabilise the economy.[155] Indeed, Carmignani found:

> ...from the point of view of Queensland, federal and state fiscal policies are jointly aligned with the Queensland business cycle only 20% of the times. Conversely, federal and state fiscal policies are jointly misaligned with the Queensland business cycle in 60 quarters out of 116, i.e. about 50% of the time. This misalignment is a factor of destabilization of the Queensland economy.[156]

This finding cautions against the use of discretionary fiscal policy to "fine tune" the business cycle, but proponents of the fiscal stimulus seen in the financial crisis have argued the possibility of destabilisation was very low given it was clear Australia would be hit by a very large adverse shock. Nonetheless, there was a recognition of the problem due to lags. Famously, Treasury Secretary Ken Henry advised the government "Go early, go hard, go households", which recognised:

1. Fiscal stimulus needs to be enacted early so it boosts the economy at the right time;

2. In the case of the financial crisis, it needed to be a large "hard" stimulus given the magnitude of the adverse shock; and

3. Stimulus should be directed at the household sector as households would be more likely to spend it in the short-term than businesses.

Another Griffith academic, Professor Tony Makin, disagreed strongly that there was a need for fiscal stimulus in response to the financial crisis. Based on his analysis of the National Accounts, Makin argued that the

---

[154] Carmignani, 2015a, op. cit.

[155] Note I am referring here to discretionary fiscal policy, such as specific new stimulus measures, which can be contrasted with the automatic stabilisers, such as the decline in tax receipts or the increase in unemployment benefit payments that naturally occur during an economic downturn.

[156] Ibid., p. 69.

depreciation of the Australian dollar and the resulting sharp reduction in imports was the main mechanism responsible for Australia enduring the financial crisis much better than other advanced economies. Makin argued this was consistent with the standard macroeconomic model for a small open economy with a flexible exchange rate, the Mundell-Fleming model.[157] A report Makin produced for the Minerals Council of Australia in 2014 that commented on the Australian government's stimulus in response to the crisis prompted a response from Treasury Secretary Martin Parkinson. The Treasury Secretary argued that, at the time of the crisis, the assumptions of the Mundell-Fleming model did not adequately describe Australia's macroeconomic circumstances. The Treasury Secretary noted:

> Specifically, the Mundell-Fleming model is based on an assumption of unilateral fiscal action, a high degree of trade openness and perfect capital mobility.[158]
>
> When these assumptions hold, the theoretical model suggests that expansionary fiscal policy will lead to a higher exchange rate, crowding out net exports and any positive aggregate demand effect from fiscal stimulus.
>
> In reality, Australia's fiscal stimulus was undertaken in concert with most other advanced economies, Australia's trade share is small enough to imply significant positive fiscal multipliers and capital was less than perfectly mobile during the GFC.[159]

The Treasury Secretary's intervention was criticised heavily at the time by leading Australian economist Henry Ergas, who noted Treasury was advancing a view that was not supported by the government of the day—the Abbott government—but instead a view favoured by the opposition.[160]

---

[157] Tony Makin, 2014, *Australia's competitiveness: Reversing the slide*, Minerals Council of Australia, Monograph no. 6.

[158] Australian Treasury, 2014, *Response to Professor Tony Makin's Minerals Council of Australia Monograph—'Australia's Competitiveness: Reversing the Slide'*.

[159] Ibid.

[160] Henry Ergas, 2014, "Treasury's conduct a disservice to public", *The Australian*, 8 September 2014, available via www.theaustralian.com.au.

In 2009, Ergas and co-author Alex Robson, later an economic adviser to PM Malcolm Turnbull, had criticised the Australian government's stimulus packages for being adopted even though no cost-benefit analysis of the measures appears to have been conducted.[161] Occasional UQ lecturer John Humphreys also criticised the Rudd government's stimulus package along similar lines in an article "The Treasury's non-modelling of the stimulus."[162]

No doubt, the debate over the efficacy of the fiscal stimulus applied in 2008-09 and for several years afterwards, owing largely to Building the Education Revolution capital works spending, will be debated for many years to come, and its resolution is outside the scope of this book.

Bligh and Fraser realise the need for course correction, but it's too late

To their credit, Bligh and Fraser saw the need to take measures that would offset the budget deterioration it was experiencing to an extent. In the 2008-09 mid-year fiscal and economic review (MYFER), which on this occasion was labelled the *Major Economic Statement*, the government announced a range of budget repair measures, including a public sector efficiency target, designed to ultimately save $200 million per annum by 2010-11, an increase in motor vehicle registration fees, increases in gambling and land taxes, and the deferral of the construction of a new Queensland Police Academy by two years.[163]

The Bligh government obviously knew the government was vulnerable when it came to economic and fiscal management. To help make the case it was acting in fiscally responsible manner, a few weeks before the 2009-10

[161] Henry Ergas and Alex Robson, 2009, *The 2008-09 Stimulus Packages: A Cost Benefit Analysis, Submission to the Senate Inquiry into the Government's Economic Stimulus Initiatives.*
[162] John Humphreys, 2012, "The Treasury's Non-modelling of the Stimulus", *Agenda*, vol. 19, no. 2, pp. 39-51.
[163] Queensland Treasury, 2008b, *Major Economic Statement*, p. 27.

state budget was handed down, the Bligh government passed a new *Financial Accountability Act 2009* and, as required by the act, adopted a charter of fiscal responsibility that set out its fiscal principles (Box 5.1).

Box 5.1 Bligh Government's fiscal principles in 2009 Charter of Fiscal Responsibility

*Fiscal sustainability

In the General Government sector, meet all operating expenses from operating revenue (where operating revenue is defined as total revenue from transactions and operating expenses are defined as total expenses from transactions less depreciation).

Growth in own-purpose expenses in the General Government sector not to exceed real per capita growth.

Achieve a General Government operating surplus as soon as possible, but not later than 2015-16.

Competitive tax regime

Maintain a competitive tax environment for business.

Managing the State's balance sheet

Stabilise net financial liabilities as a proportion of total revenue in the Non-financial Public Sector.

Source: Costello et al., 2012, p. 58.

Regarding the operating surplus target—that operating expenses were to be funded by operating revenues—expenses were to be calculated as net of depreciation, which meant that this requirement was less strict than the previous rule. As the Newman Government Commission of Audit noted in its Interim Report:

> This effectively involved achieving a positive cash inflow from operating activity only, and did not take into account any capital expenditure.[164]

---

[164] Queensland Commission of Audit, 2012, op. cit., p. 59.

That is, the government was giving itself permission to fund all capital expenditure by borrowings.

The government also adopted fiscal principles relating to (a) tax, specifically to maintain "a competitive environment for business", and (b) balance sheet management, with an objective to "stabilise net financial liabilities as a proportion of revenue", as opposed to the objective set by the Beattie government to "at least maintain and seek to increase Total State Net Worth."[165] The Queensland government no longer aspired to improve its net worth. The challenge now was to stabilise the fiscal situation and prevent things from getting worse.

No doubt to mollify the rating agencies, the 2009-10 budget strategy and outlook paper included a section titled "Path back to surplus" featuring long-term modelling of the budget balance.[166] The Bligh government set itself the target of restoring a net operating surplus by 2016-17. It needed to enact measures to ensure it could achieve this budget improvement. Controversially, it had announced a major privatisation program in the lead up to the budget, to be discussed in the next section.

Also, in its 2009-10 budget, the Bligh government included a range of fiscally responsible measures to attempt to offset to some degree the profound budget deterioration. These included the abolition of the fuel subsidy scheme. Courageously, the government also made major changes to local government subsidy programs that would re-direct funding to "councils most in need."[167] Arguably, this would have profound implications for regional Queensland, whose Councils had been benefitting from subsidies from George Street. Michael Knox, Chief Economist of Morgans Financial Ltd, a leading Australian wealth management firm, has argued that one of the consequences of budget cuts implemented

---

[165] Ibid, p. 60.

[166] Queensland Treasury, 2009b, *State Budget 2009-10: Budget Strategy and Outlook*, budget paper no. 2, p. 15.

[167] Queensland Treasury, 2009a, op. cit., p. 5.

by the Bligh government, particularly cuts to funding to local councils, was a two-speed economy in Queensland, with development in regional Queensland slowing down.[168]

While the Bligh government clearly did take measures to try to correct the fiscal situation, they were insufficient. As Figure 1.9 in Chapter 1 showed, it would not be until the Newman government that a significant net operating surplus would be run in Queensland, and during the Bligh government's final years the fiscal balance remained heavily in deficit, at around 2-2½ percent of GSP.

The Bligh government simply lacked discipline on the spending side of the budget. As highlighted in the Queensland Commission of Audit's 2012 *Interim Report*, by the end of its time in power, the Bligh government was not meeting all of its own fiscal principles, with growth in own purpose expenses exceeding inflation plus population growth, the upper limit set in the Charter of Fiscal Responsibility.[169] In its final *Mid Year Fiscal and Economic Review* in late 2011, the government reported expenses growth of 11.4 percent in 2010-11 compared with inflation plus population growth of 5.05 percent. Furthermore, it forecast expenses growth of 9.1 percent in 2011-12 compared with inflation plus population growth of 4.25 percent. Across the future years it projected that expenses growth would dramatically slow and fall below inflation plus population growth, but given the government's record to date it would have been difficult to have much faith in these forecasts (Figure 5.2).

---

[168] Michael Knox, 2012, *Queensland*, Economic Strategy note, RBS Morgans, 27 March 2012.
[169] Queensland Commission of Audit, 2012, op. cit., p. 58.

Figure 5.2 Estimates from final Bligh government MYFER showing breach of fiscal principle to keep growth in own-purpose expenses at or below inflation plus + growth rate

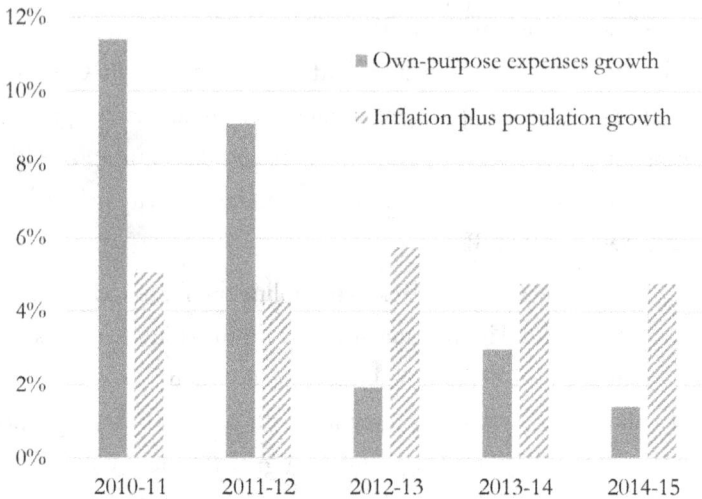

Source: Based on Queensland Commission of Audit, 2012, Interim Report, p. 58.

At least the government performed better on its taxation pledge. Taxes in Queensland remained low relative to the national average, with tax revenue per capita at around $2,271 in 2011-12, compared with a national average around $2,711—i.e. over 16 percent lower.[170]

Privatisation is not a dirty word

Bligh and Fraser's 2009-10 budget course correction involved a very large privatisation program. The privatisation program included the coal freight business of QR National, as well as Queensland Motorways, the Port of Brisbane, Forest Plantations Queensland, and the Abbot Point Coal Terminal. The privatisation plan was announced on 2 June 2009, a fortnight before the 2009-10 budget was delivered. The union movement

---

[170]   Ibid.

and the opposition argued the plan was contrary to the ALP's 2009 election platform. The Premier was accused of having a secret plan before the election to privatise state-owned assets. In her autobiography, *Through the Wall*, Anna Bligh would deny she had a "secret plan" to sell assets all along, noting:

> ...I knew drastic financial action would be necessary, and I had said this many times during the campaign. In fact, when I was asked once whether this might include asset sales, I'd replied that it could not be ruled out.[171]

The Bligh government deserves credit for advancing its privatisation program at great political risk. Arguably, the Bligh government's privatisation program ultimately resulted in the government losing the March 2012 election, at which it experienced a record swing against it, a swing which reduced the Labor caucus to seven MPs. Treasurer Andrew Fraser lost his seat of Mt Coot-tha in Brisbane's inner west. Premier Anna Bligh retained her seat of South Brisbane, but resigned as an MP very soon after the election. This provided a vacancy that was filled by then ALP organiser Jackie Trad, later Deputy Premier and Treasurer in the Palaszczuk government. Rightly or wrongly, the public perceived the privatisation program as a breach of an election commitment. Incidentally, the Bligh Government's massive election loss should probably have been a sign to the incoming Newman LNP Government that Queenslanders are difficult to convince on the merits of asset sales.

The privatisation program was highly successful, particularly the float of QR National, which raised $4.6 billion for the state government.[172] Also notable regarding privatisation was the arguably peculiar Queensland Motorways sale. As John Quiggin observed at the time, the government essentially sold Queensland Motorways to itself, as the government-owned

---

[171] Anna Bligh, 2016, *Through the wall: reflections on leadership, love and survival*, Harper Collins Publishers, p. 199.
[172] Fraser, 2010b.

funds manager QIC bought it, using funds it manages to meet the state's future superannuation liabilities. This arguably established a precedent for a fiscal trick that would be considered by both the Palaszczuk government and the LNP opposition in 2016.[173]

The Bligh government argued its privatisation program, expected to raise $15 billion, was necessary to prevent a budget deficit in the order of $14 billion.[174] One problem for the government was that because of the massive scale of the infrastructure program, the privatisations only prevented the budget deficit from blowing out massively, rather than resulting in a large reduction in debt. That is, the government took on a lot of political risk with very little to show for it. It should be noted also that privatisations are not guaranteed to improve budget outcomes, as governments forego future earnings associated with assets. Of course, that does not mean state-owned assets should never be privatised, as the budget impact is only one aspect. The important question is whether an asset should be on the government's balance sheet in the first place, or would be better owned and operated by the private sector, as noted by former Under Treasurer Doug McTaggart when interviewed for this book.

The fact that privatisations do not necessarily improve the bottom line— an issue which also plagued the Newman government as we shall see—was pointed out in a document signed off by 21 highly regarded Australian economists, including UQ Professors John Quiggin and Flavio Menezes, Australian National University Professor Andrew Leigh (now Federal Labor MP for Canberra), and Dr Henry Ergas, among others. These economists pointed out several conceptual flaws in the pro-privatisation arguments presented in the Bligh government's *Facts and Myths on Asset Sales* booklet. The statement from the 21 economists noted:

---

[173] Michael McKenna and Sarah Elks, 2016, "Secret power politics as Queensland parties plot debt deals", *The Australian*, 20 April 2016, available via www.theaustralian.com.au.

[174] AAP, 2009, *Anna Bligh defends privatisation amid Labor party row*, available via www.news.com.au.

The signatories of this statement have a range of views on the appropriate balance between the public and private sectors and on the merits of privatisation in particular cases. However, we share the view that these questions should be resolved on the basis of well-informed discussion of the economic and social costs and benefits of privatisation, and not on the basis of spurious claims that asset sales represent a costless source of income to governments.[175]

The Bligh government was unmoved by the 21 economists' critique, however. The government was not worried about losing future income streams associated with assets; it needed the cash right now to finance its huge infrastructure program and it wanted to minimise the blow out in debt.

A land of drought and flooding rains…and severe tropical cyclones

Premier Anna Bligh's finest hours were during the floods of the 2010-11 summer. The huge amount of rainfall southern Queensland experienced in December 2010 and January 2011 resulted in major flooding, with loss of life in Toowoomba, Grantham and the greater Brisbane region. It also resulted in a loss of economic activity and associated revenue, and a multi-billion dollar reconstruction bill. After heavy rainfall, several coalmines in central Queensland had filled up with water and could not be mined for many months, resulting in a fall in state government resource royalty revenue of $400 million in 2010-11.

The floods were followed in March 2011 by severe tropical cyclone Yasi in Far North Queensland, which also resulted in a major reconstruction bill, as well as wiping out most of the state's banana crop, sending banana prices soaring. In the 2011-12 budget papers, the government costed the impact of all the 2010-11 natural disasters at $6.8 billion over 2010-11 to 2013-14. Ironically, the Bligh government ended up spending money on the

---

[175] John Quiggin et al., 2009a, *Economists statement on Queensland asset sales*, 24 November 2009, available via johnquiggin.com.

reconstruction from the 2010-11 floods at the same time as it was spending money on the drought-resilient water infrastructure. For example, the 2011-12 Capital Statement, one of the budget papers, revealed the government was expected to spend $36.2 million to settle land associated with the Western Corridor Recycled Water scheme, and it would spend $16.9 million on stage 2 of the Northern Pipeline Interconnector, part of the SEQ Water Grid.[176]

The natural disasters compounded the Queensland government's fiscal deterioration, but of course the deterioration had started several years earlier. The natural disasters just made it much worse. And it should be remembered that the federal government picks up a large part of the bill for natural disasters under the Natural Disaster Relief and Recovery Arrangements. When interviewed for this book, former Under Treasurer Mark Gray succinctly explained the contribution of the natural disasters to Queensland's fiscal deterioration as follows:

> During the resources boom, ongoing expenditures were boosted in line with upside revenue rather than trend revenue growth. This happened at both state and Commonwealth levels. When upside revenues evaporated, governments discovered they hadn't stashed enough away for a rainy day. Then, when the floods and Cyclone Yasi came, Queensland had no fiscal capacity left. This exacerbated a deteriorating fiscal situation.
>
> In the 2000s, successive Queensland governments had the view that 'throwing money' at a problem would make it go away. Significant capital investment was undertaken over a number of years – irrespective of the merits or efficiency of that investment. Firstly, it was energy, then health, especially hospitals, then water infrastructure to counter the threat of the looming drought. Increasingly, this investment was funded by debt, as other funding sources were exhausted.

The former Under Treasurer's comments highlight the importance of

---

[176] Queensland Treasury, 2011a, *State Budget 2011-12: Capital Statement*, budget paper no. 3, p. 70.

prudent budget management and the need to reduce Queensland state debt to a level where there is a substantial buffer that would allow future governments to respond to disasters or crises.

Assessment of the Bligh government

Ultimately the Bligh government suffered a harsh judgment from Queensland voters. Bligh government MPs would have recognised there was a mood for change. Many Queenslanders were critical of the government's performance and its breach of promise regarding privatisation. Bligh had started out behind in the campaign, and made her position worse during the campaign with an ill-judged attack on the integrity of her LNP opponent Campbell Newman that was found to be baseless. Still, Bligh and her colleagues must have been shocked by the huge swing of over 15 percent against the government, giving the LNP around 63 percent of the two-party preferred vote, and 78 out of 89 seats in the parliament. As noted above, Labor was reduced to seven seats, and notably it had lost heartland seats such as Ipswich, held at the time by Bligh's Finance Minister Rachel Nolan, who in her former role as Transport Minister played a major role in the QR National privatisation. Two seats were won by Katter's Australian Party (KAP) and independent Peter Wellington retained his seat.

Did the Bligh government deserve such a harsh judgment from the electorate? Certainly there were several grounds for disappointment. Undoubtedly, it was during the Bligh government that Queensland's fiscal performance deteriorated (Figure 5.3 and Table 5.5), and it was the Bligh government that received the blame, even if earlier decisions by the Beattie government, such as the abandonment of the rule against borrowing for social infrastructure and arguably under-investment in public infrastructure in its earlier years, were contributing factors.

Figure 5.3 Queensland general government expenses and revenues as percentages of GSP

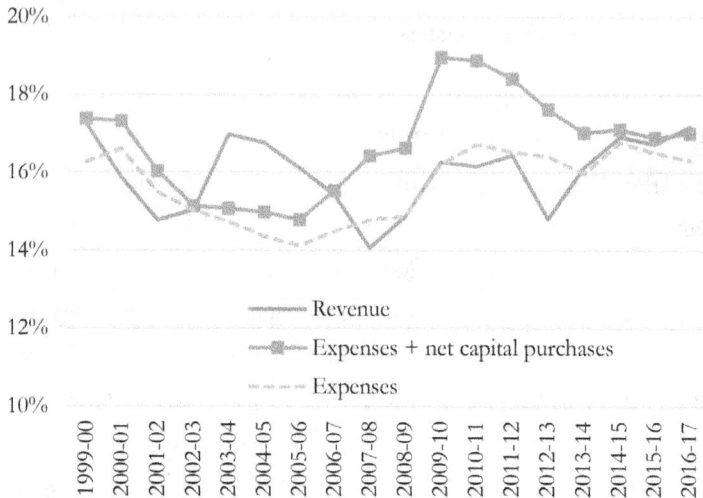

Source: Various state budget papers and ABS GFS data.

Premier Anna Bligh and Treasurer Andrew Fraser worked hard to respond to the problems handed to them by Beattie. But they failed to scale back the huge capital works program that had been put in place by policy responses shaped during the Beattie government, and the failure to do so—partly encouraged by the Rudd government which wanted Queensland to maintain its capital spending during the financial crisis—more-or-less guaranteed the loss of the AAA credit rating, resulting in higher borrowing costs, in 2009.

During the Bligh government there were both operating and fiscal deficits. In calculating the net operating balance, recurrent expenses are subtracted from revenues. The fiscal balance takes into account capital investment expenditures as well. As we shall see, there can be some justification for running a fiscal deficit if borrowings are financing infrastructure delivering a return on investment. But an operating deficit is unambiguously bad, and leaves governments exposed to the criticism they are borrowing money to pay public servants' wages.[177]

Table 5.5 Budget outcomes under the Bligh government

	2007-08 $ million	2008-09 $ million	2009-10 $ million	2010-11 $ million	2011-12 $ million
A. Revenue	31,493	37,055	39,739	41,969	45,802
B. Total expenses	33,052	37,015	39,788	43,484	46,030
C. Net operating balance (A-B)	-1,559	40	-49	-1,515	-228
D. Gross fixed capital formation	5,090	6,353	7,881	7,516	7,605
E. Depreciation (& other adjustments)	1,423	1,919	1,359	1,916	2,276
F. Net acquisition of non-financial assets (D-E)	3,667	4,434	6,522	5,600	5,329
G. Net lending (C-F)	-5,226	-4,395	-6,571	-7,115	-5,557
Indicators					
Net lending as percentage of GSP	-2.3%	-1.7%	-2.6%	-2.6%	-1.9%
Revenue growth	-1.7%	17.7%	7.2%	5.6%	9.1%
Expenses growth	9.4%	12.0%	7.5%	9.3%	5.9%
GFCF growth	37.9%	24.8%	24.1%	-4.6%	1.2%
Revenue growth - real per capita	-8.9%	12.4%	2.1%	0.0%	6.0%
Expenses growth - real per capita	1.5%	7.0%	2.4%	3.5%	2.8%
GFCF growth - real per capita	27.8%	19.3%	18.1%	-9.7%	-1.8%

Source: ABS GFS, cat. no. 5512.0, various issues.

Very few people remain who would defend the Bligh government. Even Peter Beattie, who Bligh served as Deputy Premier and Treasurer, has criticised the Bligh government. As argued through this book, the Bligh

---

[177] Note, for simplicity and so figures reported can be easily reconciled with published budget papers, I will quote dollar figures in nominal terms, not adjusting for inflation. I consider this permissible in this context, because CPI inflation would only account for a very small part of the huge increase in the debt Queensland saw. Between 2005-06 and 2015-16, total borrowings increased 421 percent from $17.3 billion to $72.9 billion, while total CPI inflation over this period only amounted to 29 percent.

government inherited a number of problems from Beattie's governments, and there were substantial capital works already underway when Bligh assumed power, so Beattie's comments must have caused the former Premier Bligh some indignation. Writing in 2016, in his book *Reform of the Federation*, Beattie contrasted expenses growth between the Beattie and Bligh governments. He compared average annual real per capita expenses growth up to the end of 2006-07 (when he was Premier) of 0.75 percent with the average growth rate of 2.3 percent over the following six years (when Bligh was Premier). Beattie observed:

> There is no doubt the GFC [global financial crisis] belted Queensland. The state's massive capital program should have been cut back when the crisis hit. I retired before the GFC in 2007 but I would have slowed the program until the budget improved.[178]

But the precedent Beattie had set with his big spending responses to various political crises and particularly commitments to a long-term program of capital works in health and water, as well as the introduction of an ambitious SEQ Infrastructure Plan, ended up have a profoundly negative influence on the Bligh government.

Political scientists may note that Premier Anna Bligh was from the Socialist Left faction of the Labor Party. Arguably the emphasis on the benefits of government infrastructure investments and programs, without much regard to the long-term budgetary implications, could be attributed partly to a left-wing ideology, which prioritises social outcomes and minimises economic and fiscal concerns. Recall that, at the end of its term, the government was no longer meeting its own fiscal principles. In contrast to the Bligh government, the Goss government had a Premier hailing from the conservative Australian Workers Union (AWU) faction. The internal factional balance of the Goss and Bligh governments may partly explain their differing governing philosophies and ultimate fiscal outcomes, but that is a matter best resolved by a political scientist rather than an economist.

---

[178] Beattie, P., 2016, op. cit.

Ultimately, it was a failure to keep control of both operating expenses and capital purchases, and to keep a buffer in the forward estimates on the operating budget, that undid the Bligh government. The increase in capital expenditure under the Bligh government was simply too large to accommodate without large increases in debt.

6

NEWMAN AND NICHOLLS—TOO MUCH TOO SOON

Newman steps up from council to state government

Before entering Queensland state politics, Campbell Newman was a hugely popular Lord Mayor of Brisbane, famous for his "can do" attitude, which saw him embark on ambitious projects such as the Clem-7 Tunnel, from Woolloongabba to Lutwyche, and the Legacy Way tunnel, from Toowong to Kelvin Grove. Fittingly, former MP for Cairns Gavin King titled his biography of Campbell Newman *Can Do*.

Newman, born in 1963 and 48 years old when he became Queensland Premier in March 2012, seemed well suited to leadership. His parents were both federal Liberal government ministers. His father Kevin Newman had served in a variety of portfolios in the Fraser government, and his mother Jocelyn Newman was Minister for Family and Community Services in the Howard government.

Newman was a graduate of the Royal Military College, Duntroon. After twelve years in the army, Newman, then a major, retired from the army to seek a corporate career. He earned an MBA from UQ and rose to become CEO of Graincorp, a grain marketing and logistics company. Newman then sought a political career and won the Brisbane Lord Mayoral election for the Liberal Party in March 2004. He served as Lord Mayor up to April 2011, when he was, unconventionally, installed as leader of the state LNP opposition—even though he was not yet in Parliament.

The Queensland Liberal and National parties merged in July 2008 to

143

become the LNP. This was considered essential to improving their chances in future elections, as it eliminated three-cornered contests in seats. This was a problem under the optional preferential voting system in Queensland that was introduced by the Goss Government. Later we will see that the Palaszczuk Government controversially reinstated compulsory preferential voting, eliminating one of the rationales for the merger of the conservative parties.

Newman replaced John-Paul Langbroek as Leader of the Opposition. While he was not yet an MP, his Deputy, Jeff Seeney, member for Callide in regional Queensland, represented him in the Parliament. Newman had replaced Langbroek because LNP members wanted to be sure they would win government at the next election. Some may have thought this was almost guaranteed, given the ALP had been in government for four terms and the Bligh government was unpopular due to its privatisation backflip, but the party switched anyway. It seemed like a good idea at the time. As noted above, the LNP under Newman won the election with a record haul of seats, with Newman winning the seat of Ashgrove in Brisbane's inner west. But by the time of the next election in 2015, many in the LNP may have regretted the switch to Newman, with opinion polls showing the government and opposition were running close together. We will consider below what led to this incredible reversal of fortune.

Newman appointed Tim Nicholls as Treasurer. Nicholls was a 46-year old urbane former solicitor and Brisbane City Councillor, who had represented the blue-ribbon ultra-safe LNP seat of Clayfield since September 2006. He was born in Melbourne, but his family moved to Queensland when he was young. Nicholl's attended the prestigious Anglican Church Grammar School, colloquially known as "Churchie", followed by QUT, from which he graduated with a law degree.

Treasurer Nicholls played a major role in the Newman government and was one of its most visible members, given the emphasis the government put on repairing the budget and paying down debt. The importance of the Treasury portfolio in the Newman government was almost guaranteed from its outset, with the new government having received a strong message from the Queensland Treasury upon assuming office.

An ominous greeting from Queensland Treasury

Very soon after an election, often the day after, newly elected Premiers (or Prime Ministers) and Treasurers are greeted by senior bureaucrats, typically the head of the Premier's (or PM's) Department and the head of the Treasury. The agency heads typically brief the newly elected leadership team on the core issues facing the government. Detailed advice from the bureaucrats on what the government should do upon assuming power is handed to the leadership team in the form of an incoming government brief. An incoming government brief offers government agencies the rare opportunity to fundamentally alter the approach of the government on particular issues. So it was regarding Queensland's public finances. Incidentally, the agency heads who would have greeted the new government, John Bradley from Premier and Cabinet and Gerard Bradley from Treasury, were soon replaced by advisers Newman and Nicholls were more familiar with, Jon Grayson and Helen Gluer respectively.[179]

Premier Newman and Treasurer Nicholls were welcomed into government by the Queensland Treasury with these ominous words in the Treasury's *Fiscal Reform Blueprint*:

> Queensland's fiscal position and outlook is unsustainable and restoration must be an urgent priority for this term of government.[180]

In the Treasury's 2012 assessment, Queensland's expenditure effort was

---

[179] Helen Gluer was replaced as Under Treasurer mid-way through the term of the Newman Government by Mark Gray.

[180] Queensland Treasury, 2012a, *Incoming Government Brief: Fiscal Reform Blueprint*, tabled in Queensland Parliament on 21 May 2015, p. ES-1.

similar to efforts in other states, but Queensland's revenue raising effort was still lower.[181] Obviously, this raised questions about the sustainability of such fiscal policy settings. The Treasury's assessment of Queensland's fiscal position being unsustainable was later supported by the Newman government's Commission of Audit (to be discussed in the next section), and in a 2015 academic study by Griffith University Professor Tony Makin and Economic Society of Australia (QLD) Vice-President Julian Pearce. Makin and Pearce found that, based on 2012-13 budget figures, and on the prevailing interest rate on government debt and the GSP growth rate, the primary budget balance (i.e. the budget balance excluding interest payments) was in deficit, whereas a small primary surplus was required for sustainability.[182]

The Newman government heeded the words of the *Fiscal Reform Blueprint*, and indeed its zealous pursuit of restoring Queensland's fiscal position arguably cost it dearly on election day, 31 January 2015. The *Fiscal Reform Blueprint* recommended the government adopt some new fiscal principles, strengthening those the Bligh government had in place—recall the Bligh government's weak operating budget requirement where expenses were net of depreciation. The blueprint also recommended strategies to move the budget back toward sustainability, including by controlling employee expenses which had grown at a very high rate over the term of the previous government, particularly across health, education and police (see Box 6.1).[183] It also made recommendations around GOC governance, essentially advocating a return to the framework the Goss government had put in place.

---

[181] Ibid., p. C-2-3.

[182] Tony Makin and Julian Pearce, 2014, "How Sustainable is Sub-national Public Debt in Australia?", *Economic Analysis and Policy*, 44(4), p. 369.

[183] Queensland Treasury, 2012a, op. cit., p. C-3-5.

Box 6.1 Queensland Treasury's Fiscal Reform Blueprint

Principles

Principle 1. Stabilise then significantly reduce the Non-financial Public Sector Debt to Revenue Ratio

Principle 2. Ensure growth in expenses does not exceed growth in revenue

Principle 3. Achieve a General Government sector net lending surplus as soon as possible but no later than 2015-16

Principle 4. Maintain a competitive tax environment for business

Principle 5. Target full funding of long term liabilities such as superannuation in accordance with actuarial advice

Strategies

Strategy 1. Protect the financial interests of the State in matters of Intergovernmental Financial Relations

Strategy 2. Set revenue and expenditure policies to achieve a sustainable budget position having regard to the implications of horizontal fiscal equalisation

Strategy 3. Control growth in employee expenses

Strategy 4. Provide agencies with the tools and flexibility they need to manage their budgets, and enforce accountability

Strategy 5. Make high quality decisions around capital spending, the State's balance sheet holdings and financing

Strategy 6. Ensure utility pricing policies are fiscally responsible

Strategy 7. Pursue ongoing commercial reform of Government Owned Corporations

Source: Queensland Treasury, 2012a, Incoming Government Brief: Fiscal Reform Blueprint.

While the Treasury made some strong recommendations, it was ultimately up to the Newman government to decide just how vigorously it would pursue budget repair and the size of the cuts to expenses and public service full-time equivalent (FTE) employees. It turns out it that it chose to prosecute the *Fiscal Reform Blueprint* with extreme vigour. To illustrate, in the 2013-14 financial year, the Queensland government experienced the extraordinary outcome of a decline in expenses—even in nominal terms (i.e. dollar terms, unadjusted for inflation)—which is typically unheard of.

Over the term of the Newman government, public service numbers were cut by around 14,000 FTE employees, with Queensland Health, Housing and Public Works, and Transport and Main Roads acutely affected (Figure 6.1). Regarding the Department of Transport and Main Roads, given it was an amalgamation of two former and separate Departments of Transport and Main Roads by the Bligh government in 2009, arguably there was lot of duplication occurring in the department that justified a large reduction in staffing.

Reflecting on the pace of the Newman government's reform efforts, the government's Minister for Transport Scott Emerson observed when interviewed for this book:

> It may be a fair criticism to say it was too much too soon. The challenge was the LNP had been out of power for most of the last two decades. Under Labor, Queensland had gone backwards. We wanted to fix things straight away. There was a failure to take people with us.[184]

In part, the government suffered because, after condemning the Bligh government for ruining public finances, it had to follow through with a major reform program. In addition to job cuts, another controversial policy was privatisation. Early in its term, on 8 October 2012, the Newman government announced it was selling down the state government's shareholding in QR National from 33 percent to 15 percent.[185] This was uncontroversial at the

---

[184] Interview by the author, 15 March 2017.
[185] Stephen Baines, 2014, *Steel on Steel*, University of Queensland Press, p. 150.

time as, since the QR National float by the Bligh government, the state government was no longer the majority shareholder. Incidentally, in what appeared to be an attempt to cast off any remaining associations with its previous public ownership, QR National rebranded itself as Aurizon on 1 December 2012. The Newman government went even further in selling down its stake in Aurizon and, by the end of the 2013, the state government owned less than 5 percent of the company.[186]

Figure 6.1 Public service cuts by agency, top 10, reduction in FTEs between June 2012 and June 2013

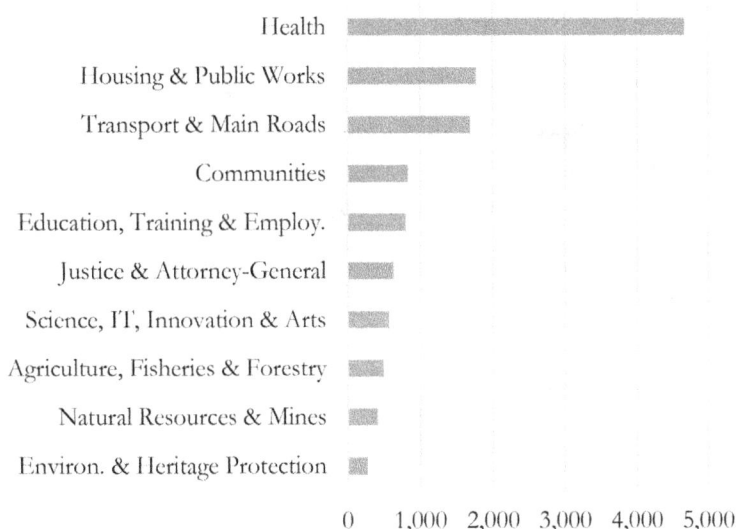

Source: Based Queensland Public Service Workforce Quarterly Profile, June 2013 and June 2012.

Based on its experience in selling down the state's shareholding in Aurizon, the Newman government may have felt further privatisation would not cause it too much political trouble. As time passed, it was obvious the government had misjudged the views of the electorate on privatisation, as the Bligh government had done in its last term.

---

[186] Andrew Fraser, 2013, "Queensland sells down stake in railways carrier Aurizon", *The Australian*, 4 December 2013, available via www.theaustralian.com.au.

A new Commission of Audit

As the previous conservative government in Queensland, the Borbidge government, had done, the Newman government appointed a Commission of Audit to advise on the state of Queensland's public finances and to recommend corrective measures. The government appointed former federal Liberal Treasurer Peter Costello to lead the Commission. Other members of the Newman government's Commission of Audit included Joan Sheldon's Under Treasurer Doug McTaggart and the Vice-Chancellor of James Cook University, Sandra Harding. Treasury stalwart, and later Under Treasurer in the Newman government, Mark Gray led the Treasury secretariat assisting the Commission.

The Commission reported in two stages. First, it issued an interim report in June 2012, around three months after the Newman government's election. The interim report argued Queensland's public finances were unsustainable and a range of reforms were needed. Second, in early 2013, the Commission issued a final report, covering the broad sweep of Queensland's public sector and containing detailed recommendations across multiple policy areas.

The Commission's interim report found:

> In recent years, the government of Queensland embarked on an unsustainable level of spending which has jeopardised the financial position of the state.
>
> Queensland has moved from a position of considerable financial strength just six years ago to a position of weakness today. Its performance has been worse than the other states over that period.[187]

In its interim report, the Commission produced some disturbing extrapolations of recent fiscal trends, suggesting the fiscal deficit could blow out to nearly $20 billion in 2015-16 and that the total government debt-to-revenue ratio could approach 200 percent.[188] Extrapolating further

---

[187] Queensland Commission of Audit, 2012, op. cit., p. 1.
[188] Ibid., pp. 48-49.

out, total debt could reach $100 billion by 2018-19.

To correct the unsustainable course resulting from past "ill-discipline", corrective actions were needed, with the Commission identifying a need to:

- review the range of services which should be provided by government
- re-prioritise and rationalise core service delivery functions
- evaluate whether there may be better ways of delivering some services.[189]

In other words, the Commission suggested a program of privatisation of government businesses—or to use the term that would come to dominate the debate, asset sales—and of contracting out or out-sourcing. This created a political challenge for the Newman government, given that, while in opposition, the LNP was critical of privatisations conducted by the Bligh government.

The Commission's interim findings and broad recommendations were used to justify strong corrective actions taken by the Newman government in its first year, discussed below. In its response to the Interim Report from the Commission on 11 July 2012, the Newman government set out its fiscal principles (Box 6.2). By targeting a fiscal surplus by 2014-15, it effectively committed itself to very strong measures in its first two budgets.

The strictness of the requirement to target a fiscal surplus was recognised at the time by the government. It noted in the media release announcing the fiscal principles that it had only committed to an operating surplus in 2014-15 during the election.[190] The government was motivated by the Commission of Audit's view that an operating surplus was insufficient to restore Queensland's public finances to a sustainable path. This view had much merit. If the government still ran fiscal deficits it would still be

---

[189]   Ibid., 2012, pp. 10-11.
[190]   Tim Nicholls, 2012, *Government's interim response to the Commission of Audit*, media release by the Treasurer, available via www.statements.qld.gov.au.

accumulating debt and not making any progress toward regaining the AAA credit rating. While it was quite possible that, if it ran relatively modest fiscal deficits (and debt grew at a slower rate than GSP and total government revenue), Queensland might eventually regain a AAA rating, this could not be guaranteed, particularly if one considered the potential for future adverse shocks, whether a recession or another financial crisis, and the looming impact of demographic change on the state budget. The impact of the latter was the focus of significant analysis by the Commission, and featured in its longer-term modelling.

Box 6.2 Newman Government's fiscal principles adopted following 2012 Commission of Audit Interim Report

To stabilise then significantly reduce debt;

To achieve and maintain a general government sector fiscal balance in 2014-15;

To maintain a competitive tax environment for business; and

To target full funding of long term liabilities in accordance with actuarial advice

---

Source: Tim Nicholls, 2012a, Government's interim response to Commission of Audit, 11 July 2012, media statement available at www.statements.qld.gov.au.

The Australian government started publishing regular so-called intergenerational reports assessing its own long-run budget position in 2002. In 2005, the Productivity Commission extended the analysis that was done for the Commonwealth to the states and territories. The Commission noted:

> On past trends, much of this could be expected to be borne by the Australian government, but there are significant potential burdens faced by State and Territory governments.[191]

The uncertainly is related to what happens to Commonwealth special

---

[191] Productivity Commission, 2005, *Economic Implications of an Ageing Australia*, research report, p. XII.

purpose payments to states and territories. Regardless, there is certainly a risk to the long-run budget positions of state and territory governments from population ageing.

The Commission of Audit's final report included an economic modelling exercise, which appears to have drawn on the expertise of staff seconded from the Treasury to the secretariat for the Commission. It adopted the same modelling framework as the Australian Treasury's Intergenerational Report, starting with demographic and macroeconomic supply-side assumptions regarding future births, deaths, migration, labour force participation, and productivity growth variables. The projected workforce and economic output values are inputted into a long-run budget model, in which expenditures are related to the age composition of the population, as well as current trends in service delivery costs, and in which government revenue is related to economic growth.

Being honest about the massive uncertainty surrounding such long-run projection models, the Commission of Audit secretariat prepared two scenarios, a lower growth scenario, with a pessimistic assumption regarding future economic growth, and a higher growth scenario with an optimistic assumption. In the lower growth scenario, revenue was projected to grow at an annual average rate of 1.7% per annum over 2015-16 to 2050-51. Based on current fiscal policy settings, the Commission projected in the low growth scenario the budget deficit would blow out to 16 percent of GSP by 2050-51. In the high growth scenario, annual average revenue growth of 2.5 percent was projected, and the budget deficit was projected to increase to 12.9 percent.[192] Of course, both the low growth and high growth scenarios resulted in an unsustainable and unimaginable budget deficit. Policies and programs would need to be adjusted long before that situation ever occurred. But the analysis was useful in highlighting the

---

[192] This discussion is based on the analysis in Queensland Commission of Audit, 2013, *Final Report—February 2013*, volume 2, pp. 2-14 to 2-16.

adverse fiscal circumstances the state government was in, and the need for strong measures.

Political controversy over the Commission of Audit

The Commission came under criticism for being politically biased, owing to the appointment of Peter Costello as its Chair. It may have been much better to have appointed as Commission head a distinguished academic or consulting economist, as the Borbidge government had done with Vince Fitzgerald. Furthermore, the assumptions made by the Commission of Audit in its economic modelling arguably led it to exaggerate the extent of the future debt burden expected based on policy settings inherited from the Bligh government. In 2016, former Premier Peter Beattie commented that regarding the Commission of Audit's analysis:

> …Adrian Noon, a smart former Queensland Treasury official, pointed out the faulty analysis underlying the Costello report. It had been constructed on highly conservative, unrealistic assumptions.
>
> The Costello audit forecast revenue of between 1.7 per cent a year as its lower growth scenario and 2.5 per cent a year as its higher growth scenario. This analysis was confirmed as overcautious as early as the 2013-14 Queensland government's mid-year fiscal and economic review, where the four-year revenue growth for the general government sector was 28.1 per cent. Annualised, revenue averaged 6.4 per cent a year, way above the ridiculous modelling in the Costello report.[193]

Beattie's point is correct for the years following the Commission of Audit report but it ignores the fact the Commission of Audit report modelled a long-run scenario out to 2050. The budget problem the Newman government had inherited had a structural, long-term dimension. While criticising what he saw as a "politically motivated audit", Beattie probably

---

[193] Beattie, 2016.

should have disclosed that Adrian Noon was a former staff member in his and Terry Mackenroth's ministerial offices. Noon was one of the key economic advisers to the Beattie and Bligh governments. That said, Noon is a highly regarded economic official, with experience that has included the Australian Bureau of Statistics and Department of Prime Minister and Cabinet.

Then Shadow Treasurer Curtis Pitt published the Labor opposition's Interim Response to the Queensland Commission of Audit in May 2013. Among other criticisms of the report, Pitt highlighted that the Commission of Audit's projections model assumed unrealistically low economic growth projections to 2050 (of 1.6-2.4 percent per annum).[194] He compared the growth projections to those contained in Deloitte Access Economics and Queensland Treasury modelling of the impacts of a carbon price on Queensland, which projected an annual average growth rate 2.8-2.9 percent growth from 2009-10 to 2049-50.[195] However, it is unclear to what extent the Queensland Treasury and Deloitte Access Economics carbon price studies took into account the impacts of expected demographic changes over the coming decades.

Pitt's interim response to the Commission of Audit argued it had exaggerated Queensland's adverse fiscal circumstances, under-estimated the state's growth prospects, and largely ignored the impact of the financial crisis on the state's economy and budget. Pitt saw the Commission of Audit report being used to justify a privatisation program, and it was in Pitt's interim response to the Commission of Audit that Queensland Labor's revised stance on privatisation was confirmed. The party that, during the Bligh government, had engaged in the largest privatisation program seen before or after in Queensland history—and without an election mandate— was now fully opposed to the Newman government doing the same thing. Pitt wrote in his foreword to the *Interim Response*:

---

194   Curtis Pitt, 2013, *Interim Response to the Queensland Commission of Audit*, p. 6.
195   Ibid. and Queensland Treasury, 2011b, *Carbon Price Impacts for Queensland*.

> The Opposition is...steadfastly opposed to the program of asset sales and mass privatisation being undertaken with no election mandate by the Newman Government.[196]

The Commission of Audit's interim and final reports were also criticised by prominent academics, including John Quiggin and Bob Walker, who prepared a detailed response to the interim report for the Queensland Council of Unions which was critical of the total debt measure used by the Commission, among other aspects of the reports.[197]

Despite generating substantial political controversy and possibly somewhat exaggerating Queensland's fiscal situation, the Commission of Audit Report nonetheless was an excellent contribution to Queensland's public policy debate. Even if some of its assumptions led it to exaggerate the fiscal problem, there is no doubt Queensland faced a major challenge at the time, as suggested by the ominous greeting to the Newman government in Treasury's Incoming Government Brief, discussed above. The three volumes of the Commission of Audit report formed an impressive guide to the reform of the Queensland government that is still relevant today. With solid analysis of policy issues across the wide range of public services in Queensland, and strong arguments in support of greater outsourcing and privatisation—arguments which still need to be prosecuted—the report will continue to have a long shelf life.

In a May 2013 presentation, head of the Commission Secretariat and later Under Treasurer Mark Gray observed that the government had accepted 118 (or 76 percent) of the Commission's recommendations in its response provided at the end of April 2013.[198] It accepted a further seven

---

[196] Pitt, C. 2013, op. cit., p. ii.

[197] See: John Quiggin, 2012, *The Queensland Commission of Audit Interim Report—June 2012: A Critical Review*; John Quiggin, 2013, "The Queensland Commission of Audit Final Report: A Critical Review", *RSMG Working Paper Series*, no. P13_1; and Bob Walker and Betty Con Walker, 2012, *Review of the Costello Report: Crude analysis. Not 'independent'. Not an 'audit'*, report prepared for the Queensland Council of Unions.

[198] Mark Gray, 2013, *Inside the Queensland Commission of Audit—The Process, Main Findings and Implications*, UQ Business School presentation.

recommendations in principle, six in part, noted 13, deferred five for further consideration, and rejected six, with the major recommendations rejected relating to the privatisation of electricity businesses.[199] The Commission of Audit had recommended the privatisation of Energex and Ergon, among other GOCs, which the Newman government initially rejected, but fatefully would come to recommend in its Strong Choices policy plan. Although some of the Commission's recommendations were rejected, the government committed to implementing a large number of them and it was expected the implementation of many of the Commission's recommendations—e.g. contestability of public transport services, commercialisation of TAFE, among others—would have had profound consequences for public service delivery and would have driven efficiency and productivity improvements. However, the implementation of a range of the Newman government's reforms were halted, as with the Public Sector Renewal Program, or largely reversed, as with the commercialisation of TAFE, when the Newman government lost power in early 2015.[200]

Slash and burn first budget

Queensland state budgets are typically handed down in June each year, but the timing of the 2012 election on 24 March meant the new government had insufficient time to have a budget prepared consistent with its priorities by June. So the release of the 2012-13 budget was deferred until Tuesday 11 September 2012.

In its first budget, the Newman government projected a very large improvement in the budget over the forward estimates, including the achievement of a fiscal surplus of $652 million in 2014-15. But, as discussed below, subsequent events frustrated the achievement of this surplus.

---

[199] Ibid. and Queensland Government, 2013, *A Plan—Better Services for Queenslanders: Queensland Government Response to the Independent Commission of Audit Final Report.*

[200] In July 2015, the Palaszczuk Government abolished the Newman Government's Queensland Training Assets Management Authority, which was seen as the precursor to privatising TAFE.

Unlike Andrew Fraser's budget speeches, there was no harking back to previous Treasurers by new Queensland Treasurer Tim Nicholls. But the Treasurer clearly had a sense of the historical importance of his first budget, and the need for strong measures to correct the budgetary situation, labelling it "the most important Budget in a generation."[201] In his speech, the Treasurer noted the traditional conservative government focal points of families, small business, and regional Queensland, and he reiterated the government's various policy priorities. These included improving "frontline" services such as health and education, lowering the cost of living, a 4 percent unemployment rate, and growing a "four pillar" economy. The so-called four pillars were agriculture, construction, resources (i.e. mining), and tourism.

Treasurer Nicholls cited the Commission of Audit's projections regarding the future trajectory of debt in support of his proposed corrective budget measures. He noted the CBRC had been assisting ministers and Director-Generals of government agencies to help identify savings. On budget day, he announced the number of FTE employees to be cut would be 14,000 in 2012-13. Taking into account that some of the cuts would come from currently unfilled positions, Nicholls noted that the public service cuts would involve around 10,600 redundancies. The cuts would save the budget around $3.7 billion over 2012-13 to 2016-17.[202] As well as showing substantial expenditure restraint, the Treasurer announced the government would also act on the revenue side of the budget, notably with a significant increase in rates for coal royalties, which was expected to raise $1.6 billion over the forward estimates.[203]

---

[201] Queensland Treasury, 2012b, *State Budget 2012-13: Budget Speech*, p. 1.
[202] Ibid., p. 7.
[203] Ibid., p. 17.

Strong Choices

Fatefully, the Newman government eventually decided to adopt the Commission of Audit's recommendations regarding privatisation of several GOCs. It started off its privatisation campaign, labelled Strong Choices, in February 2014 with what it called Community Leader Roundtables followed by a $6 million promotional campaign. In April 2014, it appealed to a wider audience, releasing an interactive website, labelled the *People's Budget Interactive Tool*, which allowed people to simulate Queensland's public finances using a simplistic model. It had the purpose of illustrating the obvious point that if a government wants to reduce debt, it either needs to raise taxes, cut spending, or sell assets. It is debatable whether the website was genuinely informative and persuasive, or just a gimmick.

On 3 June 2014, the Newman government released its draft plan *The Strongest & Smartest Choice: Queensland's Plan for Secure Finances and a Strong Economy*. The government repeated the messages from the Treasury's blueprint and the Commission of Audit's report regarding the poor state of Queensland's public finances and the need to pay down debt. Regarding the three options the government had—to cut services, increase taxes, or sell or lease out assets—it said the clear message from community consultation was that "raising taxes or reducing services were the least preferred options for achieving savings of the magnitude required."[204] Hence, in its draft Strong Choices plan, the government proposed a combination of leasing out assets, outright sale, and equity investments in GOCs.

In the draft Strong Choices plan, assets proposed for sale included the water distribution business, SunWater Industrial Pipelines, and the electricity generating GOCs Stanwell and CS Energy. The electricity transmission and distribution companies, Powerlink, Energex and Ergon, were candidates for private sector investment, in the form of what the government labelled

---

[204] Queensland Government, 2014a, *Reforming Queensland's electricity network reliability standards*, Cabinet paper lodged by the Minister for Energy and Water Supply., p. 4.

a non-share equity interest. Private sector equity investors would get a share of future profits, but would not have any control over a company in which a non-share equity interest was offered. An injection of equity from the private sector would allow the GOCs to pay down debt held on their balance sheets.

The only assets originally proposed for long-term leasing out to the private sector were those of the Gladstone Ports Corporation and the Port of Townsville Limited and the Mount Isa to Townsville rail line. Previously, the Beattie and Bligh Labor governments had leased out the Dalrymple Bay Coal Terminal, in 2002 to DBCT Management Pty Ltd for 50 years with an option for an additional 49, and the Port of Brisbane in 2009, to a consortium led by QIC and Industry Funds Management, now IFM Investors for 99 years.

In reaching the conclusion that selling or leasing out assets was necessary, the government could certainly point to an extensive community consultation process, even if the people's budget website left a lot to be desired as an informational tool. The draft Strong Choices plan noted:

> Ultimately, more than 255,000 people visited the Strong Choices website, and over 55,000 Queenslanders submitted their own 'People's Budget' online, outlining their saving and spending priorities.
>
> Almost 20,000 people attended public forums or participated in virtual town halls held around the State. Treasurer Tim Nicholls travelled more than 19,000 kilometres to meet with Queenslanders personally to discuss the Strong Choices options.[205]

Nonetheless, there was a strong adverse community reaction to its proposed privatisations, suggesting quantity was no substitute for quality in the consultation process. After experiencing the adverse public reaction the proposed asset sales had received after the release of the draft plan in June, the government changed its mind. Rather than selling many of the assets,

---

[205] Queensland Government, 2014b, *The Strongest & Smartest Choice: Queensland's Plan for Secure Finances and a Strong Economy*, p. 4.

it would lease them all out instead. This was announced in the final plan released in early October 2014. The government had dropped any notion of asset sales, including that of the non-share equity interests. It noted in the final plan that consultations on the draft plan with "business leaders, community spokespeople, independent economic analysts and members of the public" revealed:

> …while Queenslanders recognised the threat posed by the State's billion-dollar interest payments, and could see the potential for further investment if the burden of those payments could be lifted, they remained reluctant to lose a stake in these public enterprises.[206]

The Newman government obviously believed that leasing out the assets instead would be much more palatable to the public. Given that to obtain the desired proceeds the government would need to lease the assets out for very long periods (e.g. 50 or 99 years), some critics argued it was effectively selling assets anyway, although the government could technically claim the assets were remaining in government ownership. As UQ Professor John Quiggin had noted in the context of the Bligh government's large proposed privatisation program in 2009:

> The use of a 99-year lease rather than an outright sale is a device commonly used by governments seeking to make privatisation palatable, but one that makes no commercial sense for assets of this kind. The public loses the asset just as surely as if it had been sold, but gets a lower price because the buyer does not become an outright owner.[207]

By the time of its final plan, the Newman government was able to claim a higher expected value of privatisation proceeds of $37 billion, compared with $34 billion in the Draft Plan. This was due to both increases in the book values of state assets held by the GOCs and also because the government

---

[206] Queensland Government, 2014c, *The Strongest & Smartest Choice: Queensland's Plan for Secure Finances and a Strong Economy—Final Plan*, pp. 4-5.

[207] John Quiggin, 2009b, *Statement on Asset Sales*, 8 December 2009, available via www. johnquiggin.com.

had dropped its originally planned non-share equity interest investments in the electricity businesses, which were unpopular with the market, opting instead for leasing out those assets.[208]

Of the $37 billion in proceeds from leasing out the assets, $25 billion would be used to reduce State debt, $8.6 billion would be used to fund capital works (under the Strong Choices Future Investment Program), and $3.4 billion would be allocated to a Strong Choices Cost of Living Fund. The latter fund was designed to reduce electricity bills by providing the electricity distributors Energex and Ergon money to pay for the Solar Bonus Scheme introduced by the Bligh government. The Solar Bonus Scheme was highly inequitable in that it benefited those households which had installed solar panels, while disadvantaging those who had not. The households who had not installed solar PV panels under the Scheme were cross-subsidising the very high feed-in tariff of 44 cents per kilowatt hour paid to those households benefiting from the Scheme. In a memorable 2014 statement to the Queensland Parliament, Treasurer Nicholls referred to households benefiting from the Solar Bonus Scheme as "champagne sippers and the latte set."[209] The adverse equity implications of the solar feed-in tariff were later confirmed by the Queensland Productivity Commission in a 2016 report to the Palaszczuk government, in which it noted:

> While some low income households own solar PV, the overall distributional impact of solar PV subsidies is to transfer income from non-solar households to solar households, and to raise the cost of living for those on the lowest incomes...[210]

The solar bonus scheme was another foreseeable and avoidable policy problem that the Bligh government passed on to its successors.

---

[208] Queensland Government, 2014c, op. cit.

[209] Amy Remeikis, 2014a, "Solar users the champagne and latte sipping set: Tim Nicholls", *Brisbane Times*, 6 June 2014, available via www.brisbanetimes.com.au.

[210] Queensland Productivity Commission, 2016, *Solar Feed-In Pricing in Queensland: Final Report*, p. xvii.

Assessment of Strong Choices' claims regarding privatisation

There was a strong case for privatisation of many Queensland government-owned businesses based on potential efficiency gains of privatised businesses. Privatised businesses have greater incentives to become more efficient which is good for keeping prices down and the productivity of the economy. The evidence, reported by a range of independent observers such as the Productivity Commission, Grattan Institute and the World Bank, suggests that privatised businesses are more efficient than publicly-owned businesses.[211]

But there have been some poorly implemented privatisations around the world, such as of British Rail and Russian utilities, so it is understandable there was some scepticism in the Queensland community about the government's proposed privatisations.

One concern raised during the Strong Choices debate was whether consumers would have to pay higher power prices after privatisation. This ignored the large amount of economic regulation and oversight of the sector, particularly by the AER. But the government had trouble on this point, because it could not easily point to power prices being significantly higher in Queensland than States with privatised networks—that is, Victoria and South Australia.

So given that comparative power prices did not tell a nice, clear story about the benefits of privatisation, the government had to rely instead on a finding by Ernst and Young (EY) for the NSW Treasury regarding the growth of power prices and network charges (i.e. the charges by Energex, Ergon and Powerlink for the use of poles and wires, and other bits of kit such as transformers at sub-stations) since the late nineties. EY found

---

[211] This evidence is discussed in Chapter 9. The relevant references are: Productivity Commission, 2013, *Electricity Network Regulatory Frameworks*, inquiry report, vol. 1; William Megginson and Jeffry Netter, 2001, "From State to Market: A Survey of Empirical Studies on Privatization", *Journal of Economic Literature*, vol. XXXIX, pp. 321-389; Tony Wood, 2012, *Putting the customer back in front: How to make electricity cheaper*, Grattan Institute; and Sunita Kikeri et al., 1992, *Privatization: The Lessons of Experience*, World Bank.

that network costs in states with government-owned electricity network businesses grew much faster than in other states with privately-owned networks.[212] In its final plan for *Strong Choices*, the Newman government noted:

> …from 1996-97 to 2012-13, network prices in the government owned networks of New South Wales and Queensland increased in real terms by 122% and 140% respectively. During that same period in Victoria, where the networks are privately owned, network prices decreased in real terms by 18%. Additionally, in the privately owned South Australian network, from 1998-99 to 2010-11, network prices also decreased by 17%.[213]

The EY study did not necessarily support the proposition that prices would be lower after privatisation. It only suggested that, based on historical experience, prices should not increase as fast as if the assets remained operated by the government-owned business.

EY later produced a report for industry peak bodies (Infrastructure Partnerships Australia, CCIQ, Australian Industry Group, and the Property Council of Australia) that estimated the possible savings for Queensland electricity consumers from privatisation.[214] An estimated electricity bill saving of $570 per annum was reported in the *Courier-Mail*, based on historical simulation of power prices, covering 1997 to 2013, assuming Queensland experienced Victorian growth rates in network costs.[215] Households would not have got their $570 p.a. back if the electricity GOCs were privatised. The inefficiency was already largely baked in, due to network investments that have already occurred. That said, under privatisation, it is expected bills

---

[212] EY, 2014, *Electricity network services: Long-term trends in prices and costs*, report prepared for NSW Treasury.

[213] Queensland Government, 2014c, op. cit., p. 34.

[214] EY, 2015, *Network Pricing Trends: Queensland Perspective*, report prepared for Infrastructure Partnerships Australia, CCIQ, AiGroup, and the Property Council of Australia.

[215] Steven Wardill, 2015a, "Queensland election 2015: Electricity prices to fall under privatisation, says audit", *Courier-Mail*, 21 January 2015, available via www.couriermail. com.au.

would be lower than they otherwise would be, as private operators would more ruthlessly control costs, running "lean and mean."

It appears the Newman government realised that privatisation would be insufficient to lower power prices. Rather than relying on privatisation alone, the Newman government was intending to force a fall in power prices through its $3.4 billion Cost of Living Fund, funded out of asset lease proceeds. The government had committed to cutting retail prices by 6 percent in 2015-16, saving a typical household $577 over five years. In one sense, this could be seen as reversing the bad policy that was the solar feed-in tariff. But, if the government wanted to provide this relief, it should ideally have found the money in its existing budget, rather than using expected lease proceeds which would be better used for debt reduction.

Another common fear regarding privatisation relates to job losses. GOCs such as Ergon (now merged with Energex in Energy Queensland) and Gladstone and Townsville ports are significant employers in regional communities across Queensland. Undeniably there would be job losses if assets were leased out, as international evidence shows efficiency gains from privatisation typically come from shedding under-utilised labour. Of course, this labour would be better employed in other industries anyway. It is no longer the role of government to act as an employer of last resort.

Assessment of the budgetary impact of Strong Choices

Unfortunately, the debate over Strong Choices was dominated by the plan's expected budgetary impacts, without much regard to the broader issue of efficiency or productivity. In part, this was because the Newman government decided to support its privatisation program by saying it was essential for reducing debt and repairing the state budget. In the final plan for Strong Choices, the government estimated that, by reducing state gross debt from $80 billion to $55 billion, it would achieve savings on interest payments of

$1.3 billion.[216] In fact, the expected proceeds from Strong Choices, debt reduction and interest savings may well have been higher.

The Newman government would have been hoping that it would receive proceeds much higher than the $37 billion in book value for the assets which was quoted in the Strong Choices campaign. Recent privatisations in Victoria and NSW demonstrate that privatised assets can trade at high multiples of book value. For example, in 2016, the Victorian government—incidentally a Labor government—successfully leased out the Port of Melbourne's assets for $9.7 billion compared with an originally expected $6 billion.[217]

Critics, such as Professor John Quiggin, countered the government's argument with the correct observation that privatisations would result in a loss of earnings—comprising dividend and tax equivalent income—from the businesses to government.[218] Tax equivalent payments are additional to dividends and are made by GOCs to the general government sector to promote competitive neutrality with private sector businesses. As state-owned entities, GOCs are exempt from Commonwealth company income tax. Hence, they would have an unfair competitive advantage to other businesses if they did not have to provision for company income tax payments to the Australian Taxation Office.

The government had tried to evade this issue by declaring in its Strong Choices plan that, regarding GOC earnings:

> ...unlike the interest payments that would be saved by repaying debt, the earnings from these businesses are not certain, but are subject to commercial, environmental and market risks associated with any profit-making enterprise.[219]

[216] Queensland Government, 2014c, op. cit., p. 5.
[217] Steven Wardill, 2016a, "Privatisation of Queensland's assets: Why voters and some economists seem to be against it", *Courier-Mail*, 24 September 2016, available via www.couriermail.com.au.
[218] John Quiggin, 2015, *Strong Choices or weak evasions: How the effective sale of public assets will weaken Queensland's fiscal position.*
[219] Queensland Government, 2014c, op. cit., p. 36.

It went on to list these risk as including competitive forces, commodity sector conditions, energy market regulation and policies, and technological change.

The Queensland Treasury knew that the Strong Choices privatisation program would likely have an adverse budgetary impact in the short-term, but it was taking a longer-term view. According to former Under Treasurer Mark Gray, senior Treasury officials considered that the future income streams from GOCs were seriously at risk from technological change and possible policy responses to climate change. The energy assets were seen as particularly vulnerable, due largely to developments in solar and battery technologies which could reduce the reliance of households on electricity generated by the state-owned CS Energy and Stanwell and distributed by Energex and Ergon Energy, now Energy Queensland.

Furthermore, according to Mark Gray, in late 2014, at presentations on the Strong Choices privatisation program to potential investors, such as superannuation and sovereign wealth funds, Queensland Treasury officials were already being asked about the impact of technological change on the future profitability of GOCs and the risk of assets being stranded. This presented a dilemma for the government. It needed to make the best case it could for the assets it was privatising, so it could maximise sales proceeds. Hence, it could not announce publicly it was deeply concerned about the impact of technological change on future GOC earnings.

The government was correct that future GOC earnings were uncertain, particularly in the medium to long-term, but it was leaving itself exposed to criticism by not publishing estimates of the budgetary impact of the privatisations. Almost certainly, Queensland Treasury would have prepared estimates of the impact of the Strong Choices privatisations over the budget forward estimates for the government.

The government was subject to criticism relatively early in its Strong Choices campaign on the lack of information about the potential impacts of privatisation, both on the budget and also on jobs, particularly in regional Queensland. For example, Amy Remeikis reported in the *Brisbane Times* in late April 2014 that "Asset sales divide economists—but they are united in saying 'Strong Choices' is flawed." Remeikis quoted UQ Economics Professors John Quiggin and John Foster on the issue of adverse budgetary impacts, and also the author of this book, with her article noting:

> "They could have used the $6 million much more wisely and spent it on decent research, decent studies, [on] what these privatisation proposals could mean, thinking about how do we communicate this to the public," Mr Tunny said.
>
> "And that is not through PR and it is not through a flashy website, it is through well crafted speeches delivered to the public, well written opinion pieces, a genuine information campaign rather than a PR campaign."[220]

In the view of critics such as John Quiggin, the loss of GOC earnings would more than exceed any savings from a reduced interest bill from a lower level of debt achieved by using privatisation proceeds. Quiggin correctly noted that a large part of the debt reduction and related interest payments would necessarily occur in the GOC sector—as the assets of GOCs were leased out, the debt of those GOCs would be extinguished—but the saving on interest payments by the GOCs would not be available for the general government. Regarding the debt of the GOCs that would need to be extinguished after the asset leases, then estimated at $18 billion, Quiggin noted:

> The interest payments on this debt are serviced out of the gross profits (earnings before interest and tax) of the GOCs themselves. The repayment of this debt will not yield any interest saving to the general government sector (that is, to the sector covered by the state budget), since the interest was already covered by GOC earnings. Hence, the relevant figure is the reduction in general government debt is around $7 billion.

---

[220] Amy Remeikis, 2014b, "Asset sales divide economists—but they are united in saying 'Strong Choices' is flawed", *Brisbane Times*, 28 April 2014, available via www.brisbanetimes.com.au..

The interest saving to the general government sector may therefore be estimated in a range from $200 million to $300 million, far below the current flow of dividends and tax equivalent payments, which is over $1 billion per year.[221]

Overall, John Quiggin estimated there would have been an adverse impact on the budget in the order of $1 billion per annum.[222] Quiggin made a fair point regarding the budgetary impact of Strong Choices, but the government's position was justifiable when considered from an economy-wide efficiency perspective, as discussed in Chapter 9, even if some of its arguments were deficient.

Regaining a AAA credit rating for Queensland government borrowings (through paying down a sufficient amount of debt) is an important policy goal. Were Queensland to get back its AAA credit rating, the Queensland government would be able to borrow at a lower interest rate, possibly around 20 to 40 basis points (i.e. 0.2-0.4 percent) lower depending on market conditions, saving hundreds of millions of dollars per annum. That would be genuinely additional money that could actually be used to fund health and education services. Quiggin's estimate of the adverse budgetary impact of Strong Choices of around $1 billion had not included the potential budgetary benefits of getting our AAA credit rating back, which would reduce (by $100-200 million) although not eliminate the estimated budgetary loss.

By 2017-18, the Queensland government most likely would have regained a AAA credit rating if the Strong Choices plan had been implemented. Selling assets or leasing out assets on the scale of the Strong Choices plan would have been a relatively quick, no regrets way to help restore the AAA credit rating. It would have been relatively quick in the sense it would only take a few years compared with what would otherwise take up to a decade or longer by either:

[221] Quiggin, J., 2015, op. cit., p. 6.
[222] Quiggin, J., 2015, p. 10.

a) generating a string of fiscal surpluses; or

b) waiting for the economy to grow sufficiently so the ratio of debt-to-revenue would naturally revert to a level with which the ratings agencies were comfortable (so long as debt was not growing faster than revenue).

The latter approach was questioned in a section in the Final Plan for Strong Choices titled "Is there a Fourth Choice?".[223] Recall the other three choices were selling or leasing out assets, spending cuts, or tax increases. The government did not consider the so-call fourth choice a realistic option. Even though Queensland's economy was projected to grow faster than the rest of Australia's, growth was expected to be slower than the historical average due to lower working age population growth (associated with the ageing population). Also, the government foreshadowed rising demands for health, education and disability services, which would see "expenses overall outpacing revenue growth."[224]

Finally, there are important cash and debt management considerations in public finance. Currently, due to Queensland's large debt, which QTC occasionally needs to refinance as bonds of different terms and vintages mature, Queensland is highly dependent on the bond market—comprising both domestic and overseas investors—for financing.[225] This is an undesirable situation. As noted in Chapter 6, there was considerable anxiety among state Treasury officials across Australia in late 2008 and early 2009 regarding conditions in the semi-government bond market. Until the Commonwealth stepped in with a temporary guarantee of state and territory government borrowings, there was great concern around how readily (and at what interest rates) state governments would find the large amounts of money they needed to fund infrastructure and cover operating deficits. That said, in the worst case scenario, the Queensland government could always have

[223] Queensland Government, 2014c, op. cit., p. 26.
[224] Ibid.
[225] Around 30 percent of QTC's borrowing is ultimately sourced from investors located overseas according to Queensland Treasury Corporation, 2017, *Investor Booklet*, p. 42.

run down its investments at QIC, albeit realising losses as it sold assets such as shares and property in poor market conditions. Of course this would be highly undesirable, as it could mean the government no longer fully funded its defined benefit superannuation liability.

These deeper public finance considerations, which would have helped the Newman government make its case for Strong Choices, were not adequately brought out in the Strong Choices advertising campaign. In considering the merits of the Strong Choices campaign, it is necessary to consider what a first-best public policy process would have looked like. Ideally the government would have undertaken or commissioned a comprehensive analysis of the merits of any proposed asset sales, and such an analysis would take the form of a cost-benefit analysis. This point was made by the 21 economists who had criticised the Bligh government for its asset sales in 2009. This message was apparently not absorbed by members of the then opposition who would later enter the Newman government.

Unfortunately, it is not clear whether any cost-benefit analysis of asset sales (or leases) was done and, if it had been done, it was never publicly released. Rigorous analysis of the privatisation proposals would have been much better than the uninformative Strong Choices campaign. The $6 million the government spent on the Strong Choices campaign could easily have funded several comprehensive cost-benefit studies of the proposed privatisations.

Arguably, it was under-estimating the intelligence of the Queensland public to assume the opposition to asset sales was based on people being unable to grasp the simple point that, to pay down debt, the government would either need to cut spending, raise taxes or sell assets. The public appeared to have a much greater understanding of the budgetary impacts of privatisation than the government would give them credit for—that the government would be selling income-producing assets so the state's financial position would not necessarily improve. It is unfortunate the Queensland public were given Strong Choices instead of genuine information about the likely impacts of proposed privatisations. As an example of what a sound public policy campaign looks like, consider the massive economic modelling exercise Commonwealth Treasury undertook to analyse the potential impacts of carbon pricing in the late 2000s. Serious policies require serious analysis. And serious analysis is increasingly expected by a public, which is increasingly sceptical of government policies. Such analysis may well have strengthened the Newman government's case. In her book, *On Speaking Well*, former speechwriter to US President Ronald Reagan Peggy Noonan wrote:

> A good case well argued and well said is inherently moving. It shows respect for the brains of the listeners. There is an implicit compliment in it. It shows that you're a serious person and understand that you are talking to other serious persons.[226]

The Newman government was right to prioritise reducing Queensland's $80 billion debt and getting the government's AAA credit rating back. Leasing out assets would have been a good way to do this, and would have yielded wider benefits, such as more efficiently run assets, lower power prices than otherwise, and less risk on the government's balance sheet. However, the government potentially opened up a hole in the budget by using some of the lease proceeds to pay for the solar feed-in tariff and for non-commercial infrastructure that would not directly return money to the budget, as pointed out by John Quiggin. Certainly, some of the infrastructure the government was proposing to fund using Strong Choices proceeds was dubious, such as Townsville Super Stadium, which received a $150 million commitment from the Newman government.[227] From a budget management perspective, it was unfortunate the Newman government was not planning to allocate all asset lease proceeds to reducing debt and (thus)

---

[226] Peggy Noonan, 1999, *On Speaking Well: How to Give a Speech with Style, Substance, and Clarity*, Harper Perennial, p. 64.

[227] The Townsville Super Stadium was also supported by the then opposition, and $140 million funding was provided for the stadium by the Palaszczuk Government in the 2015-16 and 2016-17 budgets.

interest payments.

Contestability and public service renewal

The Newman government deserved credit for its promotion of contestability of public services: a clear focus on cost-effective service delivery, which would involve contracting out where it is more cost-effective for the private sector to deliver the services (while maintaining a particular level of service or quality). Contestability was an element of the Newman government's Public Sector Renewal Program, an innovative program designed to lead the implementation of Commission of Audit's recommendations across the government, including the application of contestability in service provision.

The program was led by Newman government Commission of Audit member and former Under Treasurer Doug McTaggart, in his role as Chair of the Public Service Commission and a member of the Public Sector Renewal Board. Other members of the high-powered board included Chancellor of the University of Western Sydney and former Secretary of the Australian Department of Prime Minister and Cabinet Peter Shergold, Adjunct Professor with the Australian New Zealand School of Government and former NSW Cabinet Secretary Gary Sturgess, and the Queensland Under Treasurer—i.e. Helen Gluer from 2012 to 2013 and Mark Gray for the remainder of the Newman government.

Former LNP MP for Cairns Gavin King, in his biography of Campbell Newman, *Can do*, nicely illustrates why such a renewal process was needed:

> Technological updates aside, the hierarchical, centralised, process-driven bureaucracy has operated much the same way it has for more than a century, so the renewal framework of the Newman Government involved looking at the public service in entirely new, creative ways. [228]

But the renewal program did not survive the change of government.

---

[228] Gavin King, 2015, *Can do: Campbell Newman and the challenge of reform*, Connor Court, p. 305.

Interviewed for this book, McTaggart said he considered that the program was starting to achieve results by the end of the Newman government's term, but it really needed a second term of government to achieve the necessary changes.

While there is no formal assessment of the achievements of the Public Service Renewal program, it appears to have had a significant impact despite its brief period of operation. It certainly oversaw a large program of change in the delivery of public services in Queensland, although it is unclear to what extent its role went beyond oversight and setting the general direction for reform. A published update report titled *Queensland's Renewal Program* in 2014 revealed a range of improvements in the delivery of health services, reforms to education services including public private partnerships (PPPs) for school construction, and to housing services, among others.[229] Another one of its legacies would be the implementation of the open data initiative, by which Queensland government data sets would be increasingly made available online where that could be done without compromising privacy or commercial-in-confidence information.

Controversies

The Newman government was not short of political controversies during its term of government. These included the controversial anti-bikies legislation called the *Vicious Lawless Association Disestablishment Act* (VLAD Act), the standing down of prominent Transport and Main Roads Director-General Michael Caltabiano after his referral to the parliamentary Ethics Committee, and controversy over the purchase of New Generation Rollingstock (NGR) trains manufactured in India by Bombardier Transportation, which proved to have a range of teething problems, which, even in 2018, are still delaying their full deployment on the rail network.

---

[229] Queensland Government, 2014d, *Queensland's Renewal Program: Achievements, January-March 2014 Quarterly Update.*

From a public finance perspective, one of the major controversies was over the commitment to build a new building to house the core public service departments and ministers at 1 William St, close to Parliament House at the southern end of Brisbane CBD. The construction cost of the building which would come to be known as the "tower of power" was around $650 million, but the Queensland government entered into a long-term lease for 15 years of 75,000m² office space in the building (i.e. a large majority of the building) valued at $1.14 billion.[230] The Queensland Auditor-General raised questions about the PPP arrangement entered into, whereby a private sector proponent would build the office tower on state government land and lease office space to the Government. The Auditor-General noted:

> A business case was not developed comparing the costs and benefits of the PPP option to alternatives such as direct public sector ownership or leasing at other locations to support the decision made to progress the construction of 1 William St. As a result, while the costs associated with 1 William St may represent value for money, it was not determined before the decision was taken, or subsequently, that it optimises value for the state. Development of a business case is an expectation under the Queensland's Government's PPP policy and value for money framework.[231]

This is another example of the failure to prepare business cases or cost-benefit analyses to support major decisions, something that, as noted above, the Beattie government had failed to do regarding its major investment in hospitals.

Two other Newman government policy decisions have become controversial, even though they may have been well motivated by a desire to cut red tape, reduce business costs and stimulate economic development.

---

[230] Kym Agius and Melissa Grant, 2013, "Auditor-General questions 1 William Street tower project", *Brisbane Times*, 10 December 2013, available via www.brisbanetimes.com.au.

[231] Queensland Audit Office, 2013, *Results of Audit: State public sector entities for 2012-13, Report to Parliament 11: 2013-14*, p. 79.

These decisions were changes to the *Vegetation Management Act 1999* which saw a surge in land clearing and the abolition of the waste levy introduced by the Bligh government, a policy change which saw large volumes of industrial waste being trucked to Queensland from NSW for disposal to avoid the levy in NSW.

Deferral of the targeted 2014-15 fiscal surplus

Recall that, in its response to the 2012 Interim Report of the Commission of Audit, the Newman Government had, rather heroically, committed itself to achieving a fiscal surplus—and not just an operating surplus—in 2014-15. That is, it would achieve a surplus not just for its operating budget but taking into account capital expenditure made that year as well. This commitment was made while the mining boom was underway, with high commodity prices and healthy royalty revenues. In the 2012-13 budget, the Government was projecting an average hard coking coal price for 2014-15 of $200/tonne. Subsequent developments, including the end of the mining boom and a crash in commodity prices, would mean the government's hopes of a surplus in 2014-15 were dashed.

The government's second budget, for the financial year 2013-14, reported on large downward revisions to revenue:

> Key revenue sources such as taxation, GST and mining royalties have fallen by $4.2 billion in underlying terms since the 2012-13 Budget, with $2.6 billion of this decline since 2012-13 MYFER. This reflects the ongoing weakness of export coal prices, downward reductions in the GST pool distributed by the Australian Government and the impact of the slower than anticipated property market recovery on transfer duty and land tax.[232]

Now the government projected a fiscal deficit in 2014-15 of $244 million, but it projected a fiscal surplus in the following year, 2015-16, of around

---

[232] Queensland Treasury, 2013, *State Budget 2013-14: Budget Strategy and Outlook*, budget paper no. 2, p. 47.

$1.1 billion. The return to fiscal surplus would be delayed by one year.

Subsequent revenue revisions, largely to royalties, cuts to Commonwealth grants to states and territories in the Abbott government's 2014-15 budget, and complications with the timing of Commonwealth Natural Disaster Relief and Recovery Arrangements payments—i.e. the Commonwealth shifting payments to Queensland forward to the 2013-14 financial year and out of 2014-15—meant that, by the time of its last MYFER budget update in December 2014, the government was forecasting a much larger fiscal deficit in 2014-15 of around $2.8 billion. And the projected 2015-16 fiscal surplus had fallen to $331 million, largely due to higher expected capital investment. As the Newman government did not survive the 31 January 2015 election, it never had the chance to demonstrate whether it would have delivered a fiscal surplus.

The black hole election

Newman returned from holidays early in the new year of 2015 and called a snap election for 31 January. It was a decisive way to end election speculation, and no doubt he was trying to catch the opposition unprepared. As expected, asset leases and the associated potential job losses, as well as the actual job losses that occurred in the public service, were prominent issues in the election campaign.

There was much talk of black holes during the 2015 election campaign, thanks in part to the efforts of the *Courier-Mail*, which on Saturday 17 January, two weeks before the election, featured a front page headline "ALP's $1.3b black hole: Debt reduction plan to gut the Budget", based on the Labor opposition's fiscal strategy announced the day before.[233] Incidentally, the same front page also noted the opposition was in the "box seat" to win the election. The government had accused the opposition of creating a $1.3

---

[233] Steven Wardill and Jason Tin, 2015, "Debt reduction plan to gut the Budget—ALP's $1.3B black hole", *Courier-Mail*, 17 January 2015, available via www.couriermail.com.au.

billion black hole. But, as noted above, the government had itself been criticised by Professor John Quiggin for creating its own budget black hole, due to the loss of earnings from income-producing assets being greater than the reduction in interest payments achieved by paying down debt.

The key features of the opposition's fiscal strategy which was so heavily criticised by the *Courier-Mail* were:

- allocating two-thirds of earnings from GOCs to debt reduction from 2018-19, channelling the money via a Debt Reduction Trust; and

- relying on savings of $150 million from the merger of Energex, Ergon and Powerlink into one big network business and CS Energy and Stanwell into one big generator.

Now, there may well be savings from merging these businesses, but in the short-run it should reasonably be expected that there would be high implementation costs from a merger, particularly in consultancy fees, that the opposition did not appear to have considered. These costs were likely to be at least $150 million, based on analysis undertaken by the Independent Review Panel on Network Costs in 2012.[234]

Also, as noted by SMART Infrastructure Senior Research Fellow Joe Branigan and the Grattan Institute's Tristan Edis, the merger of Queensland's two state-owned power businesses would massively reduce competition among Queensland generators and could result in power price increases.[235] Tristan Edis compared the merger to one between Coles and Woolworths.[236]

The Labor opposition did not provide full details of its future expenditure and revenue raising plans, meaning it was open to criticism from the government that it has a hole in its budget estimates—i.e. the $1.3 billion black hole referred to on the *Courier-Mail*'s front page. This was

---

[234] Independent Review Panel on Network Costs, 2012, *Electricity Network Costs Review Final Report*, p. 76.

[235] Joe Branigan, 2015, "Electric shock in store for voters", *The Australian*, 22 January 2015, available via www.theaustralian.com.au.

[236] Tristan Edis, 2015, "Queensland voters fooled over power bills and privatisation", *Business Spectator*, 23 January 2015.

a beat up, but the opposition left itself open to it. Technically, the Labor opposition did not propose allocating money to debt reduction that was already allocated to funding services, because it was not earmarking income from GOCs to debt reduction until 2018-19—i.e. outside of the forward estimate years for which the state budget was then planning for (2014-15 to 2017-18). That said, it was unclear how the Labor opposition would fund debt reduction of the proposed scale from 2018-19 onwards were it to win the election. Treasurer Tim Nicholls was correct to point out the opposition's plan to earmark money from the earnings of government-owned businesses did not create any new money.

The Labor opposition's Debt Reduction Trust was a gimmick (and indeed it would not be implemented by the Palaszczuk government). To pay back debt, the opposition, if it won government, would have to do the hard work of creating surpluses, by keeping expenditures below revenues. But it was unclear during the election campaign exactly how it would attain the surpluses it was effectively promising.

The Labor opposition was promising no more than a very slow path of debt reduction that was unlikely to restore a AAA credit rating to the Queensland government by the end of the decade. Also, there were no details yet of how the Labor opposition would maintain the tight expenditure control implied by its planned debt reduction, largely projected to occur beyond 2017-18 (the final year of the state budget forward estimates). The Labor opposition was essentially committing itself to very tightly managing government expenditure, and maintaining relatively low capital expenditure, which was probably unachievable and politically toxic. As we will see in the next chapter, the Palaszczuk government's record on expenditure control would be disappointing.

Overall, during the 2015 election campaign, there were significant concerns about the fiscal strategies of both major parties. Unfortunately the imperatives of politics, and the need to win marginal seats, had meant the Newman government had compromised what would otherwise have been very good economic policy. By deciding not to use all the expected *Strong Choices* lease proceeds for debt reduction, it would create a longer-term budgetary challenge. At the same time, the Labor opposition was not exactly clear on how it would fund its proposed debt reduction, which was far short of was required to restore Queensland's AAA credit rating. Queenslanders were poorly served by both major parties in the 2015 election campaign.

The election disaster

Whether because of Premier Campbell Newman's personal "can do", crash-through-or-crash style, or because the government thought it could afford to take hard controversial decisions owing to its record majority, the Newman government lost a lot of public support and narrowly lost the 2015 election.

A review of the 2015 election loss by former Premier Rob Borbidge and former Treasurer Joan Sheldon for the LNP found a range of contributing factors, including the "hubris" and "false sense of security" created by the massive victory in 2012, a "huge influx of inexperienced new MPs and a leader without parliamentary background", as well as the "perception of arrogance" and "pursuing the large scale privatisation of assets to which the majority of voters opposed".[237] As Borbidge and Sheldon observed:

> Exit polling…indicated that the plan to sell/lease the state's assets was the main reason given by 64 per cent of respondents for their protest vote.[238]

Privatisation was not just a "strong negative" with Labor and minor party voters, as some in the LNP had believed.[239]

Reflecting the importance of the state government as a major employer in Queensland, the Borbidge Sheldon election review concluded "the breaking of the promise that public servants had 'nothing to fear'" was

[237] Rob Borbidge and Joan Sheldon, 2015, *Borbidge Sheldon Election Review and Report and Recommendations*, report to the LNP, 28 May 2015, p.2.
[238] Ibid., p. 6.
[239] Ibid.

also an important factor.[240] Given there are over 250,000 people employed in the Queensland public service, the public service vote can be a decisive factor in state elections. Arguably, by increasing the public service to such a large extent during its first term in government, as we will see in the next chapter, the Palaszczuk government has realised the importance of the public service vote for its own political survival.

Assessment of the Newman government

The Newman government ushered in an extraordinary period in the history of Queensland's public finances. If the Bligh government can be considered the exemplar of loose public financial management, the Newman government can be considered the exemplar of rigorous financial management. This makes sense given the policies of the Newman government were a reaction to the policies of the Bligh government, which had largely created the fiscal challenges inherited by the Newman government. It was as if Newton's third law of thermodynamics—that for every action there is an equal and opposite reaction—was applicable to Queensland's public financial management. By reducing public service FTEs by around 14,000 and presiding over very low expenditure growth, including one year in which public expenditure did not grow and fell sharply in real per capita terms, the Newman government set a very high standard for public financial management (Table 6.1). The record is unlikely ever to be repeated in Queensland, particularly if future governments understand the political lessons of the Newman government. The Newman government was right economically to pursue its policies, but, from a political perspective, it was too much too soon.

---

[240] Ibid.

Table 6.1 Budget outcomes under the Newman government*

	2012-13 $ million	2013-14 $ million	2014-15 $ million
A. Revenue	41,889	46,894	49,945
B. Total expenses	46,271	46,271	49,285
C. Net operating balance (A-B)	**-4,382**	**623**	**660**
D. Gross fixed capital formation	6,294	6,072	4,213
E. Depreciation (& other adjustments)	2,940	2,862	3,023
F. Net acquisition of non-financial assets (D-E)	3,354	3,210	1,190
G. Net lending (C-F)	**-7,736**	**-2,587**	**-530**
Indicators			
Net lending as percentage of GSP	-2.7%	-0.9%	-0.2%
Revenue growth	-8.5%	11.9%	6.5%
Expenses growth	0.5%	0.0%	6.5%
GFCF growth	-17.2%	-3.5%	-30.6%
Revenue growth - real per capita	-12.4%	6.8%	3.9%
Expenses growth - real per capita	-3.7%	-4.6%	3.9%
GFCF growth - real per capita	-20.7%	-8.0%	-32.3%

Source: ABS GFS, cat. no. 5512.0, various issues. * NB Palaszczuk Government was elected in early 2015, and significant public service hiring in the new Government's early months are reflected in the figures for 2014-15.

7

PALASZCZUK AND PITT LEARN TO STOP WORRYING AND LOVE THE DEBT

Labor scrapes back into power

Queensland politics once again proved volatile on the day of the 2015 election, 31 January, when the Newman government suffered an 8.3 percent swing against it and the loss of 35 seats.[241] Coming into the election with 77 seats, after the election the LNP had 42 seats, three short of the 45 seats needed for a majority of the Parliament's 89 seats. Eventually, the Labor opposition, led by 45-year old former Transport Minister Anastacia Palaszczuk, with 44 seats of its own, formed minority government with the support of the independent Peter Wellington, who was appointed speaker, and two KAP members from regional Queensland.

While Palaszczuk was labelled as "Accident Anna" by some commentators, and her win was viewed as a fluke, arguably she was destined for the ALP leadership and premiership of Queensland. Since 2006, she has been the member for Inala, one of the safest ALP seats in the outer south western suburbs of Brisbane, after having followed her father Henry Palaszczuk, a Beattie government minister, as the MP. Anastacia Palaszczuk had joined the ALP in her teenage years and rose to become President of Australian Young Labor. She had studied arts and law at UQ, and political

---

[241] Joy McCann and Simon Speldewinde, 2015, "Queensland state election: an overview", *Parliamentary Library Research Paper Series*, no. 2015-16, p. 1.

science as a Chevening scholar at the London School of Economics and Political Science, and she also had experience working as a political adviser to federal and state ministers before entering parliament.

The parliamentary numbers were very tight during the Palaszczuk government's first term. Within its first two months, Labor lost Far North Queensland MP Billy Gordon as an official Labor MP after questions regarding a domestic matter, reducing their guaranteed numbers to 43. And later, in March 2016, Cairns Labor MP Rob Pyne turned independent after a dispute with Deputy Premier Jackie Trad. Given the loose ties of the KAP members to the Labor government, the Parliament was primed for upsets. One major upset was the government losing a major bill relating to sugar marketing that effectively re-regulated Queensland's sugar industry and ended up being denounced by the Productivity Commission. The bill was passed by a coalition of the LNP and KAP. The government, however, was not challenged on a vote of confidence, as it still had the KAP support in that regard, so it was able to remain in power despite losing a vote on the floor of parliament on a major piece of legislation.

Assuming the Treasury portfolio in the Palaszczuk government was the 38-year old Curtis Pitt, MP for Mulgrave in the Cairns region, who had previously served as Bligh government Minister for Disabilities, Mental Health and ATSI Partnerships. Earlier in his career, Pitt had worked as a Queensland public servant. The new government replaced Under Treasurer Mark Gray with former ANZ banking executive and Commonwealth Treasury Executive Director Jim Murphy, who had served as Chief of Staff to Kevin Rudd, when Rudd briefly resumed the Prime Ministership after ousting Julia Gillard in mid-2013.

As Treasurer, Pitt was constrained by Labor's now unequivocal opposition to privatisation, either by sale or leasing out of state assets. The lesson the Palaszczuk government learned from the Bligh and Newman governments was that, rightly or wrongly, privatisation is politically toxic in Queensland.

Incidentally, the government's unequivocal opposition to privatisation meant it was even subject to questions regarding the sale of minor assets such as pockets of under-utilised land owned by the state government. In October 2016, the Premier announced the government would sell off surplus publicly-owned land at various sites, including Mayne Rail Yards, Bowen Hills and the former Oxley Secondary College, in the interests of promoting urban renewal. Leader of the Opposition Tim Nicholls compared the Palaszczuk government to the previous Labor government of Anna Bligh's, which he alleged had "promised not to sell state assets and then did so."[242] The government attempted to explain that its pledge regarding asset sales related to "income generating assets", while the land it was selling was not income producing and had costs of upkeep that were a drain on the Treasury for no return.[243] Certainly, the attack on the government for selling surplus properties was unwarranted, as it would be absurd not to allow a government to do so, but the strong anti-asset sales language the Palaszczuk government had used while in opposition left it exposed to such an attack.

The opposition to privatisation meant that the new government had denied itself in the order of $30-40 billion of funds from the proposed Strong Choices asset leases which partly could have been used to fund $8-9 billion of new infrastructure, as discussed in Chapter 7. As it was expecting these funds to be available, the Newman government had been frugal in the forward estimates with regards to new infrastructure. At the time of the Newman government's 2014-15 MYFER in December 2014, total Queensland government capital purchases were estimated to decline from 3 percent of GSP in 2014-15 to 2.4 percent of GSP in 2017-18. Capital purchases were projected to average of 2.7 percent of GSP over these four years, compared with an average of 4 percent for the four previous years,

[242] Anthony Templeton, 2016a, "LNP accuses Palaszczuk Government of breaking promise over asset sales", *Courier-Mail*, 12 October 2016, available via www.couriermail.com.au.
[243] AAP, 2016, "Labor reveals Qld 'asset sales' plan", *SBS News*, 6 October 2016, available via www.sbs.com.au.

185

2010-11 to 2013-14.[244] The $8-9 billion of lease proceeds that would have been allocated to infrastructure under Strong Choices would have allowed capital purchases to be higher, possibly by around $2 billion per annum (or over ½ percent of GSP) for five years. As such, the election of the Palaszczuk government came as a shock to many in the local business community, particularly engineering and construction firms, which were expecting a boost from capital works funded by the Strong Choices privatisations.

Treasury's review of state finances tries to look on the bright side

While in opposition, Labor had committed to a Treasury review of state finances once it assumed power. The Treasury commenced its review of state finances in March 2015 and reported prior to the Palaszczuk government's first budget, which was shifted to mid-July from its usual timing in June, due to the disruption to the usual budget process caused by the election in January and the subsequent delay in forming government. The Treasury review report was released alongside the budget documents on budget day 14 July.

The Treasury began its Review by reporting on the economic context, which had changed substantially since the 2000s, when the state economy was powered along by the resources boom and also a construction boom induced by high state government infrastructure spending. The Treasury noted:

> The Queensland economy now faces considerable challenges in the form of a weaker outlook for Queensland's trading partners, a fall in the terms of trade and lower levels of business investment. This in turn is driving slower growth in incomes and spending.
>
> Queensland's population growth, which for some decades exceeded Australia's due to strong levels of migration, has slowed to levels more in line with the national average.[245]

These economic trends, particularly commodity prices at lower levels

---

[244] Queensland Treasury, 2014a, *Mid Year Fiscal and Economic Review*, p. 27.

[245] Queensland Treasury, 2015a, *2015 Review of State Finances*, p. 5.

than previously, meant that the revenue outlook for the government was "weak", complicating the government's fiscal strategy.[246]

Treasury then proceeded to a dispassionate analysis of the fiscal deterioration that occurred over the 2000s, noting that, at the start of the decade, Queensland had the best fiscal position in Australia, with low debt and taxes. Treasury observed, however, that:

> The policy trade-off in Queensland was levels of service, infrastructure and public sector wages that were well below national averages.
>
> Successive Queensland governments implemented policies aimed at raising service levels towards national standards in key areas and addressing infrastructure deficits. The benefit of that investment today (beyond the obvious service delivery benefits) is that Queensland is not facing the major infrastructure pressures now being experienced in many other states.
>
> Queensland's low tax settings remained in place during this period. There was a fundamental policy imbalance.
>
> In the period leading up to the Global Financial Crisis (GFC), the policy imbalance was masked by the revenue surge from the housing and mining booms and the growth in GST driven by credit expansion. However, with state fiscal capacities equalised through the Grants Commission process, it is the policy settings that are paramount. In effect, like most governments throughout the developed world, Queensland 'overshot'.
>
> Queensland also faced the added challenges of the South East Queensland water crisis and an unprecedented series of natural disasters.
>
> The net outcome was a dramatic increase in General Government debt between 2006-07 and 2013-14.[247]

The Treasury made some good points, but arguably was too lenient on the governments of the period, and its commentary could be read

---

[246] Ibid., p. 79.
[247] Ibid., pp. 5-6.

as suggesting the fiscal deterioration was largely due to the surprise of the financial crisis, drought and natural disasters. But, as argued above, successive governments should have been more prudent at the time. It was clear from Bligh's budget speeches while Treasurer that she had little regard to the long-term implications of the fiscal settings, and how robust the budget was to shocks.

The Treasury *Review of State Finances* report was also disappointing because it gave a green light to fiscal trickery, the shifting of debt from the general government sector to the GOCs, to allow the government to claim a debt reduction in the general government sector, a dubious move the Treasury should have strongly opposed, to be discussed below. That said, Treasury's analysis was generally first class. It appears to have simply made a political judgment not to upset the government of the day by being too critical of the previous Labor government led by Anna Bligh.

Finally, the *Review of State Finances* report touched on the importance of technological change, which arguably was one of the motivations for the Newman government wanting to sell some of its assets. The Treasury noted:

> Like any businesses, Queensland's GOCs face risks and will have to adapt to sectoral changes—the biggest of which is arguably the impact of new technologies on the electricity network. If these are not managed well, the costs will be borne by the Budget and taxpayers.[248]

That is, it is very possible technological change, such as cheaper solar PV and battery technology (e.g. the Tesla Power wall) will massively reduce the value of the energy businesses. It may have been wise for the government to have sold them when it could have done so at a good price. There is a large risk of so-called stranded assets.

---

[248] Ibid., p. 9.

Treasury resurrects the Golden Rule

In the terms of reference for the review of state finances, the government asked the Treasury for advice on "the appropriateness of various operating statement and balance sheet measures of state fiscal performance and sustainability."[249] The Treasury acknowledged that, under the previous Newman government, it had recommended the targeting of fiscal surpluses to reduce Queensland's high level of debt.[250] But in its advice to the Newman government, the Treasury noted the government could, "at the point at which Queensland's debt levels became more manageable", revert to the golden rule.[251] Then, it could "run modest fiscal balance deficits in recognition of future infrastructure requirements."[252] Alas, Treasury did not provide any guidance as to when in its view the debt would become more manageable, and it is not clear from the review whether Treasury thought Queensland's debt was now manageable.

In addressing the question of whether Queensland's debt was too high, Treasury suggested that a desirable level of debt was not possible to estimate, as it depended on a range of factors such as prevailing interest rates and the attitudes of rating agencies. It noted that the Queensland government was still far away from a situation where it would have to worry about a "debt spiral" where the level of interest payments leads to an exploding level of debt.[253] Typically, this can occur where the rate of interest exceeds the economic growth rate, and a government is running a primary deficit (i.e. a fiscal deficit even after excluding interest payments). In this scenario, debt increases faster than the size of the economy, an economy's public debt-to-GDP ratio (or for Queensland, public debt-to-GSP ratio) will keep increasing, obviously an unsustainable situation.[254]

---

[249] Ibid., p. 3.

[250] Ibid., p. 78.

[251] Ibid., p. 79.

[252] Ibid.

[253] Ibid., 2015, p. 79.

[254] On the arithmetic behind so-called debt dynamics, see Makin, A. and Pearce, J., op. cit.

Although Queensland was not at risk of a debt spiral, the Treasury did note that based on its analysis the "clear inference" was that "debt is too high".[255] The Treasury suggested the Queensland government balance sheet was not in a good enough state to guarantee the state would not be subject to a further downgrade from its still strong AA+ credit rating.[256] Also, it appeared to be concerned about the size of the state government's debt servicing obligations. Interest payments on general government debt had increased from 0.6 percent of revenue in 2006-07 to 4.7 percent in 2013-14. Treasury suggested this could have been much higher, were it not for the abnormally low interest rates that have prevailed in the post-financial crisis period. It noted:

> In the event that interest rates return to more 'normal' levels, this [i.e. debt servicing] would emerge as a serious issue.[257]

So Queensland Treasury needed to be cautious in its advice on an appropriate fiscal target for the government.

The advice back to the government from Treasury in the *Review of State Finances* report was a qualified restatement of the so-called golden rule of public finance, that a government must fund its recurrent expenses from current revenue, but can borrow to fund infrastructure. The Treasury was willing to entertain the state government reverting to a net operating balance target, but it appeared to still be concerned about the debt level and hence called for a fiscal principle stronger than the usual golden rule:

> The Government should target material net operating surpluses that provide an adequate buffer against adverse events and ensure that new infrastructure projects are predominantly funded from recurrent sources rather than borrowing.[258]

This provided the Palaszczuk government with the opportunity to develop new fiscal principles, which it presented in the 2015-16 budget, along with a controversial debt reduction plan.

---

[255] Queensland Treasury, 2015a, op. cit., p. 80.
[256] Ibid.
[257] Ibid.
[258] Ibid., p. 79.

The Debt Action Plan gets re-worked in the 2015-16 budget

There was lot of attention on the new Treasurer Curtis Pitt as he set about preparing the 2015-16 budget. Entering budget preparations, the Treasurer would have been conscious of the heavy criticism Labor's Debt Action Plan had received during the election campaign, particularly the front page *Courier-Mail* story referring to a "1.3 billion black hole", as discussed in the last chapter.[259]

The 2015-16 budget revealed that the government had abandoned the gimmicky Debt Reduction Trust it had proposed during the election campaign. It had also abandoned its plan to merge the power generators CS Energy and Stanwell, after it had consulted with the Australian Competition and Consumer Commission (ACCC) on the competition policy issue (i.e. the possible abuse of market power) noted in the last chapter. The ACCC advised the government the concerns over market power and price gouging expressed by economist Joe Branigan and energy expert Tristan Edis were very real.[260] However, the government still intended to combine the electricity distribution businesses Energex and Ergon. These businesses would be merged into Energy Queensland, with $680 million in savings projected to 2019-20.[261]

As in its Debt Action Plan, in the 2015-16 budget the Palaszczuk government rejected the Newman government's focus on total government debt (technically the figure labelled borrowings in the non-financial public sector balance sheet), which includes debt owed by the GOCs. Recall a focus on total debt was recommended by the Newman government's Commission of Audit. Total Queensland government debt was estimated to be just under

---

[259] Wardill, S. and Tin, J., op. cit.

[260] Incidentally, the wisdom of this advice was reinforced by the exertion of market power that occurred in early 2017 by Queensland power generators, driving up the wholesale electricity price, boosting generator earnings, and providing a windfall to the Queensland Government.

[261] Curtis Pitt, 2015, *Electricity company mergers save $680 million and drive regional jobs*, media statement by the Treasurer, 15 December 2015, available via www.statements.qld.gov.au.

$80 billion on 30 June 2015. Instead, the new government emphasised the (much lower) general government sector debt, estimated to be around $48 billion on 30 June 2015. The government had some justification for doing this, as this was standard practice in other jurisdictions.

Recall John Quiggin's point referred to in the previous chapter that GOCs pay the interest on their debt out of their own earnings. So long as GOCs are well run commercial operations, GOC borrowings should not really be a concern of government. However, that is in an ideal world. A focus on general government debt means that a government can engage in creative accounting and shift debt from one sector to the other, artificially reducing the debt level of the general government sector without really reducing the taxpayers' ultimate liabilities. Disappointingly, this dubious strategy was a major feature of the Palaszczuk government's first budget.

Instead of its originally proposed Debt Action Plan, the government proposed to shift debt from the general government sector to the GOCs, specifically the energy businesses Energex, Ergon, and Powerlink. It tried to confuse observers by presenting it as a technical financial exercise in "re-gearing" the GOCs. The re-gearing plan involved the government increasing the gearing ratio—in this context, the ratio of debt to total assets on the balance sheet—for the energy network businesses, Energex, Ergon and Powerlink, from an average of 55 percent to 70 percent for Ergon and Energex and 75 percent for Powerlink.

The Palaszczuk government suggested that shifting debt on to the GOCs was justified by analysis from KPMG, one of the big four professional services firms, purportedly showing that the energy businesses could take on higher gearing ratios, as energy businesses in other jurisdictions had higher ratios, meaning they had higher ratios of debt to equity than Queensland's energy GOCs.[262] The gearing ratio shows to what extent a business has

---

[262] KPMG, 2015, *Electricity Network Recapitalisation Strategy: Capital Structure and Dividend Benchmarking Analysis*, report prepared for Queensland Treasury Corporation.

relied upon debt to raise capital. In this context the gearing ratio is the ratio of debt to total capital (i.e. debt plus equity, which is equal to assets). It is usually optimal for businesses to have some gearing, as debt allows a business to expand its operations beyond what is strictly allowable with its own equity capital, and hence can allow the business to earn a higher return on equity. Businesses with a low level of gearing may be accused of having a lazy balance sheet.

KPMG found that the gearing ratios for the electricity network businesses, in the 47-50 percent range, were well below the benchmark gearing ratio of 60 percent used by the AER in determining the weighted average cost of capital (WACC) that regulated businesses can use to justify their prices and revenues.[263] Under the government's proposed strategy, the gearing ratios of the Queensland network GOCs would fall in the 59-65 percent range, and hence would be more comparable to the gearing ratios of their peers and the AER benchmark.

The 2015-16 budget claimed the "re-gearing plan was recommended by the Independent Review of State Finances"—that is, by the review conducted by Queensland Treasury discussed above.[264] This is a problematic claim. First, the Treasury is not independent of the government. It works for the government of the day. The Treasury may not have even considered the idea of a re-gearing if the government had not directed it towards the possibility. The Treasury of course should offer non-partisan rigorous advice and there is no reason to suggest it has not. Second, it is unclear whether Treasury actually recommended a re-gearing. There is no specifically marked recommendation to re-gear. Its language around re-gearing is very cautious. All things considered, the statement in the 2015-16 was misleading and incorrectly claimed independent support for the re-gearing plan that did not exist.

---

[263] Ibid., p. 21.
[264] Queensland Treasury, 2015b, *Queensland Budget 2015-16: Budget Strategy and Outlook 2015-16*, budget paper no. 2, p. 4.

Treasury's *Review of State Finances* report suggested there were risks to re-gearing, when it discussed the criteria for commercial sustainability of the GOCs. It appeared to be suggesting such a re-gearing assumes the GOCs are operating as independent commercial entities, and will not be subject to "non-commercial policies"—which could cover a multitude of sins such as inefficient industrial relations policies and special dividends—and "make good investment decisions", among other requirements.[265] The Treasury observed that the requirements it had identified had been breached in the past, without it detailing specific examples, but there were several it may have had in mind, as discussed in the next chapter.[266]

Treasury was trying to walk a fine line here. It worked for the government of the day, so it had to be as accommodative of the desires of the government as it could, but it also wanted to provide qualifications it could later point to so it could say it realised the debt shift was problematic. It would have been better if its advice was less ambiguous in this regard.

The Treasury did note that a re-gearing would help the government achieve its general government debt pay down objective much quicker, and that it would have "the benefit of more efficiently utilising the capital available to the State," although it is not entirely clear this is relevant to what actually occurred, the shuffling of debt from the general government sector to the GOCs.[267] It is not obvious there are efficiency gains from a reallocation of equity from GOCs to the general government sector in the public accounts. While it would reduce the general government's debt and interest payments, this would be offset by an increase in GOC debt and interest payments by the GOCs which, all else equal, reduce GOC net profit (and hence dividends).

The idea that the re-gearing would result in a more efficient utilisation of capital is contestable. The government was just moving money from one

---

[265] Queensland Treasury, 2015a, op. cit., p. 10.
[266] Ibid., p. 93.
[267] Ibid., p. 91.

part of its balance sheet to another. The government was not talking about GOCs funding new asset purchases with greater debt. It was gearing up by the transfer of debt from the general government sector to the GOCs, but, as noted above, there were not corresponding assets purchased by which it could service the burden of that debt.

Consider that a higher gearing ratio could come about if a GOC decided to take on more debt so it could fund the purchases of assets. In this case, both assets and debt would increase, equity would stay the same, but the gearing ratio has increased. This may make sound commercial sense if the assets purchased improved the business's profitability. But this was not what the Palaszczuk government proposed. Instead, the government proposed transferring debt, without any accompanying cash GOCs could use to purchase assets, meaning that its debt switch would reduce its equity in the GOCs. As is well known from the fundamental accounting equation, equity is the difference between a business's assets and its liabilities, of which debt is a component. That is, the debt switch resulted in an extraction of equity from the GOCs.

The Palaszczuk government's extraction of equity from the GOCs can be seen in the budget papers in the table detailing equity movements and in the Cash Flow Statement. The 2015-16 budget recorded a fall in equity for the public non-financial corporations (PNFC) sector (i.e. the sector comprising all the GOCs except QTC and QIC) in 2014-15 of $3.170 million, with the vast majority of that from the electricity generation and network GOCs. This was labelled in the budget papers as "the return of equity from the PNFC sector to the General Government Sector associated with the Debt Action Plan."[268] Then, in 2015-16, there was a $3.3 billion negative net cash flow out of the PNFC sector, in the line item labelled "Net cash flows from investments in financial assets for policy purposes." This would form the bulk of the positive net cash flow of $3.8 billion

---

[268]   Queensland Treasury, 2015b, op. cit., 131.

recorded by the general government sector that year (Table 7.1). This cash injection allowed the general government sector to pay back debt it owed to QTC, which, as noted above, borrows on behalf of the general government and GOCs. But to allow them to make this cash transfer to the general government sector, the GOCs had to borrow money from QTC. The debt switch was managed by QTC, which is the cash and debt manager for the general government and GOCs.[269]

Table 7.1 Net cash flows from investments in financial assets for policy purposes, actual, estimated and projected under the Palaszczuk government

	2015-16 outcome	2016-17 estimated outcome	2017-18 budget estimate	2018-19 projection	2019-20 projection	2020-21 projection
	$bn	$bn	$bn	$bn	$bn	$bn
General government	3.348	0.763	0.502	0.105	0.300	0.414
PNFC sector	-3.331	-0.755	-0.020	-0.150	-0.336	-0.414
Total PNF Sector	-0.002	-0.011	0.500	-	-	-

Source: Queensland Treasury, 2017, Budget Paper no. 2, Table 9.9, p. 169.

The debt switch is evident in the sharp reduction in general government debt in the same financial year (2015-16) as there was sharp rise in GOC debt (Figure 7.1). The reduction in general government sector debt was larger than the increase in GOC debt in 2015-16, because some of the government's measures did result in a genuine reduction in debt, although they may not have been prudent. The government had decided to now fund long service leave on an emergent (i.e. pay as you go) basis, so it took advantage of $3.41 billion that had been set aside to meet the long service leave liability.[270] This would provide a one off debt reduction but meant

---

[269]   Queensland Treasury Corporation, 2016, *Annual Report 2015-16*, p. 6.
[270]   Queensland Treasury, 2015b, op. cit., p. 5.

that in the future the government may have to dedicate cash it would rather spend on infrastructure to paying long service leave entitlements.

Compare the extraordinary changes in general government and GOC debt in 2015-16 with what occurred during the Bligh government in 2010-11, when general government and GOC debt also moved in different directions, but each in the opposite way to how they moved in 2015-16. In 2010-11, GOC debt was reduced as assets were privatised but general government debt increased due to the Bligh government's very large capital expenditure program at the time.

Figure 7.1 Annual change in Queensland general government and GOC borrowings

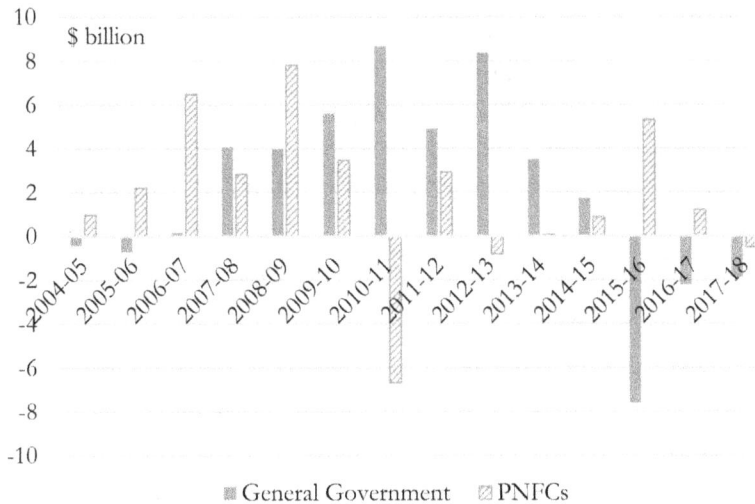

Source: Queensland state budgets, various.

At budget time 2015-16, the Treasury estimated the debt switch from the re-gearing would be worth an additional $4.1 billion to the general government sector over the forward estimates (2015-16 to 2018-19), with $600 million coming through higher dividends and tax equivalent payments—as the government now required 100 percent dividends from

Energex and Ergon rather than 80 percent—but the bulk of it coming through a $3.5 billion equity withdrawal. The government stressed that this would not impact electricity prices, a hot political issue when they are rising, as network prices were regulated by the AER.[271] The higher interest payments associated with the re-gearing would not allow the GOCs to justify higher charges in the regulatory process, which, as discussed above, assumes benchmark gearing ratios of 60 percent in estimating the WACC for the businesses and hence the return they are able to earn on their assets.

Treasurer Pitt's Debt Action Plan focussed on the general government sector, aiming to bring it down to 70-80 percent, rather than total public sector debt, including GOCs. The Treasurer noted:

> Our Debt Action Plan will deliver $9.6 billion in debt reduction by 2017-18. This is the first Queensland Budget since 1999-2000 to project a reduction in General Government debt across the forward estimates. Total borrowings are forecast to be lower over every year of the forward estimates, compared with those forecast by the previous Government.[272]

But, as discussed above, the Treasurer was reporting a debt reduction in the general government sector largely due to the debt switch.

In addition to the debt switch and funding long service leave on an emergent basis, other concerning 2015-16 budget measures included:

- as noted above, directing its profitable energy GOCs to pay out 100 percent of their earnings to the state government as dividends (up from the previous 80 percent of net profit after tax); and

- temporarily suspending contributions to the asset pool managed by QIC to meet the government's defined benefit superannuation liability.

---

[271] Ibid.

[272] Queensland Treasury, 2015c, *Queensland Budget 2015-16: Budget Speech 2015-16*, budget paper no. 1, p. 14.

Regarding the 100 percent dividend policy, this was possibly undesirable as it reduced the funds the GOCs had available for reinvestment, although the government did consider their future capital expenditure needs were lower than in the past.[273] The Queensland Treasury was very cautious about both the re-gearing discussed above and a 100 percent dividend policy for the GOCs in its *Review of State Finances* report, noting the government should "consider the risks and impacts of potential changes to the market in which these businesses operate", and later it notes technological developments in the energy sector.[274] Overall, it is difficult to read the *Review of State Finances* report as containing a clear recommendation from Treasury to the government on its 100 percent GOC dividends policy.

Also, the government would temporarily suspend contributions to the asset pool managed by QIC to meet the government's defined benefit superannuation liability, expected to result in budget savings of some $2 billion across the forward estimates. Recall that full funding of the defined benefit superannuation liability was a hallmark of the Hielscher era. The government argued, based on advice from the State Actuary, that the scheme was over-funded by $10 billion.[275] So the government arguably had some justification for this, although one may question the prudency of the measure, given asset markets can be volatile and actuarial estimates of liabilities are subject to significant uncertainty.

Overall, the 2015-16 budget proved disappointing. Reaction to the debt switch in particular was highly negative from commentators. For example, the author of this book was quoted in the *Courier-Mail* by State Political Reporter Steven Wardill as saying: "There are a lot of fiddles, a lot of accounting fiddles in this Budget, to give the illusion that they're meeting their fiscal strategy."[276] And former Queensland and federal

---

[273] Queensland Treasury, 2015b, op. cit., p. 5.
[274] Queensland Treasury, 2015a, op. cit., p. 92.
[275] Queensland Treasury, 2015b, op. cit., p. 6.
[276] Steven Wardill, 2015b, "Today's problems in Queensland bigger tomorrow after Budget, say economists", *The Courier-Mail*, 17 July 2015, available via www.couriermail.com.au.

Treasury and Queensland Competition Authority (QCA) official Joe Branigan was similarly critical, noting the budget was "...extraordinarily brazen in its disregard for public finance accounting standards."[277] The Palaszczuk government was off to a poor start in managing Queensland's public finances.

More creative balance sheet measures in the 2016-17 budget

In formulating a strategy for its second budget, the Palaszczuk government looked again to the state government's balance sheet for any funds it could use to improve its budget position. The major balance sheet measure in the 2016-17 budget was the repatriation of $4 billion of surplus funds invested with QIC to meet the defined benefit superannuation liability. Correspondence between Under Treasurer Jim Murphy and State Actuary Wayne Cameron in April 2016 (i.e. two months before the budget), which was later tabled in Parliament, illuminated the risk associated with the strategy.[278] The correspondence revealed that, while it remained more likely than not the government would not end up in a deficit regarding its superannuation liabilities (i.e. it would continue to have at least enough assets set aside to meet the expected liability), there was still a significant chance it would eventually end up in deficit (Table 7.2). Regarding the columns in Table 8.2, the funding basis assumes that assets invested earn what they are expected to earn rather than an assumed and relatively low risk-free discount rate, as the accounting basis assumes. Hence the funding basis estimates should be taken as the more probable, but a prudent government should give some regard to the accounting basis, too, as a lower bound scenario.

---

[277] Ibid.
[278] Wayne Cameron, 2016, *Actuarial Investigation of the State Public Sector Superannuation Scheme (QSuper)*, letter to Under Treasurer Mr Jim Murphy, dated 26 April 2016.

Table 7.2 Estimated probabilities of an accrued deficit regarding Queensland government's defined benefit superannuation scheme, State Actuary estimates

Surplus repatriation ($ billion)	Probability of accrued deficit	
	Funding basis	Accounting basis
0	2%	12%
1	3%	18%
2	5%	24%
3	12%	36%
4	19%	50%
5	28%	62%
6	43%	74%

Source: Cameron, W., op. cit.

Due to community concerns about the growth in public service numbers since it came into office, the Palaszczuk government introduced a new sixth fiscal principle relating to public service numbers in the 2016-17 budget:

> Principle 6 – Maintain a sustainable public service by ensuring that overall growth in full–time equivalent (FTE) employees, on average over the forward estimates, does not exceed population growth.[279]

This followed a massive increase in public service numbers since the 2015 election, which more than made up for the loss of public service jobs under the Newman government (Figure 7.2). Until mid-2016, public service numbers had been growing at a rate of 4-5 percent per annum, compared with population growth of less than 1½ percent.

[279] Queensland Treasury, 2016, *Queensland Budget 2016-17: Budget Strategy and Outlook*, budget paper no. 2, p. 68.

Figure 7.2 Queensland public service FTEs

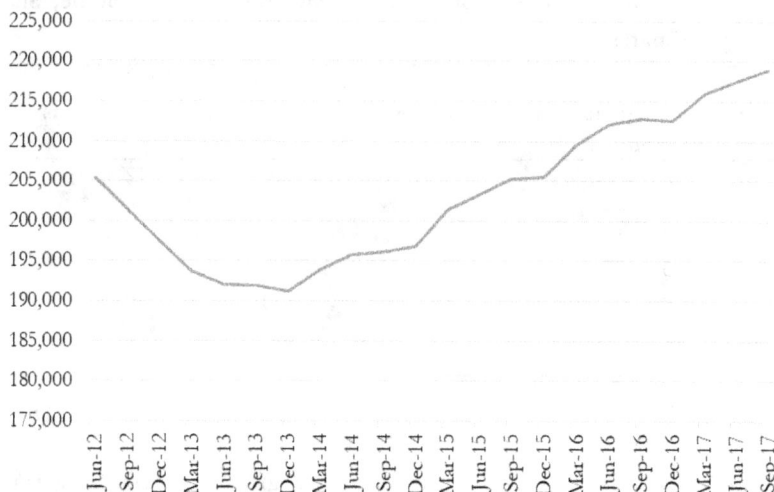

Source: Queensland government workforce statistics available via www.forgov.qld.gov.au. NB September &
December quarter 2012 estimates are interpolated.

The growth in public service numbers was associated with a surge in general government employee expenses, up 7.8 percent in 2015-16—incidentally, meaning employee expenses exceeded $20 billion for the first time—compared with the forecast in the Palaszczuk government's first budget of 5.3 percent (Figure 7.3).

It was commendable that the government introduced a fiscal principle regarding public service growth, although arguably it should have incorporated an efficiency dividend. That is, allowing the public service to grow in line with population gives no recognition to gains that could come from economies of scale, efficiency improvements or technological change. The Palaszczuk government set a principle that it should not have struggled to meet, but, as we shall see, it ended up breaching this principle by the end of its first term.

Figure 7.3 Queensland general government employee expenses growth estimated at time of each Palaszczuk Government budget

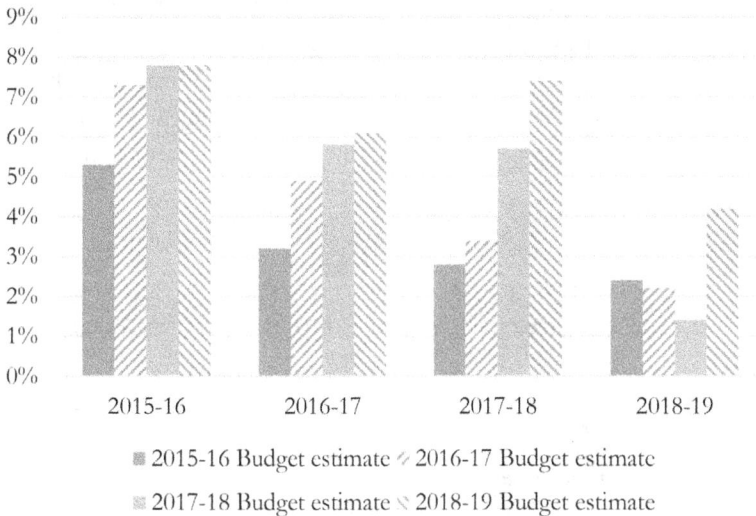

Source: *Queensland government budget papers.*

Moody's removes its negative outlook on the state's credit rating

Owing largely to stronger royalties forecast in the Palaszczuk government's MYFER for 2016-17 and the consequent improvement in the fiscal outlook, Moody's removed its negative outlook for Queensland's AA1 credit rating in April 2017. This was welcomed by the state government and commentators, although some economists remained sceptical. SMART Infrastructure Facility Senior Research Fellow Joe Branigan commented:

> The problem with Moody's analysis is that it focuses too much on the short-term boost to revenue from the recent (and welcome) increase in coking coal prices as well as the initial boost to growth from LNG exports. Moody's implicitly assumes that both of these factors will continue indefinitely. In fact, neither factor in isolation has much to do with Queensland's long-term structural budget position, especially because of the way the Commonwealth Grants Commission discounts Queensland's GST allocation every time the rivers of royalty revenue

flow a little too fast for the CGC's liking.

When you look through the fluctuating resource prices and one-off budget measures, such as the superannuation payment holiday and loading the GOCs with debt, it is clear that Queensland has a structural budget problem that can only be addressed by consistently restraining spending growth in the general government sector to below long-run average revenue growth, not just next year but for the next generation.[280]

Branigan was also highly doubtful the Palaszczuk government would keep to its budget expenses projections. He was right to be sceptical as employee expenses have typically exceeded forecasts (Figure 7.3 above).

An election winning budget

The Palaszczuk government's third budget was watched closely as it was the final budget before the next election. It delivered a politically clever budget, with funding for a range of infrastructure projects in marginal seats, including $2 billion for Cross River Rail and $225 million for the Townsville water security initiative, although one which did little to repair Queensland's fiscal position. Large fiscal deficits in the range of $2.4-3.9 billion per annum were expected over the forward estimates, and only modest net operating balances, in the $150-700 million p.a. range were expected. The 2017-18 state budget revealed the government got very lucky in 2016-17—except for the impact of severe tropical cyclone Debbie in the Whitsundays region in late March—with the government benefiting from a surge in royalties that has allowed it to generate a positive fiscal balance, not just a positive net operating balance. The government also expected a genuine fall in total debt in 2017-18, although it was expected to begin

---

[280] Joe Branigan, 2017, "Moody Blues", *Queensland Economy Watch*, posted 21 April 2017, available via www.queenslandeconomywatch.com.

climbing again in the following years (Figure 7.4).[281] The extraordinary budget outcome in 2016-17 was associated with huge estimated growth in nominal GSP of 11.75 percent, driven by higher coal prices. The *Australian* newspaper described the large net operating balance as a "coal-fuelled $2.8 billion surplus."[282]

Figure 7.4 Qld government budget balances, Treasury estimates and projections at time of 2017-2018 budget

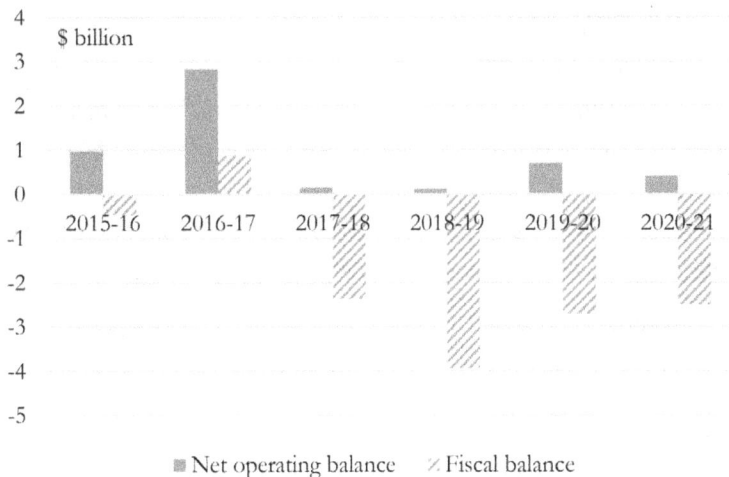

Source: Queensland government budget papers.

The Palaszczuk government was the beneficiary of a surge in coal prices in late 2016 related largely to China shutting down some of its coal

---

[281] The *Report on State Finances* released in October 2017 showed that there was actually a decline in total borrowings in 2016-17 to $71.9 billion from $72.9 billion in 2015-16, while at Budget time Treasury was expecting a slight increase to $73.1 billion. The decline in total borrowings appeared to be related to clever cash management by the Queensland Treasury. The reduction in borrowing was not due to any improvement in the underlying budget situation. Indeed, the net operating surplus was more-or-less constant and the fiscal surplus for 2016-17 actually turned out to be lower than expected. What appears to have happened is the Government received more money in advance from its government-owned corporations such as Energy Queensland than it was previously expecting.

[282] Sarah Elks, 2017a, "Queensland budget 2017: coal boosts $2.8bn surplus", The Australian, 13 June 2017, available via www.theaustralian.com.au.

mines. This meant that forecast revenue from coal royalties in 2016-17 was revised from $1.5 billion at the time the 2016-17 budget was handed down in June 2016, to $3.4 billion estimated in the 2017-18 budget handed down in June 2017. Total royalties were forecast to be $3.8 billion, compared with $1.9 billion originally forecast. Because of the sliding scale in the royalties formula, increases in coal prices tend to deliver proportionately greater increases in royalties to the government.[283]

The good luck with royalties was not expected to continue indefinitely, and Queensland Treasury estimated fiscal deficits for the years after 2016-17. So total state debt would continue to increase, and by the end of 2020-21 was expected to exceed $41 billion for the general government sector and $81 billion in total, taking into account the GOCs (Figure 7.5).

Figure 7.5 Queensland government borrowings at end of financial year, estimates and projection at time of 2017-18 budget

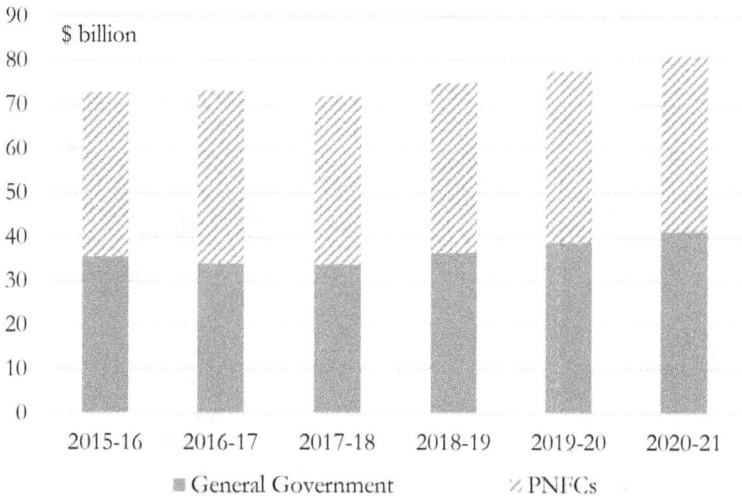

Source: Queensland government budget papers.

[283] As at June 2017, the royalty paid per tonne of coal is dependent upon its price. For the first $100, the royalty rate is 7 percent, and it increases to 12.5 percent for the next $50 (i.e. up to and including $150), and then to 15% for the balance over $150.

The Palaszczuk government was accused of pork barrelling in its 2017-18 budget, due to the location of some of the announced infrastructure projects. Extraordinarily, the Treasurer did not deny this, as *The Australian* reported:

> Mr Pitt did not deny yesterday that the $5bn regional infrastructure splash was pork-barrelling before the election — due by May next year but expected late this year — though he insisted the spending was necessary.[284]

Treasurer Pitt's honesty should be appreciated, but it is rather disturbing that a minister would be so shameless about the spending of money for political purposes.

The Queensland government's $10.2 billion capital program in 2017-18 was heavily skewed to regional areas outside SEQ, but away from other areas in SEQ with the exception of inner-city Brisbane, where Cross River Rail would be located (Figure 7.6). The large per capita funding differences between well-funded regions, such as Fitzroy and inner-city Brisbane, and relatively poorly funded regions, such as Brisbane's eastern, southern and western suburbs and Logan-Beaudesert among others, appear excessive. With money being directed to regional areas with political results in mind, there is obviously the risk of dubious projects being selected.

The government clearly had the objective of boosting its electoral prospects in the regions. The political challenge the government faced in regional areas was related in part to high regional unemployment rates after the end of the mining investment boom from the late 2000s to early 2010s. For example, in the 12 months to May 2017, the average unemployment rate was 10.1 percent in the Townsville region and 13.2 percent in the Queensland outback, compared with a state average of 6.2 percent.

Ideally, future Queensland budget papers should include additional analysis of regional per capita capital spending, explaining the reasons for

---

[284] Sarah Elks, 2017b, "Queensland budget: Curtis Pitt pours $5 billion into key seats", *The Australian*, 14 June 2017, available via www.theaustralian.com.au.

any disparities. It is possible disparities may be justifiable. For example, the state government may be funding infrastructure to complement economic development in under-populated areas such as the Queensland outback and Darling Downs-Maranoa. Also, there may be economies of scale in infrastructure provision, which could explain a relatively lower per capita spending in the Brisbane metro area and a higher per capita spending in regional areas.

Figure 7.6 Estimated capital outlays by region per capita based on Budget estimates and ABS population data, 2017-18

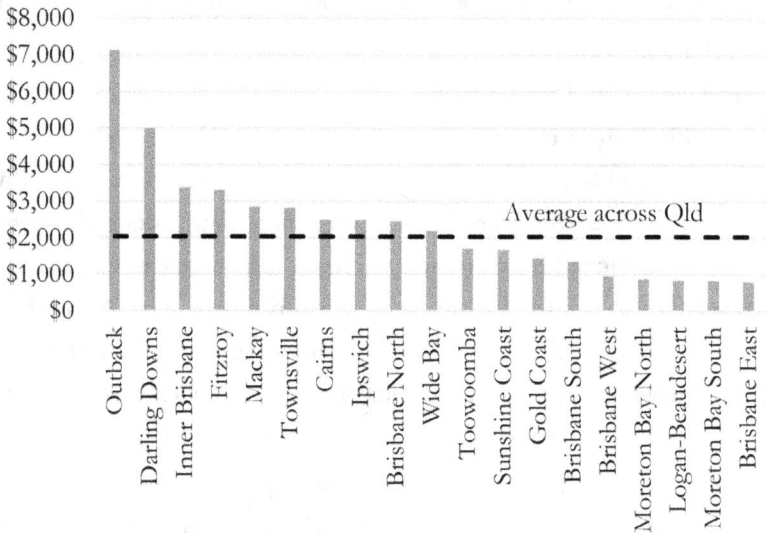

Source: Author's calculations based on 2017-18 Queensland government budget papers and ABS population estimates.

The 2017-18 budget papers revealed the Palaszczuk government was spending substantially less on capital purchases than the Newman government was forecasting to spend in its last MYFER (Figure 7.7). Assuming the proposed infrastructure spending in the Strong Choices final plan would have occurred if the Newman government were re-elected, the gap between the two governments would be even larger than shown in Figure 7.7.

Figure 7.7 Comparison of Palaszczuk government capital purchases with final budget projections of Newman government (at end of 2014), estimates and projections

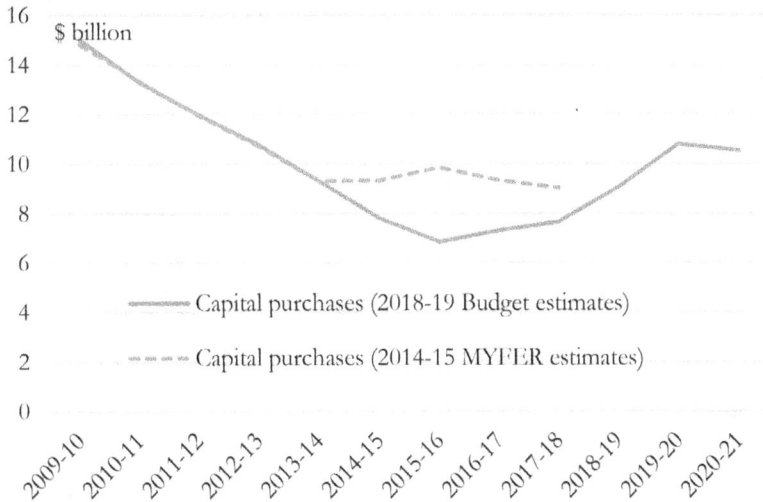

Source: Queensland government budget papers.

Partly, the lower capital expenditure under the Palaszczuk government compared with the Newman government is due to different priorities. Broadly speaking, Queensland Labor governments tend to give more priority to operating expenses than capital expenses compared with LNP governments. Recall, for example, how the Borbidge government had an explicit strategy of rebalancing the budget towards capital expenditure. Partly, Labor's budget philosophy is related to its links with trade unions, which have significant penetration in the public sector. The growth in public service FTEs and employee expenses under Palaszczuk, far in excess of what would have occurred if the Newman government were re-elected, is strong evidence of this (Figure 7.8). In 2017-18, employee expenses are estimated to be $22.4 billion, which is $1.7 billion or 8.3 percent higher than they were projected to be in the Newman government's last set of budget projections.

Figure 7.8 Comparison of Palaszczuk government employee expenses with final budget projections of Newman government

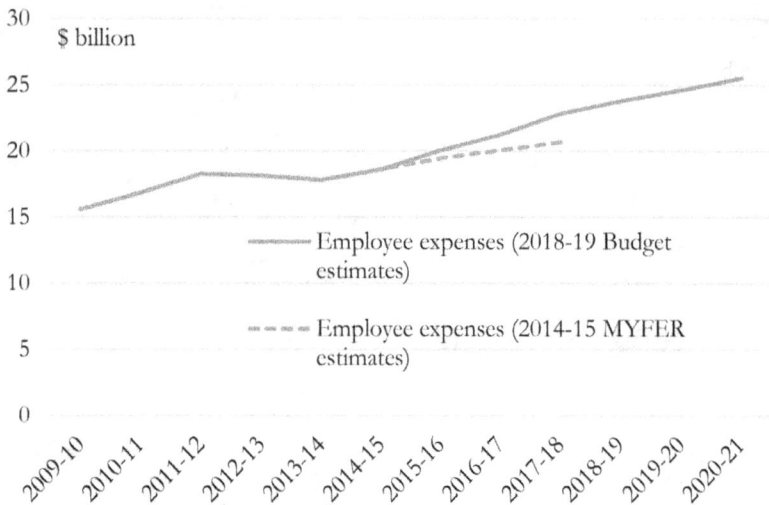

Source: Queensland government budget papers.

The surge in royalties helped the Palaszczuk government fund a boost to capital expenditure, which is expected in 2018-19 to lift it beyond the level at the end of the Newman government (Figure 8.7 above). Of course, the Newman government was counting on using $8.6 billion of proceeds from Strong Choices asset leases to fund new infrastructure, so its capital expenditure over 2015 to 2020 would likely have been much higher than the Palaszczuk government will achieve.

The surge in royalties was fortuitous for the Palaszczuk government, but as previous governments have discovered, the volatility can go the other way, and consider that the substantial royalties once predicted from coal seam gas are yet to materialise. Ultimately, the high variation in royalties which are dependent upon commodity prices makes state budget management much more difficult (Figure 7.9). The challenge of budget management is even greater when one considers any knock-on effects of changes in royalty revenues to the distribution of GST revenue in later years, as discussed in Chapter 1.

Figure 7.9 Queensland government royalties revenue

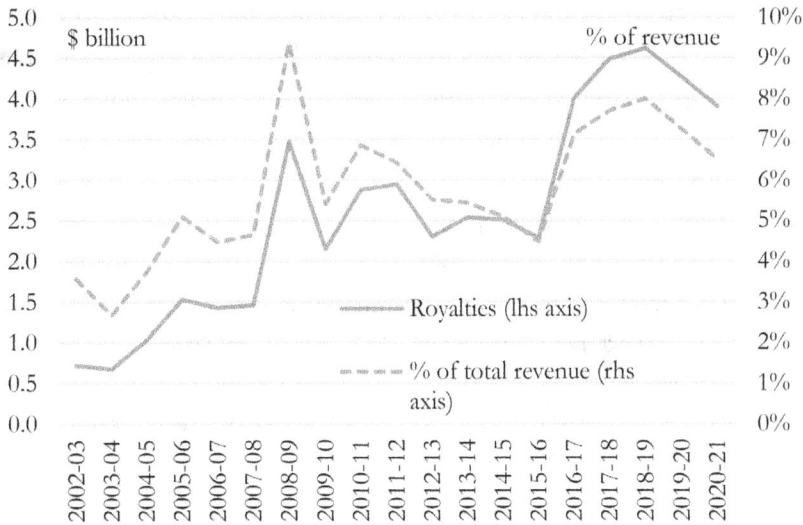

Source: Queensland government budget papers.

Ultimately, to some extent a variation of actual budget estimates from forecasts is natural. As noted in Chapter 1, readers should realise future budget estimates, particularly those 2-3 years out, are highly unreliable and little faith should be given in heroic estimates of expenditure restraint. Indeed, the 2017-18 budget illustrated a failure in fiscal discipline by the government's own standard.

The 2017-18 budget also revealed the government would breach its sixth fiscal principle, with public service numbers projected to grow at a rate of 1.7 percent over the forward estimates to 2020-21, compared with the target of 1.5 percent. It is concerning that the principle, only introduced in the previous year's budget, was so quickly breached, and it raised doubt about whether the extent of the breach may be greater in the future, considering the proverb that "one may as well hang for a sheep as for a lamb."

Restraining the growth of employee expenses, which are over 40 percent of total Queensland general government spending, is one of the major challenges facing the Queensland government. The Queensland Audit Office (QAO) has expressed concern over the growth of employee expenses, associated with growing employee numbers and average salaries, particularly as senior public service positions, from the Administrative Officer 8 (AO8) level and above, increased relative to more junior positions. The QAO found:

> ...government is employing more staff at the higher annual earnings bands to deliver on its objectives today than it did five years ago... While there may be valid reasons why agencies employ more staff in the higher job classifications, such as increased complexity of government service delivery, there is a simple but significant financial risk. With existing controls in place for managing overall public service employee costs, it will be difficult to maintain a financially sustainable public service if this long-term trend continues. Strengthening the controls around managing the public service workforce profile to meet future demand is warranted.[285]

It remains to be seen whether the Palaszczuk government will heed the QAO's advice and whether it can stick to its projected employee expenses over the forward estimates. Its record so far on both expenses and particularly employee expenses growth raise doubts about its ability to do so (Figure 8.3 above). To illustrate, employee expenses growth in 2015-16 was forecast to be 5.3 percent in the Palaszczuk government's first (2015-16) budget, but would finally be recorded as 7.8 percent in its third (2017-18) budget.

Adani mega mine sacrificed to secure re-election

In late October 2017, Premier Palaszczuk called an early election for 25 November. Going into the election the government knew it faced a political challenge over the proposed Carmichael mine to be constructed by Indian conglomerate Adani in the Galilee Basin stretching across North and Central Queensland. The so-called Adani mega mine, which was touted as

---

[285] Queensland Audit Office, 2017, *Organisational structure and accountability, Report 17 2016-17*, p. 3.

being potentially Australia's largest coalmine, had received all the necessary state and federal approvals and was supported by both state and federal governments due to the economic benefits it would bring to the region— and also arguably due to the hundreds of millions in royalty revenue it was expected to bring to the Palaszczuk government each year. Australia Institute economist Rod Campbell has estimated the mine would generate royalty revenue of over $280 million per annum by the mid-2020s.[286] But the government faced an immediate challenge in inner city Brisbane seats, including Deputy Premier Jackie Trad's seat of South Brisbane, from the Australian Greens, and it may have been looking for an opportunity to pull back from its full support for the mega mine.

The mine had already proved controversial earlier in 2017. In a surprising display of dissension in the cabinet, several weeks before the budget in June, Deputy Premier Jackie Trad protested against a royalty holiday the government was intending to grant to Adani. In the end, a deal was reached, and Adani did receive lower royalty rates for the early years of the project and the capacity to defer royalties and later pay them with interest. The extent to which this was less favourable to Adani than the original plan cannot be determined based on publicly available information, given the government's agreement with Adani is commercial-in-confidence.

An opportunity for the Palaszczuk government to pull back from its support for the mega mine presented itself at the end of the first week of the election campaign. At an unexpected Friday afternoon press conference, Premier Palaszczuk announced her government would no longer assist in the disbursement of any funds lent to Adani by the Northern Australian Infrastructure Facility (NAIF). She alleged the LNP opposition were planning to smear her with a conflict of interest charge, based on her partner Shaun Drabsch having worked on Adani's NAIF application in his position as a partner at professional services firm PwC. So to remove any

---

[286]   Rod Campbell, 2017, *Royal Pardon: How much an Adani royalty holiday could cost Queenslanders*, available via www.tai.org.au, p. 3.

concerns around probity, she would veto the NAIF loan by not allowing it to be paid to Adani using a Queensland government bank account, which was required because the federal government was relying upon section 96 of the Constitution to justify assistance through the NAIF. Section 96 allows the Australian Parliament to "grant financial assistance to any state on such terms and conditions as the Parliament thinks fit."[287] Without using section 96, it would have been more difficult, and indeed it may have been impossible, for the Commonwealth to provide NAIF loans in a valid way according to the Constitution. Normally the use of the states as a conduit for Commonwealth money would not have caused any problems. But this time was different.

The plausibility of the conflict-of-interest justification was questioned by commentators and the opposition, particularly by Rockhampton-based federal LNP Senator Matt Canavan, a strong proponent of the mega mine. Canavan noted that given the Queensland government was still a shareholder in Aurizon, the Premier faced a conflict of interest regarding Aurizon's bid, which was competing with Adani's for finance to build a Galilee basin rail line. The Palaszczuk government has not indicated whether it would veto a loan to Aurizon, and has simply noted that: "Any other NAIF matters will be given proper consideration and assessed on their merits."[288] The issue became academic on 9 February 2018 when Aurizon withdrew its NAIF loan application, due to reduced expectations regarding customer demand for its proposed rail line in the Galilee basin. Incidentally, the possibility of conflicts of interest is another reason why government ownership of businesses may not be in the public interest.

The Palaszczuk government's mega mine "back flip" was highly controversial, but it provided Labor a political wedge between itself and the

---

[287] Constitution Education Fund Australia, 2017, *Section 96 and the $900 million loan to Adani*, *2 June 2017*, available via www.cefa.org.au.

[288] Anthony Galloway, 2017, "Adani: Palaszczuk Government not ruling out loan to rival Aurizon for Galilee Basin rail line", *Courier-Mail*, 28 December 2017, available via www.couriermail.com.au.

LNP opposition, which supported the NAIF loan. It effectively allowed the government to say it was not opposed to the mega mine, just to taxpayer assistance to the mega mine. The Premier noted Adani itself had said that the mega mine was viable without the NAIF loan. This allowed it to provide different tailored messages to SEQ voters opposed to the mine and to NQ residents supportive of the mine, basically a political narrowcasting strategy. It is difficult to say to what extent the Adani loan backflip contributed to Labor winning the 25 November election and increasing its majority, so it no longer was a minority government.

In the new Parliament of 93 seats, Labor had a majority, albeit a slim one, with 48 seats. Arguably, Pauline Hanson's One Nation's (PHON's) decision to allocate preferences against the majority of sitting MPs was the most important factor that worked to the detriment of the LNP. While Labor could generally rely on Greens' preferences to help it hold its seats, the LNP could not rely on PHON preferences in a similar way. Another factor was Labor's highly effective "It'll be grim under Tim" advertising campaign, which reminded voters of Leader of the Opposition Tim Nicholl's role as Treasurer in the Newman government, focussing on public service job cuts and proposed privatisations. Nicholls did not re-contest the LNP leadership after the election loss, and his deputy Deb Frecklington, MP for Nanango, replaced him as leader.

State debt was raised as an issue several times during the election campaign, but was unable to be exploited effectively by the LNP opposition. In its economic strategy released in the lead up to the election, the opposition claimed it would eliminate Queensland's fiscal deficits, which it noted totalled around $11 billion over the four years of the forward estimates. This exposed the opposition to claims, including from UQ Professor John Quiggin, that it would cut jobs and services if it won office.

Possibly due to many stumbles by Treasurer Curtis Pitt during the term of government, and particularly during the election campaign when he referred to Queensland's projected $81 billion of debt as "magical or mythical", the Premier moved him to the position of Speaker after the election.[289] Deputy Premier Jackie Trad, who survived a strong bid from Greens candidate Amy MacMahon for the seat of South Brisbane, was appointed as the new Queensland Treasurer.

Trad's first major presentation as the new Treasurer was the MYFER for 2017-18, released in mid-December. This contained more favourable upward revisions in revenue, particularly due to higher coal royalty payments as coal prices had remained higher than forecast by Treasury. But the MYFER still showed Queensland state debt on a trajectory to around $81 billion by 2020-21.

Trad's first budget

New Treasurer Jackie Trad's first budget was an immense disappointment to those observers who were hoping for greater fiscal rigour from the Palaszczuk government. The projected operating surpluses were very thin and actually negligible when compared with gross state product and the fiscal deficits, fully taking into account capital expenditures, amounted to nearly $13 billion over the four years to 2021-22 (Table 7.3). Hence, total government debt was still on a trajectory to over $80 billion and was projected to reach around $83 billion in 2021-22, with $42 billion of that general government debt. While the government was receiving additional revenues from its new taxes announced during the 2017 election campaign and a new Waste Disposal Levy—expected to raise around $1.3 billion over four years—this was insufficient to generate material operating surpluses given continued growth in expenses and expected reductions in redistributed GST revenue and royalties over the forward estimates.

---

[289] Trent Akers, 2017, "Queensland election 2017: Treasurer says $81b debt doesn't add up", *Courier-Mail,* 3 November 2017, available via www.couriermail.com.au.

Table 7.3 Queensland Treasury estimates and projections of budget balances in 2018-19 budget

	Net operating balance ($ billion)	Net operating balance (% of GSP)	Fiscal balance ($ billion)	Fiscal balance (% of GSP)
2017-18 (estimate)	1.512	0.4%	-0.604	-0.2%
2018-19 (estimate)	0.148	0.0%	-3.033	-0.8%
2019-20 (projection)	0.160	0.0%	-3.881	-1.0%
2020-21 (projection)	0.110	0.0%	-3.400	-0.9%
2021-22 (projection)	0.690	0.2%	-2.636	-0.6%

Source: 2018-19 Queensland government budget.

Even according to the metrics the government prefers, Treasurer Trad's first budget projects a deterioration in Queensland's fiscal position. For example, p. 48 of Budget Paper 2 revealed:

- the general government debt to revenue ratio is projected to increase from 54 percent in 2017-18 to 68 percent in 2021-22, meaning the government is not expected to comply with the fiscal principle to "Target ongoing reductions in Queensland's relative debt burden..."; and

- the proportion of general government net investments in non-financial assets financed by net operating cash flows will fall below 50 percent to 40 percent in 2019-20 and 44 percent in 2020-21, meaning the government is not expected to comply with the fiscal principle that it will "ensure any new capital investment in the General Government Sector is funded primarily through recurrent revenues rather than borrowing."

This was a very disappointing budget from the new Treasurer Trad, and one which did nothing to put Queensland back on a path to regaining a AAA credit rating.

The Rail Fail

One of the major issues the Palaszczuk government faced was the deterioration in QR's reliability toward the end of 2016, with sudden cancellations of services owing to shortages of drivers. The so-called rail fail led to the resignation in late October 2016 of QR Chairman Michael Klug and CEO Helen Gluer, who was Under Treasurer in the Newman government until November 2013, when she resigned for personal reasons.

It appears there were concerns about QR for some time as the Newman government had converted it from a GOC to a statutory authority, which would mean greater ministerial oversight.[290] That said, arguably government ownership and ministerial oversight of QR contributed to the rail fail, as ministerial views on business decisions may have compromised QR's operations, as we shall see.

In late 2016, the government appointed former Rio Tinto Bauxite and Alumina CEO Phillip Strachan to investigate QR's failures. His final report, delivered on 31 January 2017, identified a range of problems afflicting QR, including:

> A coinciding 7 per cent drop in train crew productivity, due in part to more restrictive crewing rules agreed between unions and Queensland Rail's management.[291]

A Labor government, by its nature, would naturally be more receptive to unions than a conservative LNP government. Some commentators have suggested the closeness of the Palaszczuk government and unions contributed to problems at QR. Regarding new enterprise agreements negotiated between QR and unions in 2016, Kelmeny Fraser, writing in the *Courier-Mail* on 22 February 2017, observed:

> The [Strachan] inquiry found QR "may have accepted overly restrictive crewing rules because it negotiated the new train crew enterprise agreement while operating with a train crew shortfall and while implementing a major timetable change".

The *Courier-Mail* revealed this week that the board had pushed back,

---

[290] Amy Remeikis, 2014c, "New Queensland Rail boss Helen Gluer resigned two months ago for personal reasons", *Brisbane Times*, 10 January 2014, available via www.brisbanetimes.com.au.

[291] Phillip Strachan, 2017, *Queensland Rail train crewing practices commission of inquiry: Final Report*, p. 3.

refusing to endorse the driver deal because of an "excessive" pay rise for train crew. It is understood Treasurer Curtis Pitt—one of the two responsible ministers for QR—intervened to ensure the rise went ahead.

His office has denied issuing any "legally binding" directive to the QR board. But the rail inquiry found the board had not only been kept in the dark about the magnitude of the driver shortages, but had been cut out of the bargaining.[292]

There were clearly governance problems with QR, as the Strachan Inquiry acknowledged, noting that "the interfaces between Queensland Rail and the government are unclear and have limited the effective oversight of the development and implementation of major projects", and it suggested that QR's "governance and institutional arrangements now require further review and change to ensure acceptable levels of customer service."[293] One of the Strachan Inquiry's recommendations—all of which would be accepted by the Palaszczuk government, incidentally—was "a whole-of-business review of Queensland Rail to identify any systemic organisational issues and develop actions to address these issues." This would be undertaken by what the government has called the Citytrain Response Unit.[294] At this stage it is unclear what progress the Unit has made in reviewing QR's governance.

The rail fail is a good illustration of the problems that arise when GOCs such as QR are subject to ministerial interference. Regarding the current government's approach to GOCs generally, SMART Infrastructure Facility Senior Research Fellow Joe Branigan commented when interviewed for this book that:

> The treatment of the GOCs runs against the corporatisation principles established in the 1990s, which contributed towards the tremendous boost to our productivity, wages and living standards. It would appear

---

[292] Kelmeny Fraser, 2017, "Strachan inquiry finds restrictive union work rules part of problems at Queensland Rail", *Courier-Mail*, 11 February 2017, available via www.couriermail.com.au..

[293] Strachan, P., 2017, p. 50.

[294] The Strachan Inquiry suggested it be called the Rail Review Office.

we've moved away from those principles that have served us so well for the past 25 years.

The franchising model for QR, which was suggested by the Newman government's Commission of Audit, may have avoided the problems that emerged in late 2016. Under this model, the right to run rail services would be contracted out to providers, as is done in Victoria. This could be for the whole passenger rail network or particular lines. Restrictive work practices that have resulted from strong union influence in QR may not have been put in place in a privately managed rail network. To the extent that QR's problems were caused by restrictive work practices, a franchising model may have helped avoid the rail fail.

The franchising model for city passenger rail services received further support in May 2017 when Infrastructure Australia suggested it would yield efficiency gains and budgetary savings in the order of $3 billion over two decades that could help fund the Brisbane underground Cross River Rail project, the Palaszczuk government's highest priority infrastructure project.[295] Franchising would be expected to result in significant cost savings, as private sector operators would be incentivised to increase productivity, reduce costs and increase profits. International evidence suggests operating cost savings of at least 10 percent and up to 50 percent.[296]

Assessment of the Palaszczuk government so far

The Palaszczuk government has had to formulate its budgets with one hand tied behind its back, being unable to rely on privatisation proceeds to finance new infrastructure projects, as the Newman government was planning to do. And for the first half of its first term, it faced a sluggish economy, particularly in regional areas, as the economy transitions away

---

[295] Infrastructure Australia, 2017, *Improving Public Transport: Customer Focused Franchising*, pp. 4-5.
[296] Ibid., p. 13.

from the mining investment boom. As with all governments, there appears to have been a variety of questionable public expenditures and pork barrelling, particularly in the regions under the justification of job creation. Furthermore, it has not enacted the tough measures needed to repair Queensland's fiscal situation.

Overall, the Palaszczuk government has at least avoided the excesses of the Beattie and Bligh governments, but, disturbingly, it appears to have adopted the idea that active management of the state balance sheet for policy purposes, such as the transfer of general government debt to GOCs, is desirable. In doing so it is has arguably violated the principle that GOCs should be at arms-length from the government. The government appears to take the view that GOCs are simply extensions of the government for delivering its policy objectives. This runs against the principles of National Competition Policy and the principles for GOCs set by the Goss government.

The Palaszczuk government has also reduced the buffer, or margin of safety, in the asset pool set aside to meet its defined benefit public service superannuation liability, by repatriating funds to the general government sector. As discussed above, this may not have been prudent.

The second term of government won by the Palaszczuk government at the 2017 election gives it an opportunity to acquit itself far better on economic and financial management than in its first term. As noted above, however, Treasurer Trad's first budget was not encouraging in this regard. The government also faces a major challenge in resolving the bungled purchase of $4 billion of the NGR trains for the passenger rail network in SEQ, which have failed to meet Human Rights Commission standards for disability access. While the current government blames the Newman government, which was in power when the procurement was decided upon, the current opposition claims the current government has had sufficient time to resolve issues that have become apparent and it has failed to do so. Without a public inquiry into the issue, it is difficult to know where to attribute blame. But what is clear is that it is another example of the deterioration of Queensland's public administration that has occurred over the last few decades.

8

HOW WORRIED SHOULD QUEENSLANDERS BE ABOUT THE DEBT?

Does Queensland really have a problem or is it a beat up?

Queensland's total state government debt, now on a path to $83 billion, is referred to a lot in this book. This figure includes both the borrowings by the QTC, which is the government's debt management office, on behalf of general government agencies, such as the Departments of Health and Education and Training, and GOCs. The total debt measure is keenly monitored by the ratings' agencies such as Moody's and S&P, and was emphasised by the Newman government's Commission of Audit. Queensland has ended up on the path to over $80 billion of debt due to both increased borrowings by GOCs, which began to noticeably increase in the early 2000s, but also due to an increase in general government borrowings, as a huge capital expenditure program at the same time as the financial crisis contributed to massive deficits during the Bligh government (Figure 1.1 in Chapter 1).[297]

There is an important distinction between general government borrowings and borrowings by GOCs. The latter can earn income that can be used to meet interest expenses on their debt, and it may be argued that it is only general government sector debt that we should be concerned with. But as discussed below, the total debt, including that of GOCs matters, because ratings agencies are concerned with it—they take a holistic view of sub-national governments—and because, and this may be why

---

[297] See Appendix 3 for further discussion of how the Queensland government got into so much debt.

ratings agencies take that view, the distinction between GOC and general government debt can be manipulated to give the illusion of budgetary improvements. For example, debt could be shifted onto the GOC sector from the general government sector, reducing general government sector debt and improving the budget balance but reducing interest payments. Indeed, this has occurred under the Palaszczuk government.

Out of the six Australian states the Centre for Independent Studies' Senior Fellow Robert Carling assessed for his 2016 *Report Card on State Finances*, Queensland ranked fourth out of six, with a score of 5 out of 10 for current fiscal position, with only Western Australia (WA) and SA lower. However, acknowledging that the budget situation has improved in recent years, partly due to strong repair measures by the Newman government, Queensland ranks first out of six on the trend measures of fiscal performance, scoring 8 out of 10.[298] The *Report Card on State Finances* notes that Queensland:

> Once the unchallenged top of the class, has started to improve from a serious setback, but still has a long way to go.[299]

Carling acknowledged recent improvements in operating and fiscal balances, but was concerned about the total debt being high, the reversal of the Newman government's cuts to the public service, and the reluctance to privatise GOCs.

Total state government debt has increased substantially in Queensland relative to the size of the economy—i.e. as percentage of gross state product (GSP)—and in per capita terms. Regarding the debt-to-GSP ratio, Professor Fabrizio Carmignani from Griffith University noted in January 2015 that:

> ...the debt-to-GSP ratio in Queensland has increased considerably since 2006-07, and that most of this increase occurred under Anna Bligh's Labor governments.

---

[298] Robert Carling, 2017, *Report Card on State Finances*, Centre for Independent Studies, p. 12.
[299] Ibid., p. 13.

And in comparison to other states, Queensland now has the highest debt-to-GSP ratio.[300]

In per capita terms, out of the six states, state government debt in Queensland is the second highest in Australia, at over $14,600 per head compared with around $7,600 in NSW and $7,600 in Victoria, for example (Figure 8.1). Among the states, only WA is in a worse position with $17,500 in debt per capita. WA's decline has occurred much more recently than Queensland's, and was related to adverse economic conditions in the state at the end of the mining investment boom. WA's economy is much more heavily dependent than Queensland's on the resources sector, so the decline in mining investment had a very large impact in WA.

Figure 8.1 State and territory government borrowings per capita, as at 30 June 2017

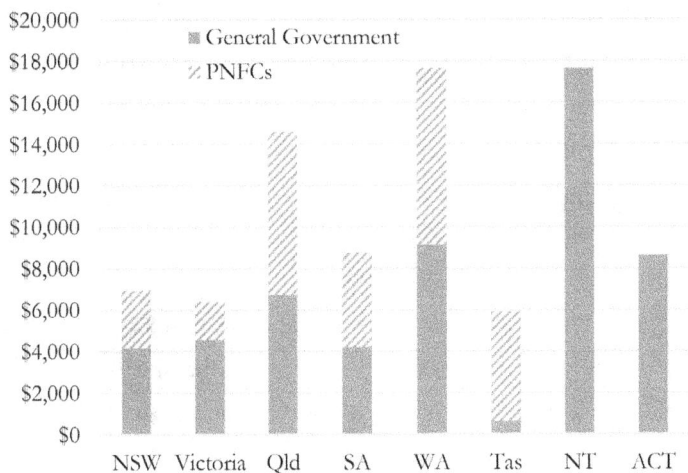

Source: ABS Government Finance Statistics, cat. no. 5512.0 and ABS Australian Demographic Statistics, cat. no. 3101.0.

---

[300] Fabrizio Carmignani, 2015b, "The true state of Queensland's debt", *The Conversation*, 29 January 2015, available via www.theconversation.edu.au.

Lest the reader considers this is all too pessimistic, it does need to be acknowledged that Queensland has time to turn this all around. After all, as Professor Carmignani noted in 2015 regarding the debt-to-GSP ratio, which is analogous to the debt-to-gross domestic product (GDP) ratio for national economies:

> ...this ratio remains relatively low in comparison to other G20 countries, including the Australian Commonwealth.[301]

For example, in the data reported in Cargminani's article, Queensland's debt-to-GSP ratio of around 25 percent was compared with that of countries such as Canada, with a debt-to-GDP ratio of 88 percent, Germany at 75 percent, the UK at 92 percent, the US at 105 percent, not to mention Japan at 245 percent.[302]

This does not mean we should be complacent, of course. Queensland's debt-to-GSP is much higher than it has been historically and it does come at a cost. Spending needs to be lower, or taxes need to be higher, for the operating budget to accommodate the higher interest bill associated with the extra debt.

In 2016-17, the Queensland general government sector's interest expenses were around $1.7 billion (out of total general government expenses of $53.6 billion). Prior to the debt build-up, interest expenses were only in the order of $200 million per annum. So the extra burden on Queenslanders is around $1.5 billion per annum, or around $310 extra per annum for every Queenslander. Consider, for example, that the Queensland government collects around $1.7 billion in motor vehicle registration fees annually. So, if Queensland had better managed its public finances, the State government could have reduced car registration fees by nearly 90 percent.

---

[301] Ibid.
[302] Ibid.

The other side of the balance sheet

So far we have discussed Queensland's debt, or its borrowings. These sit in the liabilities column of the state government's balance sheet, along with other liabilities, such as the liability for defined benefit superannuation payments for retired public servants covered by the now closed defined benefit scheme. To give a balanced perspective of the state of the Queensland government's books, we also need to consider the state government's assets.

Since the Hielscher era, Queensland has built up a treasure chest of assets to pre-fund its defined benefits superannuation liability. These assets are managed by the government-owned QIC, and include a wide variety of shares, bonds and private equity investments in infrastructure and real estate such as shopping centres. They sit on the general government and total government balance sheet and help offset total borrowings in the net debt, net financial worth and net worth calculations.

General government sector assets, such as roads, land, schools and hospitals, and GOC assets such as ports, power stations, transmission lines, and rail lines, also appear on the government's balance sheet. These assets have varying levels of liquidity—that is the ability to be converted readily into cash. These physical assets enter the calculation of net worth, but not net debt or net financial worth. So depending on what assets we count for the purposes of the relevant metric, we have a range of metrics other than total borrowings with which to assess the Queensland government's financial position (Table 8.1).

Table 8.1 Measures of the strength of the Queensland government's balance sheet, Treasury estimates for 2017-18

Metric	General government sector	PNFC sector	Total
Net worth	201.9	18.6	201.9
Net financial worth	-10.5	-45.3	-67.7
Net financial liabilities	33.3	n.p.	71.9
Net debt	1.6	36.3	37.9

Source: Queensland Treasury, 2018, Tables 9.4-9.6.

We see widely varying definitions of the strength of the government's balance sheet depending on what is included. Net worth is the most favourable measure, nearly $200 billion. This includes all government assets including land, roads and buildings, collectively worth over $265 billion, as well as financial assets of $61 billion. These financial assets include around $23 billion of equity in GOCs and other investments of $32.5 billion, the bulk of which are managed by QIC.[303] However, the physical assets are not as liquid as financial assets and hence are excluded from the other financial measures. Consider that net financial worth is strongly negative due to the high level of debt owed by the Queensland government. Net debt appears much better, because the assets the government has set aside to meet the superannuation liability can technically be counted toward reducing net debt, even though the superannuation liability itself is not counted in net debt (Figure 8.2). So net debt can be a misleading indicator, a point made by the Newman government's Commission of Audit, which preferred to focus on total debt.[304]

Figure 8.2 Understanding net debt and other metrics

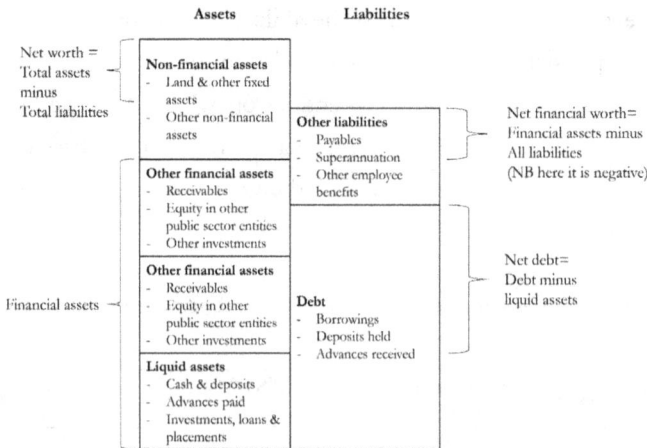

Source: Commission of Audit, 2012, op. cit. and IMF, 2001, Government Finance Statistics Manual.

---

[303] Queensland Treasury, 2017a, op. cit., p. 118.
[304] On this point see the Queensland Commission of Audit, 2012, op. cit., p. 20.

The golden rule of public finance

In assessing the state of a government's balance sheet, it is important to consider what any borrowings were used for. Was money borrowed simply to cover operating deficits, meaning the government may have been borrowing to pay for public servants' wages, or were they used to finance new infrastructure? This determines whether the debt is an unwarranted burden on future generations of taxpayers and violates the principle of inter-generational equity.

Federal Treasurer Scott Morrison notably distinguished between "good" debt and "bad" debt in the lead up to the 2017-18 federal budget. Good debt is acceptable under the golden rule of public finance, which advises against operating deficits but permits borrowing for infrastructure with a sufficient social return on investment.

The rationale for the golden rule of public finance mentioned in previous chapters is that it can make sense to finance infrastructure with borrowings, as infrastructure provides benefits over a long period, which can justify paying it off over many years. Just as households borrow to finance the purchase of a house, it can make sense for governments to purchase infrastructure assets with borrowings. Of course, an important qualification is that the infrastructure should be of sufficient quality that it justifies a government incurring the borrowing costs. As the Queensland Treasury noted in the 2015 *Review of State Finances*:

> Debt in itself is not 'bad'. It is widely accepted that Australian state governments should not borrow for recurrent expenditure, including maintenance of the existing capital stock. However, it is entirely appropriate for government to borrow for infrastructure that will service this and future generations of Queenslanders.

> Borrowing to invest in infrastructure does not violate the principle of intergenerational equity so long as: (a) the infrastructure is high quality in terms of the social return it generates (just as not all debt is 'bad', not all infrastructure is 'good'); and (b) the debt associated with that infrastructure has been repaid by the time it needs to be replaced.[305]

---

[305] Queensland Treasury, 2015a, p. 79.

But, as we have seen, there are reasons to be concerned about whether much of the infrastructure built in Queensland is yielding the social return necessary to justify it. Regrettably, governments have not always required a rigorous business case—i.e. including cost-benefit analysis—of proposed infrastructure projects. It is widely acknowledged that there were some white elephants among capital works projects in the last decade, particularly the Western Corridor Recycled Water scheme and the Tugun desalination plant. That said, it is also asserted by many that Queensland has received benefits from some valuable new pieces of infrastructure funded by the borrowings, particularly in road transport and in the health system, which saw a major rebuilding program.

Also, the full whole-of-life costs of infrastructure need to be considered and properly factored in to businesses. Regrettably they often are not, and this means infrastructure investments often turn out to be significantly more costly over their life cycle than expected. As Mark Gray noted when interviewed for this book:

> It is often not fully appreciated that capital expenditures usually give rise to additional operational expenditures. Governments commit to capital expenditures at budget time, but often do not allow for sufficient operational expenditures in the forward estimates. Treasury is as much at fault here as the politicians, in not making adequate provision for full whole-of-life costs.

In summary, we should recognise that the government has invested in assets at the same time as its debt build-up and that it does have some balance sheet flexibility due to the large investment pool it has. That is, if the Queensland government was unable to borrow on favourable terms, something the Queensland Treasury and QTC were worried about in 2008-09, it could sell off some of its assets to bring in much needed cash. Of course, it would be imprudent to touch its treasure chest at QIC, as it is meant to fund the state government's defined benefit superannuation liability, but it is comforting to know that it is there and could provide somewhat of a buffer during a future fiscal crisis.

Implications of the debt for infrastructure spending

Debt servicing costs have to be met out of the budget and hence constrain a government's options. The Queensland government's interest expenses (for the general government sector) is an estimated 3 percent of revenue, compared with around ½ percent in the mid-2000s.[306] Queensland's high debt burden and reluctance to embrace privatisation has meant that infrastructure spending has had to be constrained and has not met the expectations of the Queensland business community. Privatisations, which could provide a large source of funds for rapid debt-pay down is now seen as politically toxic in Queensland, after both the Bligh Labor and Newman LNP governments suffered electorally as a result of privatisation programs—an actual program that went ahead under Bligh, and a proposed program from Newman, Strong Choices, that never went ahead, as the government was not returned for a second term. As we shall see, while privatisation was a popular source of finance for Labor and LNP governments over the late 1990s to 2000s, currently both major parties have ruled out future privatisations.

In its September 2016 update to its Major Projects Report, BIS Shrapnel highlighted the large decline in infrastructure spending, of around 50 percent, which occurred in Queensland in 2015-16, largely associated with the end of the mining boom. Queensland was also performing poorly in terms of planned major projects ($100M+).[307] The state government has not been in a position to do much to offset the decline due to a lack of funds.

The lack of so-called asset recycling means genuinely new

---

[306] Based on Table 9.1 on p. 161 in Queensland Treasury, 2017a, op. cit. and Queensland Treasury, 2015a, p. 80.

[307] Templeton, A., 2016b, "Infrastructure spending plummeting in Queensland", *Courier-Mail*, 23 September 2016, available via www.couriermail.com.au.

infrastructure in the Queensland budget is relatively low.[308] The current Queensland government refers to a $45 billion infrastructure program over four years, which is based on gross infrastructure investment figures.[309] In net terms, allowing for the fact depreciating infrastructure needs to be refurbished or replaced, infrastructure expenditure is substantially lower (Figure 8.3). As a percentage of GSP, gross infrastructure spending is expected to remain relatively low (Figure 8.4). While the late 2000s and early 2010s were unusual in that they featured very high infrastructure spending, particularly on water sector assets, this chart suggests there may be scope to significantly boost infrastructure spending in Queensland. Of course, any new infrastructure spending should pass a cost-benefit analysis.

Figure 8.3 Gross and net Queensland government acquisitions of non-financial assets, estimates and projections

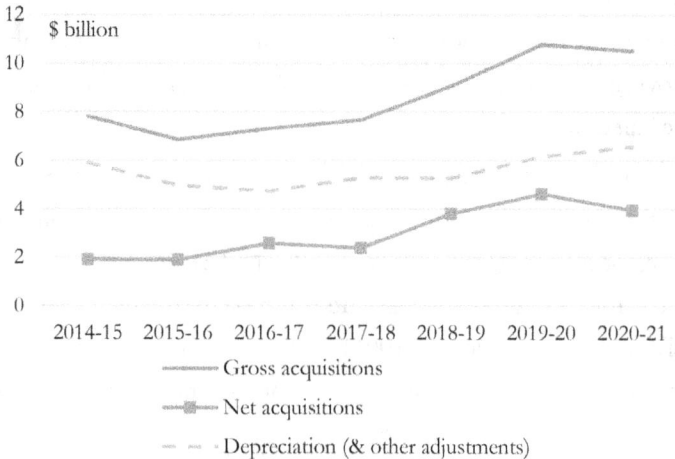

Source: Queensland government budget papers.

---

[308] Asset recycling is the clumsy terminology now used in Australia for using privatisation proceeds to purchase new capital assets. From an economic perspective, there is no reason to link the sale of old assets with the purchase of new ones. Money is fungible, and proceeds from asset sales are not "tagged" so they can only be used be for new capital investment.

[309] For example, see www.budget.qld.gov.au

Figure 8.4 Queensland government capital purchases as a percentage of GSP, estimates and projections

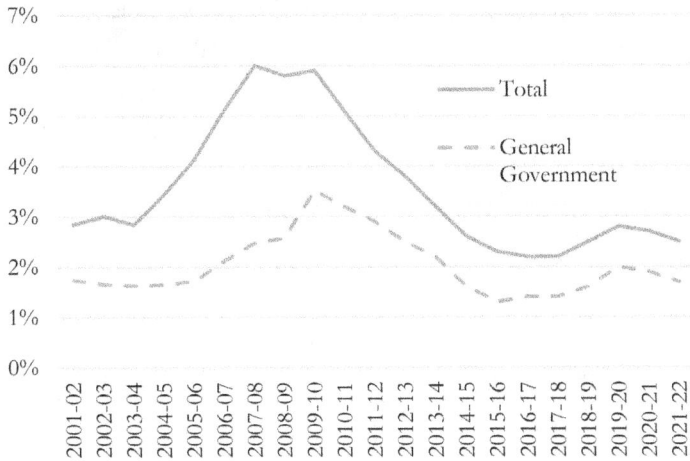

Source: *Queensland government budget papers and ABS GSP estimates for Queensland.*

Note that I have been assuming there is little scope for Queensland governments to fund new infrastructure by cutting back on recurrent expenses. The challenge the government has, of course, is that half of the budget is in the politically sensitive areas such as health and education (Figure 8.5), in which fiscally responsible measures will require great political nous to introduce. That said, the next chapter considers some options for trimming state government expenses.

Vertical fiscal imbalance

We have seen that the debt is problematic in that not only does it impose an ongoing burden in interest expenses, it limits the government's budgetary flexibility. It makes the government's budget management challenge even greater. The Queensland government, like other state and territory governments around Australia, are already severely constrained due to VFI. The Queensland government only raises around one-half of the revenue and income it needs to fund its expenses, and the other half comes from the Commonwealth. Like other states and territories, Queensland is highly dependent on the doling out of GST revenue as "general revenue assistance" by the Commonwealth, and on other grants from the Commonwealth under federal funding agreements covering policy areas such as health and education, for example (Figure 8.6).

Figure 8.5 Queensland general government expenses by purpose, 2016-17

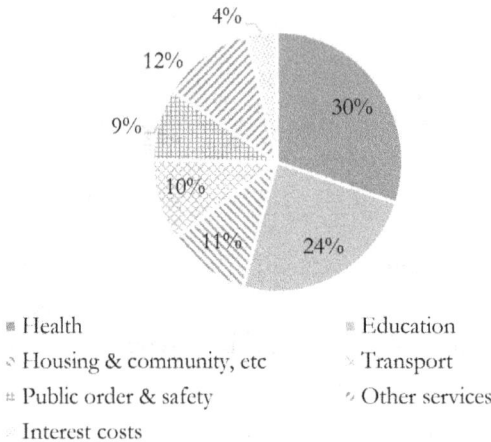

- Health
- Housing & community, etc
- Public order & safety
- Interest costs
- Education
- Transport
- Other services

Source: Queensland Treasury, 2017a, op. cit., p. 112.

Queensland's grants revenue from the Commonwealth is far in excess of any revenue in any other category. Queensland's other revenue sources include own-source taxation—comprising payroll tax, stamp duty on transfers of assets such as houses and motor vehicles, resource royalty revenue, and other items—and earnings from GOCs, both dividends and tax equivalent payments. The tax equivalent payments are a payment the GOCs make to the state government for National Competition Policy reasons, so GOCS, which are exempt from Commonwealth company tax, have "competitive neutrality" with private sector businesses that have to pay company tax.

Figure 8.6. Share of Queensland general government sector revenue by item, 2017-18 estimates

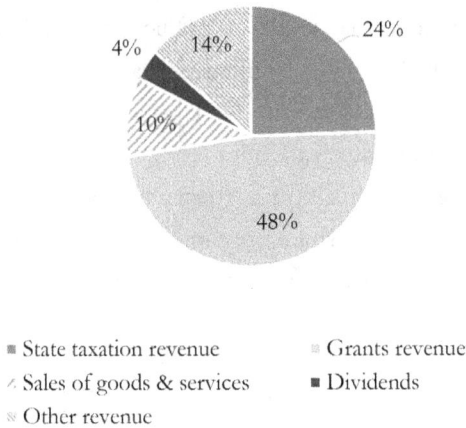

- State taxation revenue
- Grants revenue
- Sales of goods & services
- Dividends
- Other revenue

Source: Queensland Treasury, 2017a, op. cit., p. 161.

The mismatch between expenses of state and territory governments and their expenditure responsibilities is referred to as vertical fiscal imbalance (VFI). For decades, VFI has been blamed for blurring accountabilities and creating a situation of learned helplessness and an unedifying blame game. The states and territories blame the Commonwealth for not providing sufficient funding to deliver quality services, while the Commonwealth blames the states and territories for poor service delivery. The VFI sets up a patron-supplicant relationship between the Commonwealth and the states and territories. Premier Wayne Goss once compared the relationship to "a dialogue between a begging bowl and a baseball bat", with the Commonwealth obviously the one holding the baseball bat.[310]

As well as being subject to Commonwealth arm-twisting over so-called National Partnership Agreements, the states and territories are subject to

---

[310] Wayne Goss, 1999, "The Republic and the States", *UQ Law Journal*, vol. 20, no. 2, pp. 294-300.

the vagaries of the HFE methodology employed by the CGC. HFE occurs in a number of other federations around the world, including Canada and Germany. It is designed to guarantee that the states and territories have the fiscal capacity to provide similar levels of public services. The HFE methodology was once applied to general, untied assistance payments from the Commonwealth and since 2000 to the GST revenue pool, which is redistributed to the states and territories. Under HFE, states and territories which have higher income residents, and a greater tax capacity, such as NSW and Victoria, receive a smaller share per capita of GST revenue than states and territories with less capacity for taxation—or greater expenditure responsibilities due to the presence of remote communities, for example. Queensland has typically been a net beneficiary of HFE, although at times Queensland has received below its population share.

HFE is aimed at ensuring a level playing field, but can penalise Queensland at times of high commodity prices, particularly for coal, which is Queensland's most valuable export. As the Queensland Treasury explained in its Fiscal Reform Blueprint presented to the newly elected Newman government in 2012:

> Although the bulk of mineral production in Australia is generated in Queensland and Western Australia, the net impact of the HFE process is that royalty revenue is redistributed between all the states and territories through their GST distribution. Higher royalty revenue in Queensland and Western Australia simply means less GST revenue for Queensland and Western Australia.
>
> Therefore, mining royalties do not provide states such as Queensland or Western Australia with the capacity to provide additional services or infrastructure or reduce taxes relative to other states. Non-mining states such as Victoria and Tasmania benefit as much in fiscal terms from mining as Queensland and Western Australia. [311]

The CGC's HFE formula could mean massively fluctuating levels of

---

[311] Queensland Treasury, 2012a, op. cit., p. C-2-4.

revenue from year-to-year in Queensland as the formula is adjusted for capabilities or disabilities. The formula is partly responsible for the large fluctuations in revenue in recent years. For example, general revenue assistance from the GST revenue pool increased 18 percent in 2008-09. In this year, Queensland had received a boost from higher coal prices, but the backward looking HFE formula did not yet reflect Queensland's recent good fortune with coal royalty revenue, so GST revenues distributed to Queensland were not adjusted downward. Compare the high rate of revenue growth in 2008-09 to the later decline of 8.8 percent in 2012-13, when Commonwealth payments to Queensland were estimated to fall by 17.1 percent at budget time. This was because the HFE formula was now recognising the high commodity prices of the last few years, and the Queensland government was penalised for this good fortune (Figure 8.7).[312]

Figure 8.7 Yearly growth rates of Queensland general government revenue and expenses

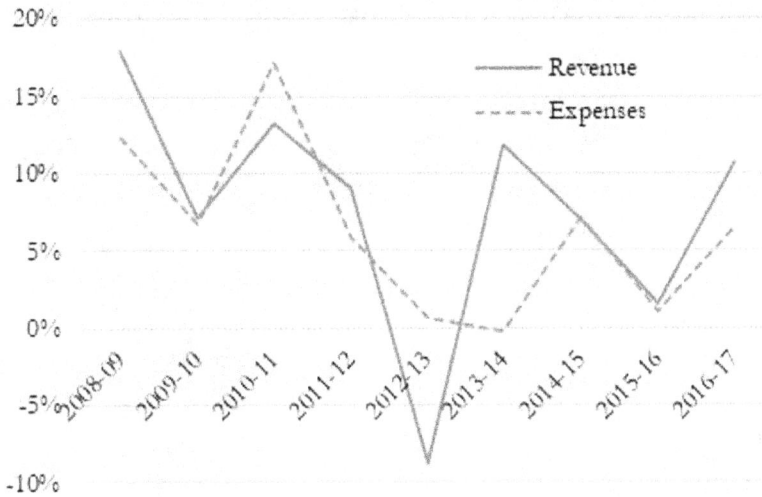

Source: Queensland government budget papers.

---

[312] Queensland Treasury, 2012c, *State Budget 2012-13: Budget Strategy and Outlook*, budget paper no. 2, p. 109.

The volatility in general revenue assistance from the Commonwealth makes the Queensland government's task of budget management significantly more difficult. Given expenses are typically more stable, so the volatility in revenue is not typically offset by changes in expenses and results in a fluctuating budget balance (i.e. the surplus or deficit).

Finally, regarding Commonwealth-state relations, another complicating factor in the preparation of recent budgets has been the timing of Natural Disaster Relief and Recovery Arrangements, under which the Commonwealth picks up 75 percent of the cost of natural disasters, such as the 2011 Cyclone Yasi and state-wide floods. By varying the timing of payments for its own budgetary purposes, the Commonwealth can substantially impact the achievement of state budget forecasts, as both Queensland Treasurers Tim Nicholls and Curtis Pitt discovered.[313]

Population pressures in the 1990s and 2000s

Finally, in assessing Queensland's current level of debt and the extent of blame that should be apportioned to different parties, it is important to consider the broader economic and social context. Over the 1980s, 1990s and much of the 2000s, Queensland had a strongly growing population, with a large contribution made by interstate migration from NSW and Victoria. Queensland's population was 2.86 million when Wayne Goss came to power at the end of 1989. It grew to 3.45 million when Peter Beattie became Premier in June 1998, and was at 4.13 million when Beattie handed over the Premiership to Anna Bligh in September 2007.[314] Interstate migration has been much lower in recent years, and this has resulted in the Queensland population growth rate falling to around the national growth rate (Figure 8.8).

---

[313] See Chapters 6 and 7 and Steven Wardill, 2016b, "Federal Budget exposes Queensland's flimsy accounts", *Courier-Mail*, 7 May 2016, available via www.couriermail.com.au..

[314] These figures are sourced from the ABS publication *Australian Demographic Statistics*, cat. no. 3101.0.

Figure 8.8. Queensland and rest of Australia population growth rates

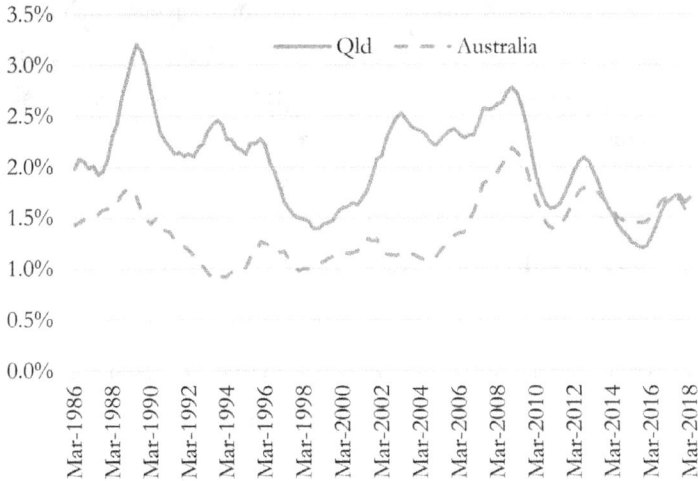

Source: ABC cat. no. 3101.0.

The previously mentioned abolition of death duties in 1978 was an important stimulus to growth in the late 1970s and early 1980s, but Queensland had much more to offer than just low taxes. Southerners were attracted by a combination of better climate, better employment opportunities, and cheaper housing.[315] At its peak in the mid-1990s, interstate migration was running at around 50,000 people per year. At the time, it was often observed that 1,000 people were crossing the NSW-Queensland border each week to become new Queensland residents.

Queensland's rapid population growth over the 1990s and 2000s created pressures on public services, including roads, hospitals, electricity and water supplies among others, and arguably these were not planned for well enough in advance, resulting in massive catch up investment by the Beattie and Bligh governments over the 2000s. However, as argued in this book, it is highly likely this catch up investment was far in excess of what would have been

---

[315] For example, see the Queensland Treasury econometric study by Christine Williams, Jim Hurley and Beverley Morris, 1999, "An economic model of interstate migration", *Economic Analysis and Policy*, Special Edition May 1999, pp. 93-112.

optimal. Much of it is was formulated in an atmosphere of crisis, and later turned out to suffer cost blowouts or to have been unnecessary, such as the Tugun desalination plant or the Western Corridor Recycled Water scheme. Furthermore, in Anna Bligh, Queensland had a Treasurer and then Premier with a desire to massively expand infrastructure spending, without apparent regard for financial sustainability. Queenslanders have been burdened with much higher debt, and not all of it was incurred to finance the creation of valuable assets that would allow the state to service the additional debt.

Summing up

All things considered, the concern over Queensland's high level of debt is warranted. While it is important not to over-react, as critics would argue the Newman government did, it is nonetheless important to prioritise debt reduction over the forward estimates. The state government needs to make up for the fiscal follies of previous administrations, and get the state's balance sheet back to a position where it is in good shape to weather future shocks.

9

IS PRIVATISATION STILL AN OPTION IN QUEENSLAND?

Wise words from a former Labor Treasurer

The Palaszczuk government came into office with ambitious plans for new infrastructure, including the $5-10 billion Cross River Rail, but it was severely lacking in available funds to pay for its plans. It has had to commit funding to Cross River Rail spasmodically, with the largest amount, around $2 billion, only committed after a royalty revenue windfall in 2017.[316] The government had tied its hands by ruling out privatisation, via asset sales or asset leases, of government-owned businesses such as Energex and the Port of Gladstone. It has ruled out the Strong Choices asset leases the previous government would have used to fund over $8 billion of new infrastructure. This meant the new government faced a big challenge in finding alternative ways to fund the new infrastructure expected by the business sector and community.

The Palaszczuk government's aversion to asset sales is peculiar to it, and was not shared by previous Labor governments. Queensland's history, particularly the experience of the Beattie government, suggests privatisations

---

[316] Queensland Treasury, 2017a, op. cit., p. 2. The $2 billion of funding announced in the 2017-18 budget was additional to around $900 million of funding that had been announced previously.

can be undertaken at a gradual pace without causing too much adverse political reaction. In the inaugural Hayden oration, Beattie's first Treasurer David Hamill argued that what is important is that a public service or utility is provided in a cost-effective manner, not whether it is provided by the public or private sector. Where public ownership is not the best means to deliver desired outcomes, it should not be favoured. Hamill observed:

> We are saying that spending on our preferred programs and services is more important than other options. Resources, even for governments are finite. Our challenge is to determine which policy outcomes are most desirable and set our budgetary and legislative priorities accordingly.
>
> Public enterprises can provide a tool to overcome market failure. Public enterprises can be used to deliver service outcomes, but we must always be alert to any less expensive or more efficient alternatives that will achieve an identical or preferably, a better outcome.
>
> Let's look at the same issue from a different perspective. By delivering a service more effectively and at a lesser cost to budget enables government to use the savings to support important programs that it could not otherwise afford to fund. Hanging on to "so-called assets" simply because they are currently in public possession is not only a nonsense, it represents an abdication of responsibility and missed opportunity to act in the interests of achieving greater fairness and equitable access to services on the part of those who are most in need.[317]

This was a bold speech from Hamill, and the topic was well chosen. Privatisation has always been a vexing issue for Labor. Indeed, the organiser of the Hayden oration, former Ipswich MP and Bligh Transport and Finance Minister Rachel Nolan, lost her safe seat partly due to local community dissatisfaction with the Bligh government's privatisation program. After her defeat, Nolan became a cafe owner in Ipswich among other pursuits, and was willing to strongly defend her record, including in a letter she wrote to

---

[317] David Hamill, 2016, *The Inaugural Bill Hayden oration, by The Hon Dr David Hamill AM at The Ipswich Club Gray Street Ipswich 13th August 2016.*

the Quarterly Essay in response to Laura Tingle's *Great Expectations* essay. Nolan provided an excellent perspective from a former minister, and one managing QR's freight network prior to the float, regarding the problems with government ownership and why privatised assets may be preferable:

> ...in my first year as transport minister I had a different rent seeker at my door every day of the week. The mining industry said it couldn't afford Queensland Rail's shift to the more commercial "take or pay" contracts, the beef barons didn't want to be bound by real cost pricing—or indeed by any kind of contract at all—and the unions came to me because they were unable to negotiate with Queensland Rail on even the most basic industrial issues. I once found myself being heaved to intervene on whether or not workers at the Rockhampton Railway Workshops should be allowed to wear shorts. Seriously.[318]

Despite corporatisation, stakeholders still saw Queensland Rail as being subject to government control. As the former minister's comments suggest, this could have led to undesirable and absurd outcomes. This is additional evidence to support the wisdom of the Bligh government's privatisation program. It may have been done largely to fix the Bligh government's budgetary problems, but it was good policy nonetheless.

Even though assets had been privatised throughout the Beattie and Bligh governments, the combination of the massive 2012 election loss and the political opportunity to attack the Newman government over Strong Choices, meant that Queensland Labor reverted to its traditional ideological position in favour of public ownership.

What have other States done on asset recycling?

The current Queensland government's reluctance to privatise assets stands in stark contrast to the willingness to privatise assets shown by other state governments, particularly NSW and Victoria, under Liberal-National and Labor rule, respectively.

---

[318] Rachel Nolan, 2012, "Great Expectations: Correspondence", *Quarterly Essay*, no. 48, p. 103.

The NSW government has committed to a $20 billion infrastructure plan, Rebuilding NSW, which was made possible by leasing out 49 percent of NSW electricity network assets.[319] Under its Rebuilding NSW Plan, the NSW government will invest in new transport, water and social infrastructure, including WestConnex and the Western Harbour Tunnel ($1.1 billion), Sydney Metro ($7 billion), schools and hospitals ($2 billion), among other investments.

NSW has also taken advantage of $2 billion that was made available from the Commonwealth government's Asset Recycling Initiative, introduced by the Australian government in the 2014-15 budget but now closed. The justification for a Commonwealth incentive for asset recycling is that once assets are sold or leased, and the revenues associated with them are no longer earned by a GOC, tax-equivalent payments no longer flow to a state government but, instead, company income tax payments will flow to the Commonwealth government. The Palaszczuk government had argued that it being denied access to the Asset Recycling Initiative was unfair, but it misunderstood the original justification for the initiative.

The Victorian government has also recently prosecuted a successful privatisation. In September 2016, the Victorian government leased out the Port of Melbourne for 50 years to the Lonsdale Consortium for an unexpected high value of $9.7 billion. This demonstrated the high value that private sector operators can place on state-owned assets they expect they can run more efficiently and profitably than public sector managers. The Victorian government was expecting a 15 percent bonus from the Asset Recycling Scheme of $1.45 billion, but this has been subject to a dispute with the Commonwealth. The Commonwealth has argued Victoria did not complete the transaction in the two years the Scheme was operating, and it did not support its use of the funds to remove railway level crossings.

---

[319] 100 percent of Transgrid which manages the high-voltage transmission network, 50.4 percent of distribution companies Ausgrid and Endeavour Energy, with distribution company Essential Energy remaining not subject to a lease.

Nonetheless, the leasing out of the Port of Melbourne will provide the Victorian government with substantial proceeds and is a testament to the large values that assets currently owned by the public sector can sell or be leased out for, particularly to consortia looking for long-term assets with relatively reliable earnings.

State-owned assets may well be suited for superannuation funds to invest in as suggested by various advisors including PwC in a report prepared for the Business Council of Australia. PwC noted:

> Superannuation and pension funds are now major investors in infrastructure and are looking to acquire more of these assets, due to the close alignment of returns from infrastructure and their financial objectives. The demand for sound, stable investments from these private sources is expected to increase substantially.[320]

This suggests the potential for governments to receive very favourable terms in privatisations of government-owned businesses.

Productivity is almost everything in the long-run

As we have seen, one of the most effective criticisms of proposed privatisations by Queensland governments has been the potential adverse budgetary impact. This is obviously of relevance to decision makers, but can distract us from the most important issue: whether the productivity of our economy is improved by privatising state assets. Nobel Prize winning US economist Paul Krugman once wrote about productivity that "it's not everything but in the long-run it's almost everything."[321] Ultimately, our economic performance and wellbeing depend on how effectively and efficiently we use the resources, natural, human and man-made, at our disposal.

---

[320] PwC, 2013, *Securing Investment in Australia's Future: Infrastructure Funding and Financing*, report prepared for the Business Council of Australia, p. 14.

[321] Paul Krugman, 1994, *The Age of Diminished Expectations: US Economic Policy in the 1990s*, MIT Press.

Australia's productivity growth has been significantly lower in recent years than the strong growth rates achieved in the 1990s, which, as the Productivity Commission has argued, were due to a large extent to microeconomic reforms in the 1980s and 1990s—reforms that included the privatisation or corporatisation of many government-owned enterprises (Figure 9.1).

Figure 9.1 Productivity growth, through-the-year, Australia

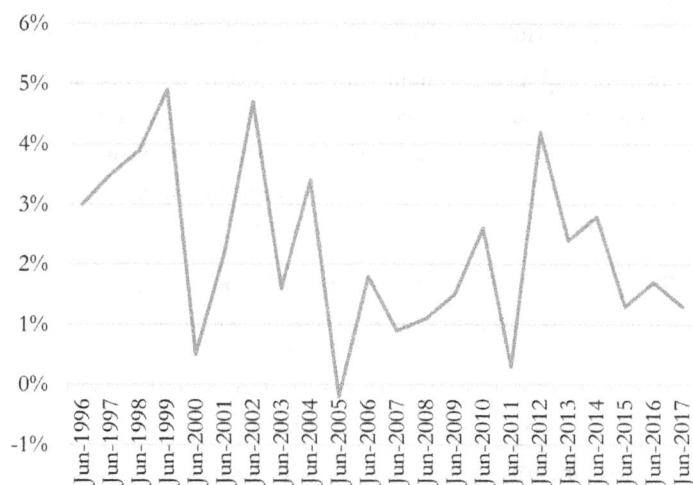

Source: ABS cat. no. 5206.0.

Clearly there was huge scope for reform of government-owned businesses in the 1980s and 1990s. Back in the post-war boom from the end of World War II to the mid-1970s—when Australia was finally mugged by economic reality—the country enjoyed a very low unemployment rate, typically 1½ to 2½ percent.[322] By many accounts, this owed a lot to state-owned businesses such as railways acting as employers of last resort.[323] Eventually, Australians figured out this was not a recipe for a dynamic economy, but it instead condemned Australia to falling down the league

---

[322] Based on historical economic statistics available at www.rba.gov.au.

[323] For example, see Warwick Smith, 2017, *Unemployment Policy in Australia: A Brief History*, Per Capita, p. 14.

246

ladder of OECD nations in terms of living standards.

Since the 1990s many government-owned businesses have been corporatised, including Queensland's electricity businesses, and you may well ask whether there remains any scope for further efficiency gains. It is very likely there are, particularly for efficiency gains resulting from further reductions in X-inefficiency: the specific inefficiency identified in 1966 by Harvard economics professor Harvey Leibenstein where slack exists from resources not being worked hard enough.[324]

There potentially is scope for further efficiency gains and the evidence supports this. For example, in its 2013 report on the regulation of electricity networks, the Productivity Commission observed significantly lower costs of operation for privately owned electricity transmission and distribution businesses than publicly-owned businesses. This is likely because privately-owned businesses have a clearer profit motive than publicly-owned ones. Also, boards of GOCs may take into account a range of considerations, possibly including pressure from unions for favourable workplace agreements. The Commission observed:

> While analysis of relative efficiency is difficult given the number of other differences between network businesses, the empirical evidence suggests that, although some perform relatively well, as a group, the aggregate productivity outcomes of state-owned businesses are poorer than their private peers...This is likely to reflect the mixed incentives they face. Some participants in this inquiry claim that a risk-averse focus on 'building things for the future' still permeates some of these businesses.[325]

Productivity in the private sector is driven by the strong private sector desire to minimise costs and maximise profits. Evidence from the UK reported in the highly regarded peer-reviewed *Journal of Economics, Law and Organization* supports this, and that a corporatised entity cannot match the

---

[324] Harvey Leibenstein, 1966, "Allocative Efficiency vs. "X-Efficiency"", *American Economic Review*, vol. LVI.

[325] Productivity Commission, 2013, op. cit., pp. 24-25.

incentives for efficiency and financial performance in a privatised firm. The researchers noted:

> Using data from large firms in the United Kingdom, we find no relationship between compensation and financial performance in state-owned firms, both before and after corporate governance reforms. In contrast, we find a strong sensitivity in privatized firms both immediately and in more mature privatized firms driven largely by stock options and shareholding.[326]

International evidence is undeniable that privatisation generally yielded efficiency gains, and therefore is ultimately good for the economy and living standards. The most comprehensive and authoritative review of the impacts of privatisation was published in 2001 in the American Economic Association's *Journal of Economic Literature*, the world's leading journal for reviewing and summarising the findings of economic literature. The review by US economists William Megginson and Jeffry Netter found:

> Research now supports the proposition that privately owned firms are more efficient and more profitable than otherwise comparable state-owned firms...We know that privatization "works," in the sense that divested firms almost always become more efficient, more profitable, and financially healthier, and increase their capital investment spending.[327]

A 1998 World Bank study shows the balance of evidence around the world is that privatisation results in significant efficiency gains, though often through the shedding of excess labour that was employed in inefficient, government-owned businesses.[328] This is obviously a politically contentious aspect to privatisation, but is often unavoidable and essential to yielding efficiency gains. It suggests a possible need for transitional or structural adjustment assistance directed at displaced workers.

[326] Michael Cragg and Alexander Dyck, 2003, "Privatization and management incentives: Evidence from the United Kingdom", *Journal of Law, Economics and Organization*, vol. 19, no. 1, p. 176.
[327] Megginson, W. and Netter, J., op. cit., p. 381.
[328] Sunita Kikeri, 1998, "Privatization and Labor: What Happens to Workers When Governments Divest?", *World Bank Technical Paper*, no. 396.

Regarding specific Queensland businesses, based on a benchmarking exercise taking into account the performance of domestic electricity distribution businesses across Australia, in 2012 the Newman government-commissioned Queensland Independent Review Panel on Network Costs found capital expenditure per customer for Energex and Ergon higher than expected based on customer density. Also, operating expenditure was higher than efficient levels for Ergon, although not for Energex.[329] These higher than expected costs result ultimately in higher electricity prices than would occur under private ownership. This concurs with the analysis by EY cited previously, showing electricity prices grew at a lower rate than they would have otherwise in Victoria due to privatisation of the electricity network.

The experience of Aurizon has clearly shown the benefits of privatisation in Queensland, with the share price having risen from around $3.50 in 2012 to a high of nearly $5.70 in Mid-2017, although it is currently trading at around $4.40 per share, owing partly to a regulatory decision by the QCA that was not in its favour.[330] Post-privatisation, Aurizon has shed hundreds of jobs across Queensland in an effort to improve efficiency. The experience of Aurizon shows just how substantial X-inefficiency can be, with Aurizon Chief Innovation Officer Stephen Baines noting in his book *Steel on Steel*:

> The old QR could boast many highly skilled people who wanted to do a worthwhile job. It was also home to many who had a strong sense of entitlement, and believed the company owed them a living, and indeed a 'job for life'. Inefficiencies were tolerated and ignored. Materials would regularly disappear from storerooms.

The fuzzy reporting lines encouraged a culture of 'optionality'—where employees always felt they had the option of refusing to comply with instructions from management.[331]

Another excellent example of a privatisation that was very successful

---

329 Independent Review Panel on Network Costs, op. cit., pp. 35-36.
330 As at 16 March 2018.
331 Baines, S., op. cit., p. 152.

in Australia was Qantas, which yielded $2.1 billion to the Australian government in the mid-1990s, although Qantas continues to be constrained by the Commonwealth *Qantas Sale Act 1992* regarding possible mergers. In the years prior to the privatisation, there was an increase in competition from international carriers and Qantas needed to upgrade its fleet. But the Australian government was reluctant to provide capital to invest in vital upgrades to deal with an industry in transition. Post-privatisation, the company went from 30,000 staff servicing 16 million passengers with 136 planes in 1995, to 38,000 staff servicing 50 million passengers with 297 planes in 2005. These productivity gains very likely would not have been achieved if the government had retained ownership.[332]

Finally, it should be made clear that as well as increasing efficiency, privatisation typically produces better services for consumers and providers that are more responsive to consumer needs. In early 2018, highly regarded Financial Times columnist Martin Wolf reflected on what state-owned businesses were like in the UK prior to the Thatcher Conservative government, in comments that could have applied to the Australian situation, too:

> Some of us remember what the nationalised industries were like…they were most definitely not in the hands of people who used them. They were in the hands of the ministers and civil servants who controlled them and the people who staffed them. They were chronically overmanned and heavily politicised. They either underinvested or made poor investment decisions…Not least they treated users with indifference.[333]

While there have undeniably been some botched privatisations around the world, largely privatisations have been successful, and Queensland governments should maintain privatisation as a legitimate policy option.

---

[332] Lisa Allen, 2015, "How Qantas landed a privatisation success", *The Australian*, July 24, available via www.theaustralian.com.au.
[333] Martin Wolf, 2018, "Nationalising utilities is the wrong answer to a real question", *Financial Times*, 12 January 2018, available via www.ft.com.

Regulation and the role of government

Based on the discussion in the previous section, privatisation of government-owned businesses appears desirable, with the caveat that the privatisation is well-managed and monopoly businesses are (or remain) appropriately regulated. As observed by Charles Darwin University economist Rabindra Nepal and UQ Economics Professor John Foster in 2015:

> ... international empirical evidence indicates that the efficiency gains to consumers from electricity networks privatization will depend on the underlying regulatory regime and regulatory institutional framework.[334]

By a well-managed privatisation, it is meant that the government needs to ensure it gets a good price for the business, as privatising an income-generating business obviously affects the budget. It is also meant that the impacts of any job shedding on local economies are considered—and appropriate labour market and training programs are introduced, if necessary.

Job losses are often raised as a concern regarding privatisation. But the government could make the case that the community will be better off and that we should not be protecting jobs by maintaining inefficient government-owned businesses. Governments did that once in Australia, but those days have passed. Now it is recognised among policy advisers that the proper role of government is to provide the right policies and frameworks to promote a highly productive and innovative economy, as well as to provide the public services with public good (e.g. defence) or merit good (e.g. health and education) aspects.[335] It is not seen as the role of government to directly create jobs beyond those needed to efficiently deliver public services.

---

[334] Rabindra Nepal and John Foster, 2015, "Electricity network privatization in Australia: An overview of the debate", *Economic Analysis and Policy*, vol. 48, p. 12.

[335] See, for example, budget statement 4 in Australian Treasury, 2005, *Budget Strategy and Outlook 2005-06*, budget paper no. 1.

This brings us to an important philosophical question: exactly what activities in an economy should a Government undertake? Clearly no one anymore believes we should have state-owned butcher shops, as Queensland did in the early twentieth century, and no one would expect the Government to run McDonald's better than it is being run now.

So should any businesses be government-owned? Some will argue that natural monopolies—such as electricity or water distribution networks—should be government-owned, both because they are essential services and because otherwise there is the potential for consumers to be exploited.

But, here, there does not appear to be a logical case for government ownership, but rather for the regulation of natural monopolies. In Australia, we have a significant overlay of economic regulation, administered by bodies such as the QCA, the ACCC and the AER, that is designed to protect consumers from price gouging. Hence, there is not necessarily a case for government-ownership of businesses. After an extensive examination of the pros and cons of government ownership of electricity network businesses, the Productivity Commission noted in its 2013 report on electricity network regulation:

> While governments have a legitimate role in owning and operating many services in Australia, the rationale for state-ownership of electricity network businesses no longer holds. This reflects the development of sophisticated incentive regulations that function best when the regulated businesses have strong cost-minimising and profit motives.

State governments often impose multiple constraints on state-owned corporations that are incompatible with maximising returns to their shareholders.[336]

This logic is applicable not just to Energy Queensland, but also to other government-owned businesses, including the power generators and ports that are proposed for sale or long-term lease. For example, the Queensland Interdepartmental Committee on Electricity Sector Reform noted in 2013 that:

---

[336] Productivity Commission, 2013, op. cit., p. 24.

...the government owned generators have additional constraints that further impede their operations in the current market, including a policy of no new investment in Queensland, legacy agreements and workforce restrictions.[337]

Appropriate regulation is the important precursor to efficient outcomes for natural monopolies, not government ownership. Also important is the issue of market design or structure. It is important to work out whether an asset should be sold whole, or as a vertically or horizontally separated set of businesses. This issue has been an important consideration in debates over the privatisations of Telstra and British Rail, and indeed of QR, among other government-owned businesses. Allowing a business to remain as a vertically-integrated business could provide an unfair advantage to the part of the business competing with other businesses and bidding for use of the underlying network asset. But so-called Chinese walls within the company and appropriate regulation can help prevent any inappropriate related party transactions. Selling a vertically integrated asset is likely to maximise the overall sale proceeds to a government, but there are also economic advantages, as pointed out by a study by former ACCC Chief Allan Fels which recommended QR National be sold as a vertically integrated business. A vertically integrated entity was more likely to have sufficient incentive to maintain rail tracks and to invest in new capacity. Also, it was the model used in the US and Canada, which arguably has had the most successful railway privatisation.[338]

This also goes to show the importance of doing the detailed analysis of privatisation proposals and ensuring that, first, the sale maximises the return to the community and, second, the post-sale regulations will promote efficient outcomes.

---

[337] Queensland Interdepartmental Committee on Electricity Sector Reform, 2013, *Report to Government*, p. 36.

[338] See Adele Ferguson, 2010, "Vertical integration gets support", *Sydney Morning Herald*, 23 March 2010, available via www.smh.com.au and Douglas Young, 2010, "Vertical integration delivers the goods", *The Australian*, 15 June 2010, available via www. theaustralian.com.au.

Conclusions regarding potential asset recycling in Queensland

There remain several valuable Queensland GOCs that could be suitable candidates for privatisation, namely the GOCs that were previously proposed to be leased out by the Newman government, noting Energex and Ergon have now merged to become Energy Queensland (Table 9.1). These candidates could raise many billions of dollars, and substantially more than the equity estimates reported in annual reports. This is because private owners would be expected to undertake efficiency measures and to improve governance and management, increasing the value of the companies, and they would base their bids on their expected net earnings. Of course, as noted above, proposals to sell or lease out the assets of these GOCs, and to use the proceeds to pay down debt or invest in infrastructure, would inevitably raise objections about the loss of earnings to the government or job losses.

Table 9.1. Potential GOCs for asset recycling, 2016-17 financial performance

GOCs	Equity, $ million	Net profit after tax, $ million	Return on assets*	Return on equity
Energy businesses				
Energy Queensland	3,571	881	7.8%	n.p.
Powerlink	1,714	351	10.0%	21.2%
Energy generators				
CS Energy	480	283	17.9%	n.p.
Stanwell	1,289	375	n.p.	30.4%
Ports businesses				
Gladstone Port Corporation	1,068	72	5.8%	7.0%
Port of Townsville	191	15	n.p.	3.4%

* or return on capital employed. Source: various annual reports.

The appropriate framework for assessing asset-recycling proposals is cost-benefit analysis. An appropriate cost-benefit analysis would be from the perspective of the Queensland population, rather than the perspective of the Queensland government. Unfortunately, much of the debate on asset recycling has been conducted with reference to Queensland government budget impacts. That is, the debate has simply been a comparison of the gain to the government from savings in interest payments with the loss of dividends and tax equivalent payments. In an economic environment where interest rates have been low, undertaking this comparison would likely show savings in interest payments less than the reduction in dividends and tax equivalent payments. However, there is no guarantee that future interest rates will be at low levels. Further, a simple comparison of interest savings with the loss of dividend and tax equivalent payments ignores the risk that is placed on the government's balance sheet from owning GOCs. As discussed in Chapter 6, there is a large risk that technological developments, particularly in renewable energy and battery technology, will reduce future levels of demand for the services of government-owned energy generators and distributors.

It appears it is time to reconsider privatisation in Queensland. Arguably the public can be persuaded of its merits, where the government makes a strong evidence-backed case for it. As IAQ Chief Executive Steve Abson noted when interviewed for this book:

> Experience from relevant Australian jurisdictions indicates that when the public has the matter explained in terms it can relate to, vast numbers of the citizenry not only support this type of reform, they often demand an explanation as to why sluggish politicians have sat on their hands for so long. The asset recycling, debt reduction and reinvestment program in New South Wales is a case in point.

Particularly given the state government's current fiscal predicament, privatisation has much to recommend it in Queensland. Of course, governments need to be careful selling income-generating assets to get proceeds to invest in new infrastructure, which has been labelled asset recycling, as the new infrastructure should earn at least the same return to the community as the asset sold. With congestion ever increasing on our transport networks and other pressing needs, there may well be opportunities for asset recycling, so the government should definitely consider it.

At the same time, there is a need to repair the state budget, so the Queensland government can start genuinely paying down debt. A large share of any privatisation proceeds could and, indeed, should be used to pay down state debt, which is still on the path to over $80 billion. The Queensland government needs to pay down $10-20 billion of debt if it is to get back and entrench its AAA credit rating and achieve the lower ongoing borrowing costs and confidence boost it would bring. Regarding the debt-to-revenue ratio, in its interim report, the Newman government's Commission of Audit referred to "the trigger band of around 100-110% for a AAA credit rating."[339] The Queensland government needs to convince the ratings agencies the debt-to-revenue ratio is on a path to 100-110 percent (and preferably that it will fall below that). On current projections, the Queensland government is falling short (Figure 9.2).

That said, the Queensland government may eventually regain a AAA credit rating, after 5-10 years on business-as-usual settings, which would be assuming everything goes well and the state does not face a recession or financial crisis during that period. It would be a risky strategy.

Privatisation would bring a double dividend, as many state-owned assets would be better managed by the private sector. Privatisation of electricity businesses would result in lower growth of electricity network costs, and hence lower growth in electricity prices, according to EY, as noted in Chapter 6. And privatisation would also help us avoid the risk of losses in asset values that could arise if improvements in battery technology are so great that households can rely upon solar power, stored in batteries, rather than on the electricity grid. That is, Queenslanders would likely be better off if the state government sold its electricity businesses now, rather than running the risk they will be worth much less in the future.

---

[339] Queensland Commission of Audit, 2012, op. cit., p. 4.

In summary, from an economic perspective, there is much upside and little downside risk in privatisation. As the NSW government's recent successful $10 billion privatisation of NSW's Transgrid electricity business has shown, privatisation can bring in many billions of dollars that can help finance essential infrastructure and contribute to debt reduction. Indeed, the previous government's Strong Choices privatisations were estimated to bring in $37 billion. The current Queensland government should shake off its ideological opposition to asset sales and leases.

Of course, embracing privatisation would be politically difficult, but then so are all of the genuine choices for repairing the Queensland state budget or boosting long-term economic growth, such as restraining health spending or cutting business regulation and regional or industry assistance measures. Such measures are considered in the next chapter.

Figure 9.2. Queensland Treasury 2018-19 projections of debt-to-revenue ratio for Queensland non-financial public sector

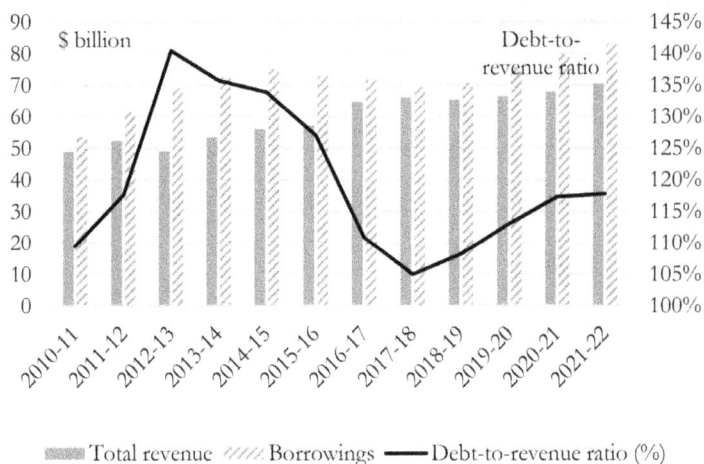

Source: Queensland government budget papers.

10

WHAT ELSE CAN BE DONE OTHER THAN ASSET SALES AND LEASES?

Introduction

The Queensland government needs to take a range of measures to, first, pay down the debt and restore the AAA credit rating and, second, prevent a fiscal deterioration such as that in the late 2000s from occurring again. Former Under Treasurer Mark Gray noted in an interview with the author:

> Governments need to leave capacity to respond to a rainy day. That's why the Commission of Audit argued for doing more than what was necessary to get the AAA credit rating back. A debt-to-revenue ratio of 100 to 110 percent is required for AAA, but the Commission argued Queensland needs to get debt down to 60 to 80 percent of revenue to provide a buffer for shocks.

Based on current budget figures, that would mean reducing total debt to around the $40-50 billion range.

In addition to the leasing out or sale of some state assets, discussed in the previous chapter, measures to improve Queensland's public finances, to create a "capacity to respond to a rainy day" in Mark Gray's words, include:

- the adoption of sound fiscal principles;
- trimming unnecessary expenditures;
- introducing new user pays and value capture mechanisms;
- pushing for reforms to intergovernmental financial relations along with comprehensive tax reform;
- restoration of arms-length relationships with GOCs;
- institutional reforms related to the Parliament and its Committee System; and

259

- greater transparency and independence in budget analysis and forecasting.

These measures are considered below.

Fiscal principles

Evidence from OECD economies is that clear fiscal rules—e.g. expenditure should not grow at more than 2 percent per annum in real terms—can be effective in disciplining governments and ensuring sound public finance. Switzerland has had great success in reducing debt by the implementation of the so-called debt-brake rule, which requires Switzerland to balance its general government budget (in terms of the fiscal balance) over the business cycle.[340] This means that any deficits during recessionary periods would need to be offset by surpluses during expansionary periods. The OECD considers that, along with the rule the budget should be balanced over the economic cycle, an expenditure growth rule of some kind (e.g. real growth in expenses to be no higher than 2 percent annually) is highly desirable.[341]

The so-called golden rule of fiscal policy is insufficient to guarantee desirable fiscal policy outcomes. As we have seen in the case of Queensland, the adoption of the golden rule and the abandonment of the previous strict rule from the fiscal trilogy only to borrow for economic infrastructure, arguably contributed to Queensland's fiscal deterioration.

The golden rule does not guarantee optimal fiscal policy. As Robert Carling, a leading Australian public finance expert and Senior Fellow at the Centre for Independent Studies has observed:

> The states could draw some comfort from the golden rule, as the build-up of debt in recent years has—at least for the states in aggregate—not reflected net operating deficits, but rather an elevated level of capital expenditure. However, the golden rule is subject to major

---

[340] OECD, 2015a, *Government at a Glance Country Fact Sheet: Switzerland.*
[341] OECD, 2015b, "Achieving prudent debt targets using fiscal rules", *OECD Economics Department Policy Note*, no. 28.

qualifications in its practical application. Much of what is classified as government capital expenditure has little or no connection to future economic growth or state revenue, and even genuine economic infrastructure projects are not necessarily rigorously selected according to cost-benefit criteria or implemented at an efficient cost.[342]

This relates to the point made earlier about the three hospitals that were committed to without cost-benefit analysis studies being conducted. Drawing on comments from former IMF Director of Fiscal Affairs and internationally renowned public finance expert Vito Tanzi, Carling suggested:

> Operating surpluses should be the norm, and should be large enough to finance what Tanzi describes as 'routine public investment spending (spending which does not change much year after year)'. Borrowing should only be used to finance large, one-off economic infrastructure projects with a demonstrable link to future economic and revenue growth.[343]

It is necessary to guard against financing so-called "white elephants" or "roads to nowhere" that may be politically opportunistic but to the detriment of the budget, given that, as Vito Tanzi has noted:

> Not all *public investment* is productive, and not all of it contributes to economic growth and to future tax revenue.[344]

When interviewed for this book, former Queensland Under Treasurer Mark Gray commented:

> When it comes to debt, there is a dilemma. Debt is not necessarily a bad thing, as there can be good debt if money is borrowed to invest in projects with a net benefit to the community. But governments cannot always help themselves, and may invest in politically attractive projects that do not pass the cost-benefit test. Hence, it's good to make government fiscal principles stronger than commercial approaches to debt, as there is not the same commercial discipline to guide the

---

[342] Carling, R., op. cit., p. 4.
[343] Ibid., p. 4.
[344] Vito Tanzi, 2016, *Pleasant Dreams or Nightmares in Public Debt Scenarios?*, Centre for Economic Studies, p. 40.

responsible use of debt.

The current government's fiscal principles should be strengthened. Recall the Palaszczuk government's fiscal principle is to: "Target net operating surpluses that ensure any new capital investment in the General Government Sector is funded primarily through recurrent revenues rather than borrowing."[345] In practical application, the metric the government uses to measure this is "General Government operating cash flows as a proportion of purchases of non–financial assets."[346] For 2017-18, this is estimated by Queensland Treasury to be 69 percent, but it is forecast to drop to below 50 percent for 2018-19 and 2019-20, to 49 percent and 40 percent respectively, meaning that arguably the government would not be achieving its fiscal principle in those years.[347] Also consider that, by excluding depreciation from this metric, as it is a non-cash expense, the government's principle is requiring insufficient prudency, as the government is not making any allowance for future refurbishments of assets.

There would be merit in Queensland introducing a rule restraining the growth of expenditure below a certain rate in real terms over the economic cycle. Of course, whether the government abides by a rule is another matter, and we have seen the Queensland government has breached its own rule around the growth of FTE employees. That said, an additional rule around total expenditure would provide additional pressure on the government to restrain its expenses growth.

Trimming unnecessary expenditure

Health is the largest area of Queensland government expenditure, and one that is growing at a high rate. It would make sense to begin here. Thankfully, the current Queensland government has managed to negotiate a not unreasonable pay deal with public servants, at 2.5 percent growth per

---

[345] Queensland Treasury, 2016, op. cit., p. 70.
[346] Ibid.
[347] Queensland Treasury, 2017c, *Mid Year Fiscal and Economic Review 2017-18*, Table 6, p. 20.

year over the three years from 2016-17. This is within the RBA target range for consumer price index (CPI) inflation, although it is a fraction higher than the average inflation rate in recent years. Also note the Palaszczuk government granted public servants a one-off bonus of $1,300, which it argued was necessary given negotiations for a public service pay deal stalled during the Newman government's term.[348]

Successive Queensland governments have attempted to control the growth of health costs, such programs as clinical services redesign, and such efforts have had some success. But to achieve substantial savings, the Queensland government will need to work closely with the Commonwealth and other state and territory governments through COAG to fix the health system. Centre for Independent Studies Senior Research Fellow Jeremy Sammut recently argued:

> The problem is that we spend too much on some kinds of care that are very expensive, and not enough on different kinds of care that could reduce costs and improve outcomes for patients.
>
> We spend more than we should on costly hospital-based care for chronic disease patients, and not enough on non-hospital based primary care that could prevent them from having to be admitted to hospital.[349]

Addressing this problem will require reforms to Medicare, so that health professionals are incentivised to keep people with complex health conditions out of hospital, rewarding outcomes rather than activity as the current system does.[350]

There is substantial scope to cut expenditures in areas in which state government intervention lacks a clear rationale, such as market failure. Following a recommendation of its Commission of Audit, the Newman government instituted a review of state government industry assistance, often pejoratively referred to as "corporate welfare". The review was

---

[348] Jason Tin, 2016, , "Queensland public service: New pay deal and special $1300 bonus", *Courier-Mail*, 29 April 2016, available via www.couriermail.com.au.

[349] Jeremy Sammut, 2016, "Silicon Valleys for Health", in *Politically-Feasible Health Reform: Whatever Will it Take?*, Centre for Independent Studies, p. 1.

[350] Ibid., p. 3.

conducted by the QCA, which commenced work on the review in early 2014, but it would not issue its final report until well into the term of the Palaszczuk Government in mid-2015.

After the QCA published the final report of its Industry Assistance Review, the Queensland government was quick to reject its recommendations regarding a cut to drought assistance and the further review of subsidised regional electricity prices. So these costly policies which lead to inefficient outcomes will continue, as will unjustifiable industry assistance in many other sectors as well. The QCA identified $25 billion worth of industry assistance measures over 2013 to 2018, and, given the QCA's strong criticism of such assistance, the Queensland government should have been able to find, at a minimum, hundreds of millions of dollars of savings by abolishing assistance with no legitimate rationale. The QCA noted:

> The evidence that is available suggests that, although a number of industry assistance measures are beneficial, many others are ineffective and result in a range of costs, including resource allocation distortions, lower productivity, lower household incomes and harmful environmental impacts.[351]

The QCA was strongly critical of the lack of evidence regarding the impacts of industry assistance, particularly the lack of proper monitoring and evaluation of assistance provided and a lack of published cost-benefit analysis reports demonstrating that programs provide net benefits. It noted "there is limited transparency in the provision of significant amounts of public resources to the private sector."[352] For example, in 2014, the government provided an undisclosed assistance package to attract the Walt Disney *Pirates of the Caribbean 5* production to Queensland. Secret deals with an industry of this nature should be a major cause for concern. Unfortunately, the current government has continued the tradition of providing undisclosed industry assistance to other film productions, such as

---

[351] Queensland Competition Authority, 2015, *Industry Assistance in Queensland, Final Report, Volume 1*, p. vi.
[352] Ibid., p. vi.

Aquaman, Thor: Ragnarok and *Dora the Explorer*, and to Scottish craft brewer BrewDog, which is establishing a factory at Murrarie in Brisbane's eastern suburbs. The assistance to BrewDog was especially egregious, as noted by Director of Queensland Economic Advocacy Solutions Nick Behrens in a post on his blog:

> ...has anyone within Government bothered to ask how the 20 plus breweries already established in Brisbane and on the Gold Coast feel about a new competitor launching underpinned by State Government funding? Yes that's right, taxpayer dollars are being used to set up an overseas company in Brisbane to compete against an already mature Queensland run and owned industry in SEQ.[353]

The QCA has sensibly recommended that the government not provide financial incentives to attract international film productions such as *Pirates of the Caribbean 5*, observing the benefits of such packages are largely captured by foreign production companies, such as Walt Disney. It also recommended re-focussing state government film industry assistance on activities providing cultural benefits to Queensland, and that any such assistance should be provided transparently.

The QCA also found that assistance to another industry favoured by recent governments, tourism, was futile, with the QCA noting:

> While it could be the case that tourism expenditure in Queensland would have been lower without destination marketing, it is losing market share to other states and territories.[354]

The Queensland Treasury should keep this in mind for the next time it sees a funding submission regarding Tourism and Events Queensland, the state's tourism promotion agency, which currently receives over $100 million of state government funding per annum.[355]

---

[353] Nick Behrens, 2018, "Why the State Government is 'NUTS' to offer Scottish beer giant BrewDog industry assistance", *Queensland Economic Advocacy Solutions blog*, 14 February 2018.
[354] Queensland Competition Authority, op. cit., p. 111.
[355] Queensland Treasury, 2017d, *Queensland Budget 2017-18 Service Delivery Statements: Department of Tourism, Major Events, Small Business and the Commonwealth Games*, p. 36.

User pays and value capture mechanisms

There is large scope for introducing or increasing user charges for government services in Queensland. This is especially so in education, for example. A report from Domain on 7 February 2017 considered the impact of school catchment areas on house prices:

> Despite a 3.5 per cent decrease in Brisbane city price growth last year, top performing primary and secondary catchment areas in south east Queensland have seen between 19 and 40 per cent growth in prices...Some of Brisbane's best performing schools made the top 10 list for catchment zone house price growth, including West End State School (up 21.7 per cent), Brisbane State High School (up 11.1 per cent) and Indooroopilly State High School (up 9.6 per cent).[356]

Rigorous academic studies confirm that property prices are affected significantly by school catchment areas, as was found for the ACT by Ian Davidoff and Andrew Leigh.[357]

Given the extent to which house prices are being bid up in the catchment areas of desirable schools, it is clear parents have the capacity to make a greater contribution to the costs of running state schools. Currently, existing property owners in desirable catchment areas are capturing a monetary benefit that could be captured by the state government, through higher parental contribution charges at popular schools, to help it cover the costs of education provision. Of course, the state government may need to make some concessions for poorer households living in desirable school catchment areas. Ideally, we would have a means-tested school voucher scheme across Australia. But in the absence of that, appropriate user charges for state schools in high demand would be desirable.

---

[356] Ellen Lutton, 2017, "House prices in some Queensland state school zones rise by up to 40 per cent", *Domain*, available via www.domain.com.au.

[357] Ian Davidoff and Andrew Leigh, 2008, "How much do public schools really cost? Estimating the relationship between house prices and school quality", *Economic Record*, vol. 84, no. 265, pp. 193-206.

In health, there are also substantial opportunities for greater cost recovery, although such measures may need to be enacted at the Commonwealth level. But, as with the controversial Medicare co-payment proposed in the 2014-15 federal budget, they may be politically toxic and considered inequitable, suggesting changes to health policies will not come easily.

As opposed to the concept of user pays, which has influenced Australian public policy since the 1980s, value capture is a concept that has emerged more recently. In the Queensland policy debate it arose during the term of the Palaszczuk government, particularly in regard to the Cross River Rail project in inner city Brisbane. It is a form of what economists call "beneficiary pays." The idea is that landowners and businesses which stand to benefit from new infrastructure being provided, either through higher property prices or greater turnover and profit, should be required to contribute to the funding of infrastructure. Such benefits can be substantial. UQ economist Cameron Murray estimated the $1.2 billion first stage of Gold Coast Light Rail—a tram running from Griffith University, Gold Coast through to Surfers Paradise and Broadbeach—provided an uplift in the value of land in the vicinity of light rail stations of around $300 million in total.[358]

In jurisdictions with value capture, the charges are typically called betterment levies. There is a sound public policy rationale for such levies, given they tax windfall gains and hence should not distort economic behaviour. As such, the possibility of value capture should be explored for any new state government infrastructure project. However, value capture should be carefully applied, as noted by SMART Infrastructure Facility Senior Research Fellow Joe Branigan when interviewed for this book:

> Care is required to ensure value uplift is not a spurious source of additional benefit used to improve the benefit-cost ratio of an

---

[358] Cameron Murray, 2016, "Gold Coast light rail study helps put a figure on value capture's funding potential", *The Conversation*, 20 September 2016.

unviable project. Estimates of value uplift should be conservative, and net out uplift caused by exogenous factors, such as population growth.

It is well known that optimism bias can creep into cost-benefit analysis assessments of infrastructure projects, so analysts need to be careful not to add another source of possible error in their cost-benefit analysis of projects.

Comprehensive reforms to federal financial relations and taxation

Queensland should continue to push for reform of federal-state financial relations, possibly through prosecuting the case for state-based income tax. After all, the Queensland Treasury appeared supportive of such a measure in the *Fiscal Reform Blueprint* it handed to the Newman government in 2012. The Treasury noted:

> The ability of states to impose a surcharge on top of the Australian Government's income tax schedule would allow states to access a robust, stable and broad revenue base that would increase the state's capacity to reform and strengthen their revenue systems.[359]

Alas, state and territory governments missed a recent opportunity to bring in a sub-national income tax. Prior to the 2016 Council of Australian Government's meeting on Friday, 1 April 2016, Prime Minister Malcolm Turnbull raised a constructive suggestion that the States could take over a share of the income tax, but this was derided as a "thought bubble" and did not proceed. From a public policy perspective, it may be desirable for the Commonwealth to cut its income tax rates and make room for state income tax to piggyback on the Commonwealth tax. This would start redressing the imbalance that arose when in 1957 the High Court, in the case *Victoria v Commonwealth*, commonly known as the second uniform tax case, refused to restore the States' income tax powers the Commonwealth had taken over during World War II.

---

[359] Queensland Treasury, 2012a, op. cit., p. C-1-11.

Also, Queensland needs to continue to push for reforms to Commonwealth-state financial relations that properly recognise the contribution the state Government makes to the development of the resources industry, particularly due to any expenditure requirements associated with population expansions in mining regions. This was an issue raised by the Queensland Treasury at the time of the last GST distribution methodology review. In September 2014, in response to a draft report from the CGC, the Treasury commented:

> The Terms of Reference require the Commission to develop a new assessment of mining revenue. This is in recognition of the serious problems with the current approach whereby a state's own policy decisions can have significant impacts on their GST outcomes. The Draft Report proposes to assess each mineral type individually, which exacerbates these problems. This could result in the GST distribution methodology distorting government decision-making related to the setting of royalty rates.
>
> The proposed methodology will have an even more detrimental impact on states' ability to obtain an appropriate return for the state from its resources assets. Queensland argues for the aggregation of minerals, which would help address these policy neutrality concerns.
>
> Despite evidence of additional expenditure incurred by mining states in support of their industries, the Commission has proposed a minimal adjustment (for regulation expenses). The expenditure incurred by states in support of their mining industries should be recognised, rather than just the royalties.[360]

This is still a substantial policy concern—and one that is being considered in the current Productivity Commission HFE review discussed in the previous chapter—because it means state governments are penalised to an extent for actions that complement the development of particular industries. The methodology certainly requires more adjustment, but Queensland

---

[360] Queensland Treasury, 2014b, *Queensland Treasury Response to Commonwealth Grants Commission 2015 Methodology Review*, p. 7.

appears better off with HFE than without it, as on average, over the years, Queensland has been a net beneficiary of the GST redistribution, with an average relativity of 1.028 over 2000-01 to 2017-18 (Figure 10.1). That is, on average, Queensland received 2.8 percent more GST revenue than it would be entitled to per capita. In the 2016-17 budget papers, Queensland Treasury expressed the view that:

> In the longer-term, Queensland's fiscal capacity can be expected to be nearer to the average of states (that is, a relativity of 1).[361]

This view appears to be based on an assumption that the factors which boost Queensland's relativity and hence GST entitlement, particularly the "higher than average expenditure needs, owing to the state's higher proportions of remote and Indigenous populations", will be offset by "a higher capacity to raise revenue from mining royalties and lower assessed public sector wage costs".[362]

Nonetheless, for the time being, HFE appears still to be in Queensland's interest, although some adjustments to the methodology, along the lines suggested by Queensland Treasury in the extract above, may be necessary to avoid HFE reducing the incentive for states and territories to promote economic development.

Along with reforms of federal financial relations, Australia needs comprehensive tax reform along the lines suggested by the 2008-09 tax review led by then Treasury Secretary Ken Henry, *Australia's Future Tax System*. Such a reform program would include the abolition of inefficient state and territory revenue sources such as mining royalties and stamp duties. This would necessarily involve adjustments to current federal financial relations due to the need to replace these revenue sources.

---

[361] Queensland Treasury, 2016, op. cit., p. 154.
[362] Ibid.

Figure 10.1 Per capita relativity for GST revenue redistribution

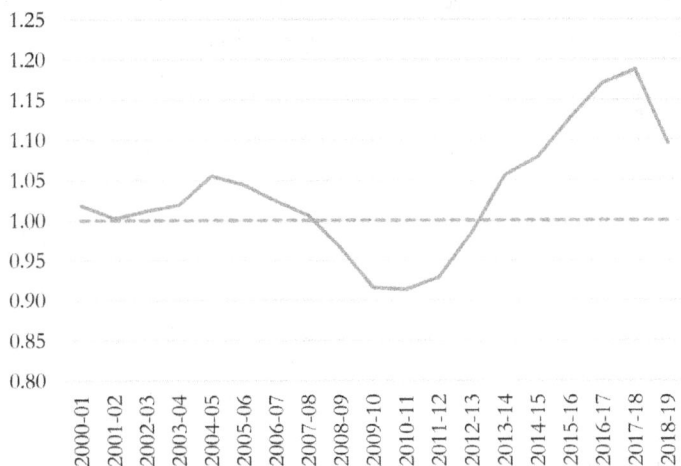

Source: Australian Government Budget papers.

Restoration of arms-length approach to GOCs

In 2001, Keith De Lacy had raised issues with GOCs that arguably should have been heeded by the Beattie government at the time and by subsequent governments. De Lacy was concerned about the over-turning of principles that he had established for GOCs while Treasurer, and noted at the time:

> ...in the last year or so GOCs have had an ever increasing list of public policy interventions—executive salaries, approvals for overseas travel, State purchasing policy, the Building Code, IR policies, redundancy policies and so on—all policies that don't apply to our private sector competitors, and inconsistent with the fundamental principle of competitive neutrality.[363]

It may prove difficult for GOCs ever to be given the freedom from interference they need. As De Lacy noted, important stakeholders, including

---

[363] Keith De Lacy, 2001, *Corporate Governance—GOCs*, speech delivered on 11 July 2001.

ministers, unions and the media, had not appreciated the need for the reforms he had implemented. Earlier in the speech he had observed:

> A good example was the unedifying spectacle we witnessed some time ago when there was public criticism of a pay rise given to the CEO of Energex. In the media feeding frenzy that followed, GOC executive salaries were compared with those of politicians, public servants, blue collar workers and even pensioners—indeed with everyone except that of their commercial peers in the industry!

Political interference means there is a lack of a clear line of accountability, which is contributing to poorer outcomes for GOCs. The crises we have seen in Energex and QR, for example, may not have come as a surprise to anyone who listened to De Lacy's words in 2001.

Reforms to Parliament and the public service

Vital reforms are needed to Queensland's Parliament and possibly to the public service, although the need for reform here is more debatable. The major concerns, to be considered in turn below, are:

- the lack of an upper house of review;
- the related issue of a weak committee system overseeing government business; and
- arguably, a public service that has lost capability and is less frank and fearless than it was in the Hielscher era.

Consider that the Queensland government is not subject to oversight and scrutiny by an upper house of review, such as the Senate for the Commonwealth government or the Legislative Councils for other state governments such as NSW and Victoria. Originally, Queensland did have a Legislative Council, but a suicide squad of Labor members of the Council voted to abolish it in 1922. The Labor government of the time saw the Legislative Council as a constraint on its agenda. So Queensland's parliament is unicameral rather than bicameral, with only a lower house, the Legislative Assembly. The beautifully decorated Legislative Council chamber in Queensland's Parliament House in Brisbane is reserved for ceremonial duties and functions only.

The lack of a Queensland upper house has arguably led to poorer governance ever since its abolition, as it entrenched the power of the government winning election to the lower house. Unlike in other states and territories and at the federal level, there is no upper house of review that scrutinises and proposes amendments to new legislation. One may conjecture that, to some extent, the poor governance outcomes experienced in Queensland in recent decades, including corrupt government ministers and officials, and multiple crises in the provision of utilities and public services, may be related to the lack of an upper house of review. As Professor Scott Prasser of the Australian Catholic University observed in 2009:

> Recent scandals enveloping the Beattie and Bligh Labor governments, concerning Ministers, former Ministers and staff and lobbying, independence of the Auditor-General, and the operations of the public hospitals system and rushed legislation, have highlighted the continuing executive dominance of Parliament, the lack of accountability, and the limitations of the many new external review mechanisms that Queensland, post-Fitzgerald had established. As a consequence there has been renewed interest in establishing an Upper House in Queensland.[364]

The lack of an upper house could make large swings in economic policies and fiscal outcomes more likely. Students of political science may well ask whether the changing political ideologies of governments in Queensland have impacted the fiscal outcomes observed. In Queensland's case, it is very possible, as up until the end of the Beattie government, Queensland had typically had fiscally conservative Premiers and Treasurers. But former Premier Anna Bligh, who served as Beattie's

---

[364] Scott Prasser, 2009, "The virtues of upper houses", Chapter 6 in *Proceedings of the Twenty-first Conference of The Samuel Griffith Society*, p. 50.

last Treasurer before taking up the Premiership, was from the Socialist Left of the ALP and had a different perspective, as discussed earlier in this book.

Turning to the second major concern above, UQ Emeritus Professor Kenneth Wiltshire has suggested a core problem in Queensland is the lack of an effective system of parliamentary committees as there is at the Commonwealth level. There appears to be a need for the Queensland Parliament to be revamped, with proper staffing for committees, and consideration given to the need for a parliamentary budget office, which is accountable to the parliament rather than the executive government, similar to the Commonwealth body.

What is also urgently needed is a system of rigorous Treasury-led internal reviews that can act as an internal warning system in government, such as the system with which the Goss government was successfully experimenting. It is unclear to what extent the Newman government's Public Sector Renewal initiative may have helped in this regard. Also, rigorous *ex ante* and *ex post* reviews of major capital works projects should be conducted to assess whether money spent on different projects should actually have been spent.

Wiltshire, in a 2004 speech, was also critical of the fact that the role of the Auditor-General has been diminished and is not defended by parliamentary committees.[365] Regarding Queensland committees, Wiltshire noted in 2004, in a statement that he considers still applies today, that:

> The committee system is not brilliant. It is better in Canberra than it is here. The estimates committees I find very sad here in Queensland. Ministers keep fronting the estimates committees. It should be public servants. This is the one place where parliament and public servants can actually meet in the committee system, but what do we have in Queensland? We have the ministers answering all the questions and refusing, most of the time, to allow public servants to answer those

---

[365] Wiltshire, K., 2004, op. cit., p. 5.

questions.[366]

In such a situation it is even more important to have professional public servants offering frank and fearless non-partisan advice, whose advice is influential in government decision making. This is what Queensland had in the Hielscher-era. Arguably, this characterisation has been less applicable since then.

Instead of a Westminster system with professional non-partisan public servants, we have a "Washminster system", according to Emeritus Professor Ken Wiltshire, a mixture of Whitehall and Washington, DC, in which agency heads are now appointed by the government of the day on contracts, and there is a risk of politicisation.[367] In a 2016 op-ed for the *Courier-Mail* on governance in Queensland, Professor Wiltshire wrote:

> Perhaps the key symbol of the politicisation and hence fall in standards, is the decline of the powers of the Public Service Boards which have morphed into tame Public Service Commissions. They were once the buffer between politicians and public servants, serving to protect public servants from ministers who play the blame game and also try to influence appointments thus corrupting the system – the sort of behaviour we condemn in other countries.[368]

There are arguments against permanency in the public service, however, relating to the public choice critique of government that emerged in the 1970s, associated with economists such as James Buchanan and Gordon Tullock, who pointed out the incentive for bureaucrats to build public service empires and the bias in representative government toward bigger government, among other findings.[369] It may hence be unwise to give

---

[366] Ibid.
[367] Kenneth Wiltshire, 2004, in Australasian Study of Parliament Group (Queensland Chapter), *Parliament and Public Servants—Separate or United in 21st Century Westminster Practice?*, Queensland Parliament, p. 7.
[368] Kenneth Wiltshire, 2016, Take the politics out of policy", *Courier-Mail*, 2 November 2016, available via www.couriermail.com.au.
[369] James Buchanan and Gordon Tullock, 1977, "The expanding public sector: Wagner squared", *Public Choice*, vol. 31, pp. 147-150.

bureaucrats too much power.

SMART Infrastructure Facility (University of Wollongong) Senior Fellow Research Joe Branigan notes:

> If there is a change of government and no department head is sacked it indicates that the former opposition hasn't done its homework, has no real agenda, and don't know what they are doing. On the other hand, if they sack a dozen Directors-General it looks vindictive and petty. In my view, at the very least, an incoming government should have done enough homework to know who could run the Premier's Department and implement its reform agenda with distinction. In addition, given its central importance, if there is any question mark over the performance of the Under Treasurer, he or she should be replaced immediately. I also think that any blatantly political appointments from the previous government, whether at the Director-General level or even much lower should be moved on. The bottom line is that an incoming government must always reserve the right to appoint the most capable people to key roles to implement its agenda without being accused of petty vindictiveness.

In other words, there is no easy way of going back to the previous era of permanent public service heads. That world is gone, and we need to accept the reality of governments that more directly interact with their public services.

So the best bang-for-buck in reforms is likely to occur in relation to the Parliament and the committee system. Queenslanders should consider what reforms are necessary, possibly including the re-establishment of an upper house, to promote a more vigorous committee system and greater oversight of the Parliament. While proposing solutions is probably best left to political scientists rather than economists, I can confidently conclude there is a clear problem with our governance settings given the range of crises and scandals still vivid in the memories of Queenslanders: the health, electricity and water crises, the Queensland Health payroll debacle, the 1 William St leasing controversy, and the rail fail, among others.

The need for greater transparency and medium-term budget modelling

The large build-up in debt that began in the mid-2000s underlines the need for rigorous medium-term budget modelling, beyond the forward estimates, which does not appear to have been done at the time. It is not apparent that the Beattie or Bligh governments understood the risks they were taking when they committed to such high expenditures. It took the financial crisis to provide much needed clarity. After the financial crisis, concerns about fiscal sustainability started to be expressed by the Bligh government, in what looked like an attempt to mollify the ratings agencies, which downgraded the state's credit rating in early 2009. That said, Queensland budgets still do not present projections of Queensland's public finances beyond the forward estimates. In contrast, the federal budget includes a projection of the budget balance a decade into the future.

Arguably, an independent panel of budget experts and economists to review Treasury budget forecasts and projections—or to actually produce the official forecasts—would be desirable. As Harvard economist Jeffrey Frankel has identified, across countries there is a tendency for government budget agencies to produce overly optimistic forecasts and for this to lead to poorer fiscal outcomes in the long-run.[370] Frankel notes that Chile, which is highly dependent on copper exports with volatile prices, has successfully implemented independent institutions to produce forecasts. With a government budget also influenced by volatile commodity prices, Queensland would do well to follow Chile's example.

---

[370] Jeffrey Frankel, 2011, "Over-optimism in forecasts by official budget agencies and its implications", *Oxford Review of Economic Policy*, vol. 27, no. 4, pp. 536-562.

11

CONCLUSION

In the three decades since Sir Leo Hielscher retired as Under Treasurer, Queensland went from being the exemplar of sound public finance in Australia, to having the highest level of public debt among the States and a downgraded credit rating. When Sir Leo left Treasury in 1988, he became Chairman of the QTC and his legacy of fiscal discipline lived on for some years, mostly intact, although future Queensland governments, beginning with Peter Beattie's (1998-2007) abandoned the rule against borrowing for social infrastructure, such as schools and hospitals—as opposed to economic infrastructure such as ports, toll roads or bridges. Fiscal management remained commendable, however, up until the mid-2000s. Notably, Beattie government Treasurer Mackenroth presided over the three largest recorded budget surpluses. However, the abandonment of the rule against borrowing for social infrastructure meant there was always the risk that Queensland's public finances could deteriorate in the future. Indeed, they did so, once Mackenroth was no longer Treasurer, and Anna Bligh had taken over.

Queensland has also lost its crown as the low tax state, although taxes are still lower per capita than in NSW, Victoria, WA and ACT. The build up of debt was only partly justifiable by the need to build infrastructure with net benefits to the community. It is likely much of the money borrowed was used to fund projects of dubious value. Alas, the poor decisions of past governments continue to cost Queensland taxpayers, as the state government's debt imposes an ongoing burden. It means taxes and charges have to be higher than otherwise, or services and new infrastructure cannot be funded as much as otherwise.

A review of the last three decades of Queensland's public financial management reveals a range of factors that were relevant to Queensland's fiscal deterioration. Undoubtedly the deterioration occurred over the mid-to-late 2000s, at the end of the Beattie government and during the Bligh government. While these governments deserve a large share of the blame, they were, to some extent, the victims of events—a financial crisis and natural disasters—and a deterioration in the capability and quality of Queensland's public administration that has occurred over a relatively long period.

The Bligh government lost its way partly because there were insufficient mechanisms to keep it on course. First, there was no longer a rigorous fiscal trilogy, with a strict rule against borrowing against social infrastructure, which would keep governments in line. Second, Queensland no longer has tenured public servants of the calibre of Sir Leo Hielscher and Sir Charles Barton with the autonomy that they had. Instead we have senior public servants on contracts who can be dismissed by their political masters and may not survive a change in government. Certainly the position of Under Treasurer has become subject to political vagaries, and the Treasury has arguably lost the power that it had in the days of Hielscher. With the decline in the relative power of the public service, the politicians and their advisers exerted greater control over the state's public finances. In the mid to late 2000s, this resulted in budgets being produced that were increasingly divorced from economic reality.

Under the Bligh government, partly due to decisions made during the Beattie government, Queensland's state debt grew to tens of billions of dollars more than was desirable. General government interest expenses blew out to be comparable with motor vehicle registration revenue at over

$1½ billion, and the prized AAA credit rating on Queensland government bonds was lost. State debt, currently around $70 billion, remains on a path to over $80 billion, and there is little prospect in the foreseeable future of the state government paying down sufficient debt to regain a AAA credit rating.

Queensland's debt needs to be paid down to well below the level at which we could possibly get our AAA credit rating back—i.e. well below 100-110 percent of total government revenues (i.e. including that of GOCs), currently around $65-70 billion—so there is a large buffer in which the state's public finances can temporarily deteriorate in the event of a recession or financial crisis. But, instead, Queensland's state debt is heading in the other direction.

Strong measures and reforms, such as those advocated in the previous two chapters, are required. It is clear is that Queensland needs to urgently reform its parliamentary and public service institutions. For a long time now, Queensland government fiscal outcomes and service delivery have been far short of community expectations. Queenslanders deserve far better.

Although the Hielscher era has now passed, and the state's public finances are not in the outstanding position they once were, Sir Leo's legacy is still important. He is the supreme example of fiscal discipline for future Treasurers and Under Treasurers to emulate.

POSTSCRIPT

Sir Leo Hielscher broke his long post-retirement public silence on Queensland's state debt problem when he delivered the annual McIlwraith Lecture for the Australian Institute for Progress at the Tattersall's Club, Brisbane on 18 July 2018. The former Under Treasurer and QTC Chairman observed:

> We must really worry about this $80 billion debt...
>
> ...Unfortunately also, there seems to be no plan or program to pay off the debt. It is still growing. Sorry kids....sorry grand kids...
>
> We have lost our AAA credit rating. A lot of our cash reserves, superannuation surpluses and such like have been tapped and the debt is still rising.

Regrettably, despite Sir Leo's observations and those of various other experts concerning Queensland's state debt problem, the Palaszczuk government is yet to demonstrate it is similarly concerned. As noted in Chapter 7, Treasurer Trad's first budget projected total state government debt is now on a path toward $83 billion. I live in hope of an eventual return to fiscal discipline in Queensland, but it may be a long time coming.

APPENDIX 1

QUEENSLAND TREASURERS AND UNDER TREASURERS SINCE SIR LEO HIELSCHER BECAME UNDER TREASURER

Treasurers

Treasurer	Party	Premiers	Years
Sir Gordon Chalk	Liberal	Nicklin, Pizzey, Bjelke-Petersen	1965-1976
Sir William Knox	Liberal	Bjelke-Petersen	1976-1978
Sir Llewellyn Edwards	Liberal	Bjelke-Petersen	1978-1983
Sir Joh Bjelke-Petersen	National	Bjelke-Petersen	1983-1987
Mike Ahern	National	Ahern	1987-1989
Russell Cooper	National	Cooper	1987-1989
Keith De Lacy	Labor	Goss	1989-1996
Joan Sheldon	Liberal	Borbidge	1996-1998
David Hamill	Labor	Beattie	1998-2001
Terry Mackenroth	Labor	Beattie	2001-2005
Peter Beattie	Labor	Beattie	2005-2006
Anna Bligh	Labor	Beattie	2006-2007
Andrew Fraser	Labor	Bligh	2007-2012
Tim Nicholls	Liberal National Party	Newman	2012-2015
Curtis Pitt	Labor	Palaszczuk	2015-2017
Jackie Trad	Labor	Palaszczuk	2017-

Under Treasurers

Under Treasurer	Years
Sir Leo Hielscher	1974-1988
John Hall	1988-1989
Henry Smerdon	1989-1994
Gerard Bradley	1994-1996
Doug McTaggart	1996-1998
Gerard Bradley	1998-2012
Helen Gluer	2012-2013
Mark Gray	2013-2015
Jim Murphy	2015-2018

APPENDIX 2:

CAVEATS REGARDING BUDGET DATA

Over the time period considered in this book, there have been substantial changes in budgetary accounting standards, which make it very difficult to precisely compare budget outcomes across governments. Nonetheless, the changes seen over time in the major budget aggregates (e.g. the fiscal deficit or the level of debt) are of such a large magnitude that the intricacies of accounting and reporting can be put largely in the background. That said, one major change, the switch to accrual accounting from cash accounting in the late 1990s may have had a substantive impact on budgetary outcomes, as discussed below. The switch to accrual accounting was necessary for a range of reasons, including that it was best practice in the private sector and for consistency with IMF Government Finance Statistics (GFS) standards. As opposed to cash accounting, where transactions are recognised in the accounts when an actual cash payment is made or received, accrual accounting recognises transactions in the time period to which they relate. Also, adopting accrual accounting standards meant recognising the non-cash depreciation expense in the operating balance, which has implications for defining the government's fiscal principles, as discussed above.

The switch to accrual accounting means we cannot precisely compare budget results from the late 1990s with those from earlier years, as reflected in the break in the time series in Figure 3.1 in Chapter 3. While the surpluses not measured according to accrual accounting for 1997-98 and prior years are not strictly comparable with GFS net lending, which corresponds to the concept of the fiscal balance, in 1999-00 and beyond, they are sufficiently similar that the Newman Government's Commission of Audit treated them as one consistent time series in its *Interim Report*.[371] Thus the fiscal balance surpluses in the general government sector under the Goss government are seen to be comparable as a share of GSP to the large fiscal surpluses recorded during Terry Mackenroth's time as Queensland Treasurer during the Beattie government. These were the high points for Queensland's public finances in the readily available historical data, while the huge fiscal deficits of over 2 percent of GSP during the Bligh government in the late 2000s were the low points.

Throughout this book I have often distinguished between the forecasts of revenues, expenditures and surpluses (or deficits) at budget time, and those that actually occurred. The Bligh government especially found its budget estimates revised substantially at the mid-year update, the so-called *Mid Year Fiscal and Economic Review* (MYFER), and in the next budget. Outcomes differ from forecasts, not because Treasurers and Treasury officials are trying to mislead the public at budget time, but because key economic and demographic assumptions, particularly around GSP growth or coal prices, can differ from what was forecast. Treasury does not have a crystal ball after all.

Usefully, the Queensland state budget provides advice on the sensitivity of important budget items to relevant variables, such as the estimates provided in Table A.1. The major factors leading to divergences between Queensland budget forecasts and outcomes in recent years have tended to be coal prices, the exchange rate, the relativity estimated by the CGC, public sector wage costs and interest rates. Sometimes these factors work in Queensland's favour, sometimes not. Also consider that Queensland is at risk from natural disasters, particularly tropical cyclones that may be becoming more prevalent due to climate change. Of course, the frequency and severity of cyclones, and their budgetary impacts, are inherently unpredictable at budget time.

---

[371]   Queensland Commission of Audit, 2012, op. cit., p. 60.

Table A.1 Sensitivity of Queensland budget items to parameter changes, 2017-18 Budget estimates

Parameter	Variable affected	Change in parameter	Impact on variable
Wages growth	Payroll tax	1 percentage point	$38 million
Employment	Payroll tax	1 percentage point	$38 million
Average value of property transactions	Transfer duty	1 percentage point	$32 million
Volume of property transactions	Transfer duty	1 percentage point	$32 million
A$-US$ exchange rate	Coal royalty revenue	One cent	$49 million
Export coking and thermal coal volumes	Coal royalty revenue	1 percent	$23 million
Average price of export coal	Coal royalty revenue	1 percent	$37 million
Public sector wage outcomes	Expenses	1 percent	$220 million

Source: Queensland Treasury, 2017a, op. cit., pp. 242-244.

It is important to consider both the budget forecasts and outcomes as it can inform our judgments regarding the proficiency of various governments in public finance matters. This involves considering the reasons behind the variation between forecasts and outcomes. If the budget deteriorates due to factors beyond the government's control, we should be more sympathetic. We need to ask to what extent were they justified to pursue a particular course of action based on the best forecasts at the time. Should they have exercised more caution given the inherent volatility? As argued, in this book, the decisions made that led to the loss of Queensland's AAA rating were deliberate and unjustifiable even at the time they were made. We should have little sympathy for the relevant decision makers, although it needs to be acknowledged Premier Bligh and Treasurer Fraser did try to turn things around in their final term, at great political cost, but by then the fiscal damage had been done.

APPENDIX 3: BREAKING DOWN THE DEBT BUILD UP

It is worthwhile summarising just how the Queensland government accumulated so much debt in the first place. To do so, we analyse the ten years from 2006-07 to 2015-16, which cover the period from when the debt started surging to when its growth slowed substantially, due to measures taken by the Newman and Palaszczuk governments. Over this period, total Queensland government debt increased by $54.6 billion, with $31.2 billion in additional general government debt and $23.4 billion in additional PNFC debt. Obviously, governments borrow money and accumulate debt when they need cash. Hence it is important to analyse the cash flows of the Queensland government. Analysis of the net cash flows reveals the general government sector was responsible for around 53 percent of the total $64.3 billion of the cash flow deficits (prior to borrowing) for the whole Queensland government over this period (Figure A.1). The non-financial GOCs (the PNFCs) were responsible for the other 47 percent.

Figure A.1 Cash flow surplus(+)/deficit(-), Queensland government, 2006-07 to 2015-16

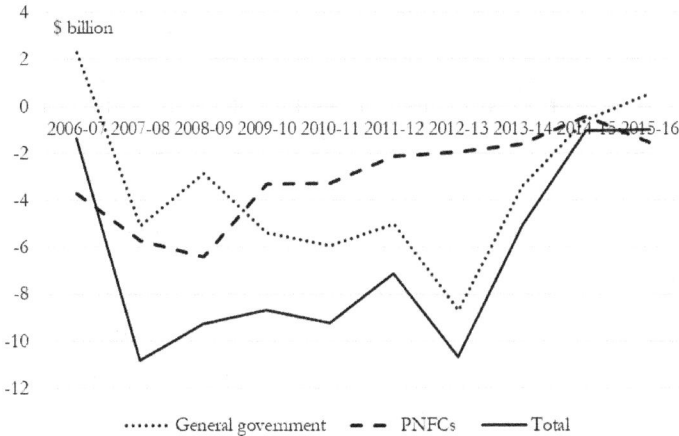

Source: ABS Government Finance Statistics, cat. no. 5512.0.

At the start of the period, the general government sector was in cash surplus but the heavy capital investment requirements, particularly on transport and water infrastructure, pushed it into deficit. For both the general government and PNFC sectors it was the capital expenditures that led to cash flow deficits, as the sectors were always in cash flow surplus on operating activities over this period, with the exception of 2012-13 for the general government sector. In 2012-13, the state government suffered a large reduction in grants received due to the Rudd government having brought forward payments into 2011-12 for its own budgetary purposes.

While the additional capital expenditures were largely responsible for the $64 billion in cash deficits, a substantial contribution was made by the additional interest payment associated with higher debt. As suggested in the discussion on the sustainability of debt in Chapter 7, interest expenses associated with previously incurred debt can add to government deficits and lead to more debt being incurred, and higher interest payments. Over the ten years to 2015-16, additional interest payments, relative to the level in 2005-06 amounted to around $19 billion or 29 percent of the total cash deficits. In other words, additional expenditures, mostly capital expenditures, contributed 71 percent to the deficits over this period.

The $64 billion in cash deficits over 2006-07 to 2015-16 were financed largely by borrowing but also by privatisations, both asset sales (e.g. Aurizon, Queensland Motorways) and lease (e.g. Port of Brisbane). Consider how the total financing requirement of the Queensland government, to cover its cash deficits on operating activities and capital expenditures, and also to set aside money to meet long service and superannuation liabilities, was met by borrowing and privatisations in Table A.2. This shows over one-quarter of the estimated financing requirement of the Queensland government was met by the proceeds of asset sales or leases. The government's financing need was so great it still ran up a large amount of debt even with a large-scale privatisation program.

Table A.2 How the Queensland government met its financing needs over 2006-07 to 2015-16

ABS GFS item	Cash flows $ billion
Surplus(+)/deficit(-)	-64.3
Investments in financial assets for liquidity purposes*	-9.4
Total financing need	**-73.7**
Investments in financial assets for policy purposes**	19.7
Total borrowing required	**$54.0**

Source: ABS Government Finance Statistics, cat. no. 5512.0.
*i.e. setting aside money to meet future liabilities such as superannuation and long service leave.
**This is positive in the case of privatisation proceeds, as is the case here.

So what was the all the additional borrowing spent on? Consider the breakdown of capital outlays over the period by broad category (Table A.3). The water infrastructure expenditure was illustrative of the breakdown of financial discipline in Queensland but it only accounted for around 7 percent of the total capital program over the period. That said, in hindsight, the water infrastructure investments were much less justifiable than many other items of expenditure, and they also did not receive funding contributions from the federal government, unlike major road projects.

Capital outlays by the Department of Transport and Main Roads made up the largest share of capital outlays. Over the period, major projects included the Tugun bypass, Ipswich Motorway upgrade, and Airport Link, to which the Queensland government made a contribution via a PPP. Electricity GOCs also made a large and sustained contribution to total capital outlays over the period.

Table A.3 Queensland government capital outlays, totals over 2006-07 to 2015-16 by broad category

Category	Capital outlay $ billion	Percent of total
Transport & Main Roads	35.5	28.9
Electricity GOCs	27.2	22.1
Health	11.4	9.3
QR	10.8	8.8
Water infrastructure	8.5	6.9
Education	8.2	6.7
Ports	4.3	3.5
Other	17.1	13.9
Total	122.9	100.0

Source: Author's calculations based on data in Queensland government budget papers.

REFERENCES

AAP, 2009, "Anna Bligh defends privatisation amid Labor party row", *www.news.com. au*, 17 August 2009.

AAP, 2016, "Labor reveals Qld 'asset sales' plan", *SBS News*, 6 October 2016, available via www.sbs.com.au.

ABS, 2009, *Qld Stats*, cat. no. 1318.3, available via www.abs.gov.au.

Agius, K. and Grant, M, 2013, "Auditor-General questions 1 William Street tower project", *Brisbane Times*, 10 December 2013, available via www.brisbanetimes. com.au.

Akers, T., 2017, "Queensland election 2017: Treasurer says $81b debt doesn't add up", *Courier-Mail*, 3 November 2017, available via www.couriermail.com.au.

Allen, L., 2015, "How Qantas landed a privatisation success", *The Australian*, July 24, available via www.theaustralian.com.au.

Australian Government, 2009, *Guarantee of State and Territory Borrowing Scheme Rules*.

Australian Treasury, 2005, *2005-06 Budget*, Budget Statement 4.

Baines, S., 2014, *Steel on Steel*, UQ Press, Brisbane.

Barbeler, D., 2009, "Qld loses AAA credit rating after budget blow-out", *Brisbane Times*, 21 February 2009, available via www.brisbanetimes.com.au.

Beattie, P., 2005, *Queensland Government takes lead on urban drought*, media release of the Queensland Premier and Treasurer, 23 August 2005, available via www. statements.qld.gov.au.

Beattie, P., 2005, *Queensland Government takes lead on urban drought*, media release of the Queensland Premier and Treasurer, 23 August 2005, available via www. statements.qld.gov.au.

Beattie, P., 2016, "Peter Beattie book extract: Reform of the federation", *Sydney Morning Herald*, 20 February 2016.

Behrens, N., 2018, "Why the State Government is 'NUTS' to offer Scottish beer giant BrewDog industry assistance", *Queensland Economic Advocacy Solutions blog*, 14 February 2018.

Bjelke-Petersen, J., 1987, *Ministerial Statement*, 14 October 1987.

Bjelke-Petersen, J., 1987, *Ministerial Statement*, 14 October 1987.

Bligh, A., 2015, *Through the wall: reflections on leadership, love and survival*, Harper Collins Publishers.

Borbidge, R. and Sheldon, J., 2015, *Borbidge Sheldon Election Review and Report and Recommendations*, report to the LNP, 28 May 2015.

Branigan, J., 2015, "Electric shock in store for voters", *The Australian*, 22 January 2015, available via www.theaustralian.com.au.

Branigan, J., 2016, *Value capture in the Australian Federation—issues*, submission to House of Representatives Standing Committee on Infrastructure, Transport & Cities Inquiry into Transport Connectivity.

Branigan, J., 2017, "Moody Blues", *Queensland Economy Watch*, posted 21 April 2017.

Buchanan, James and Tullock, Gordon, 1977, "The expanding public sector: Wagner squared", *Public Choice*, vol. 31, pp. 147-150.

Burke, C., 1993, "Education: Promise, Policy and Performance", in Stevens, B. and Wanna, J. (eds.), *The Goss government: promise and performance of Labor in Queensland*, Macmillan Education.

Cameron, W., 2016, *Actuarial Investigation of the State Public Sector Superannuation Scheme (QSuper)*, letter to Under Treasurer Mr Jim Murphy, dated 26 April 2016.

Campbell, R., 2017, *Royal Pardon: How much an Adani royalty holiday could cost Queenslanders*, The Australia Institute, available via www.tai.org.au.

Carling, R., 2017, *Report Card on State Finances*, Centre for Independent Studies.

Carmignani, F., 2015a, "Can public expenditure stabilise output? Multipliers and policy interdependence in Queensland and Australia", *Economic Analysis and Policy*, vol. 47, pp. 69-81.

Carmignani, F., 2015b, "The true state of Queensland's debt", *The Conversation*, 29 January 2015, www.theconversation.edu.au.

Chandler, J., 2005, "The scandal of 'Dr Death'", *The Age*, May 28 2005.

Colley, L, 2005, "Reworking merit: Changes in approaches to merit in Queensland public service employment 1988 to 2000", in Baird, M., Cooper, R. and Westcott, W. (eds.) *Reworking work: proceedings of the 19th conference of the Association of Industrial Relations Academics of Australia and New Zealand*.

Colley, L., 2009, "The politics of an apolitical public service", in Bowden, B., Blackwood, S., Raferty, C. and Allen, C., *Work and Strife in Paradise*, Federation Press.

Commonwealth of Australia, State of New South Wales, State of Victoria, State of Queensland, State of Western Australia, State of South Australia, State of Tasmania, Australian Capital Territory and Northern Territory of Australia, 1999, *Intergovernmental Agreement on the Reform of Commonwealth-State Financial Relations*.

Constitution Education Fund, 2017, *Section 96 and the $900 million loan to Adani*, 2

June 2017, available via www.cefa.org.au.

Courtney, P., 2015, "Mary Valley revival: Last of properties sold during Traveston dam project back in private hands", *ABC News*, 19 April 2015, available via www.abc.net.au.

Cragg, M.I. and Dyck, I.J.A., 2003, "Privatization and management incentives: Evidence from the United Kingdom", *Journal of Law, Economics and Organization*, vol. 19, no. 1, p. 176.

Darby, P., 2013, Australia's credit rating, Australian Parliamentary Library.

Davidoff, I. and Leigh, A., 2008, "How much do public schools really cost? Estimating the relationship between house prices and school quality", *Economic Record*, vol. 84, no. 265, pp. 193-206.

Davies AO, Hon. G, 2005, *Queensland Public Hospitals Commission of Inquiry Report*, p. 6.

De Lacy, 2001, *Corporate Governance—GOCs*, speech delivered on 11 July 2001.

Edis, T., 2015, "Queensland voters fooled over power bills and privatisation", *Business Spectator*, 23 January 2015.

Elks, S., 2017a, "Queensland budget 2017: coal boosts $2.8bn surplus", *The Australian*, 13 June 2017, available via www.theaustralian.com.au.

Elks, S., 2017b, "Queensland budget: Curtis Pitt pours $5 billion into key seats", *The Australian*, 14 June 2017, available via www.theaustralian.com.au.

Ergas, H. and Robson, A., 2009, *The 2008-09 Stimulus Packages: A Cost Benefit Analysis, Submission to the Senate Inquiry into the Government's Economic Stimulus Initiatives.*

Ergas, H., 2014, "Treasury's conduct a disservice to public", *The Australian*, 8 September 2014, available via www.theaustralian.com.au.

EY, 2014, *Electricity network services: Long-term trends in prices and costs*, report prepared for NSW Treasury.

EY, 2015, *Network Pricing Trends: Queensland Perspective*, report prepared for Infrastructure Partnerships Australia, CCIQ, AiGroup, and the Property Council of Australia.

Ferguson, A., 2010, "Vertical integration gets support", *Sydney Morning Herald*, 23 March 2010, available via www.smh.com.au.

Fishpool, M., 1997, "Departure of senior PS women sparks row", *Courier-Mail*, 7 March 1997.

Frankel, J., 2011, "Over-optimism in forecasts by official budget agencies and its implications", *Oxford Review of Economic Policy*, vol. 27, no. 4, pp. 536-562.

Fraser, A., 2009, *Statement—Treasurer*, media statement by the Queensland Treasurer, 21 February 2009, available via www.statements.qld.gov.au.

Fraser, A., 2010a, *Ministerial Statement by the Treasurer on the retirement of Sir Leo Hielscher*, Media Release of the Treasurer and Minister for Employment and Economic Development The Honourable Andrew Fraser.

Fraser, A., 2010b, *QRN Share offer raises more than $4 billion in proceeds for Queensland*, Media Release of the Treasurer and Minister for Employment and Economic Development The Honourable Andrew Fraser.

Fraser, A., 2013, "Queensland sells down stake in railways carrier Aurizon", *The Australian*, 4 December 2013, available via www.theaustralian.com.au.

Fraser, K., 2017, "Strachan inquiry finds restrictive union work rules part of problems at Queensland Rail", *Courier-Mail*, 11 February 2017, available via www.couriermail.com.au.

Galloway, A., 2017, "Adani: Palaszczuk Government not ruling out loan to rival Aurizon for Galilee Basin rail line", *Courier-Mail*, 28 December 2017, available via www.couriermail.com.au.

Goss, W., 1989, quoted in Ryan, C., 1993, "Financial and budgetary management", in Wanna, J. (ed.), 1993, *The Goss Government: Promise and Performance*, Macmillan, Melbourne, p. 136.

Goss, W., 1999, "The Republic and the States", *UQ Law Journal*, vol. 20, no. 2, pp. 294-300.

Gray, M., 2013, *Inside the Queensland Commission of Audit—The Process, Main Findings and Implications*, UQ Business School presentation.

Hamill, D., 2007, "W(h)ither Federalism?", *Proceedings of the Nineteenth Conference of the Sir Samuel Griffith Society*, Chapter 5.

Hamill, D., 2016, *The Inaugural Bill Hayden oration*, by The Hon Dr David Hamill AM at The Ipswich Club, Gray Street Ipswich 13th August 2016.

Herald Sun, 2012, "Use fiscal stimulus again: Henry", *Herald Sun*, 16 May 2012, available via www.heraldsun.com.au.

Hielscher, L., 2011, *Queensland Speaks interview*, interviewed by Brian Head and Chris Salisbury, 23 August 2011, available at http://www.queenslandspeaks.com.au/.

Hielscher, L., 2013, *Inaugural Parliamentary Oration—Sir Leo Hielscher: Queensland's economic history and how the State's economy was transformed from the early 1960s onwards*, Queensland Parliament, Transcript of Proceedings, 18 October 2013.

Holliman, J., 2014, *Sir Leo Hielscher: Queensland Made*, UQ Press.

Houghton, D., 2013, "Beattie-era Western Corridor Recycling Scheme a $2.7b white elephant", *Courier-Mail*, 13 September 2013, available via www.couriermail.com.au.

Humphreys, J., 2012, "The Treasury's Non-modelling of the Stimulus", *Agenda*, vol. 19, no. 2, pp. 39-51.

Independent Review Panel on Network Costs, 2012, *Electricity Network Costs Review Final Report.*

Infrastructure Australia, 2017, *Improving Public Transport: Customer Focused Franchising.*

Interdepartmental Committee on Electricity Sector Reform, 2013, *Report to Government*, Queensland Government.

International Monetary Fund (IMF), 2001, *Government Finance Statistics Manual.*

Kikeri, S., 1998, "Privatization and Labor: What Happens to Workers When Governments Divest?", *World Bank Technical Paper*, no. 396.

Kikeri, S., Nellis, J. and Shirley, M., 1992, *Privatization: The Lessons of Experience*, World Bank.

King, G., 2015, *Can do: Campbell Newman and the challenge of reform*, Connor Court.

Knox, M.J., 2012, *Economic Strategy: Queensland*, RBS Morgans, 27 March 2012.

KPMG, 2015, *Electricity Network Recapitalisation Strategy: Capital Structure and Dividend Benchmarking Analysis*, report prepared for Queensland Treasury Corporation.

Krugman, P., 1994, *The Age of Diminished Expectations: US Economic Policy in the 1990s*, MIT Press.

Lancaster, D. and Dowling, S., 2011, "The Australian Semi-government Bond Market", *RBA Bulletin*, September quarter 2011.

Lee, D., 2016, *The Second Rush: Mining and the Transformation of Australia*, Connor Court.

Leibenstein, H., 1966, "Allocative Efficiency vs. "X-Efficiency"", *American Economic Review*, vol. LVI.

Lloyd, G., 2016, "Energy security: Peter Beattie, like Jay Weatherill, learned the hard way", *The Australian*, 8 October 2016, available via www.theaustralian.com.au.

Lutton, E., 2017, "House prices in some Queensland state school zones rise by up to 40 per cent", *Domain*, available via www.domain.com.au.

Makin, A and Pearce, J 2014, "How Sustainable is Sub-national Public Debt in Australia?", *Economic Analysis and Policy*, 44(4), 364-375.

Makin, A., 2014, *Australia's competitiveness: Reversing the slide*, Minerals Council of Australia, Monograph no. 6.

Mayne, S., 2000, "Queensland's $800 Million Power Disaster", *Crikey*, 27 February 2000.

McCann, J. and Speldewinde, S., 2015, "Queensland state election: an overview", *Parliamentary Library Research Paper Series*, no. 2015-16.

McKenna, M. and Elks, S., 2016, "Secret power politics as Queensland parties plot debt deals", *The Australian*, 20 April 2016.

McMonagle, H., 2012, "Queensland's Public Sector Management Commission: Goss's Governmental "Reformation"?", *Centre for the Government of Queensland Summer Scholar Journal*, 2, pp. 1-9.

Megginson, W.L. and Netter, J.M., 2001, "From State to Market: A Survey of Empirical Studies on Privatization", *Journal of Economic Literature*, vol. XXXIX, pp. 321-389.

Moore, T., 2009, "Rail depot closures will be tip of the iceberg: union", *Brisbane Times*, 30 July 2009, available via www.brisbanetimes.com.au.

Moore, T., 2016, "Second route to Gold Coast should be considered: Tom Tate", *Brisbane Times*, 2 February 2016, available via www.brisbanetimes.com.au.

Mulgan, R., 1998, *Politicising the Australian Public Service*, Parliamentary Library Research Paper no. 3, 1998-99.

Murray, C., 2016, "Gold Coast light rail study helps put a figure on value capture's funding potential", *The Conversation*, 20 September 2016.

Nepal, R. and Foster, J., 2015, "Electricity network privatization in Australia: An overview of the debate", *Economic Analysis and Policy*, vol. 48, no. 12-24.

Nicholls, T., 2012a, *Media Statement: Government's interim response to Commission of Audit*, 11 July 2012.

Nolan, R., "Great Expectations: Correspondence", *Quarterly Essay*, no. 48, pp. 103-106.

Noonan, P., 1999, *On Speaking Well: How to Give a Speech with Style, Substance, and Clarity*, Harper Perennial.

Novak, J., 2011, *Queensland the low tax state: The birth and death of an idea, and how to bring it back to life*, Institute of Public Affairs.

OECD, 2015a, *Government at a Glance Country Fact Sheet: Switzerland*.

OECD, 2015b, "Achieving prudent debt targets using fiscal rules", *OECD Economics Department Policy Note*, No. 28.

Owen, J., 2013, "Big spending Beattie and Rudd perfect partners", *The Australian*, 26 August 2013, available via www.theaustralian.com.au.

Pitt, C., 2013, *Interim Response to the Queensland Commission of Audit*.

Pitt, C., 2015, *Electricity company mergers save $680 million and drive regional jobs*, media statement by the Treasurer, 15 December 2015, available via www.statements. qld.gov.au.

Prasser, S., 2009, "The virtues of upper houses", chapter 6 in *Proceedings of the Twenty-first Conference of The Samuel Griffith Society*.

Productivity Commission, 2005, *Economic Implications of an Ageing Australia*, Research report.

Productivity Commission, 2013, *Electricity Network Regulatory Frameworks*, Inquiry report vol. 1.

PwC, 2013, *Securing Investment in Australia's Future: Infrastructure Funding and Financing*, report prepared for the Business Council of Australia.

Queensland Audit Office, 2003, *Auditor-General's Report No. 7 2002-03*.

Queensland Audit Office, 2005, *Auditor-General's Report No. 7 2004-05*.

Queensland Audit Office, 2013, *Results of Audit: State public sector entities for 2012-13*, Report to Parliament 11: 2013-14.

Queensland Audit Office, 2014, *Hospital Infrastructure Projects*, Report 2: 2014-15.

Queensland Audit Office, 2017, *Organisational structure and accountability*, Report 17 2016-17.

Queensland Commission of Audit, 2012, *Interim Report*.

Queensland Commission of Audit, 2013, *Final Report—February 2013*, volume 2

Queensland Competition Authority, 2015, *Industry Assistance in Queensland*, Final Report, Volume 1.

Queensland Department of Premier and Cabinet, *Annual Report 2013-14*.

Queensland Government Statistician's Office, 2018, *Exports of Queensland goods overseas*, February 2018.

Queensland Government, 1987, "Credit rating of Queensland", *Cabinet Minute*, no. 51715.

Queensland Government, 2013, *A Plan—Better Services for Queenslanders: Queensland Government Response to the Independent Commission of Audit Final Report*.

Queensland Government, 2014a, *Reforming Queensland's electricity network reliability standards*, Cabinet paper lodged by the Minister for Energy and Water Supply.

Queensland Government, 2014b, *The Strongest & Smartest Choice: Queensland's Plan for Secure Finances and a Strong Economy*.

Queensland Government, 2014c, *The Strongest & Smartest Choice: Queensland's Plan for Secure Finances and a Strong Economy—Final Plan*.

Queensland Government, 2014d, *Queensland's Renewal Program: Achievements, January-March 2014 Quarterly Update*.

Queensland Parliament, 1990, *Record of Proceedings (Hansard)*, 7 March 1990.

Queensland Parliament, 1993, *Record of Proceedings (Hansard)*, May 12 1993.

Queensland Parliament, 1996, *Record of Proceedings (Hansard)*, 11 July 1996,

Queensland Productivity Commission, 2016, *Solar Feed-In Pricing in Queensland: Final*

Report.

Queensland Treasury Corporation, 2016, *Annual Report 2015-16.*

Queensland Treasury Corporation, 2017, *Investor Booklet.*

Queensland Treasury, 1986, *1986-87 Estimates of the Probable Ways and Means and Expenditures of the Government of Queensland.*

Queensland Treasury, 1987, *1987-88 Estimates of Receipts and Expenditures.*

Queensland Treasury, 1991, *1991-92 State Budget, Budget Paper no. 4: Supplementary Budget Information.*

Queensland Treasury, 1993, *Interim Budget Statement: State Budget 1993-94.*

Queensland Treasury, 1995, State Budget 1995-96, *Budget Paper no. 2: Budget Overview and Statement of Receipts and Expenditure.*

Queensland Treasury, 1996a, *State Budget 1996-97: Budget Overview,* budget paper no. 2.

Queensland Treasury, 1996b, *State Budget 1996-97: Budget in Brief,* budget paper no. 4.

Queensland Treasury, 1997a, *State Budget 1997-98: Budget Overview,* budget paper no. 2

Queensland Treasury, 1997b, *State Budget 1997-98: Budget in Brief,* budget paper no. 4.

Queensland Treasury, 1998, *State Budget 1998-99: Budget Overview,* budget paper no. 2.

Queensland Treasury, 1999a, *State Budget 1999-2000: Budget Overview,* budget paper 2.

Queensland Treasury, 1999b, State Budget 1999-2000: Budget Speech, budget paper 1.

Queensland Treasury, 2000, *State Budget 2000-01: Budget Overview,* budget paper no. 2, p. 22.

Queensland Treasury, 2001, *State Budget 2001-02: Budget Statement,* budget paper no. 2, p. 17.

Queensland Treasury, 2004, *State Budget 2004-05: Budget Strategy and Outlook,* budget paper no. 2.

Queensland Treasury, 2005, *2005-06 State Budget: Budget Speech,* budget paper no. 1.

Queensland Treasury, 2006, *State Budget 2006-07: Budget Strategy and Outlook,* budget paper no. 2.

Queensland Treasury, 2006, *State Budget 2006-07: Budget Strategy and Outlook,* budget paper no. 2.

Queensland Treasury, 2007, *State Budget 2007-08: Budget Speech,* budget paper no. 1.

Queensland Treasury, 2008a, *State Budget 2008-09: Budget Speech,* budget paper no. 1.

Queensland Treasury, 2008b, *Major Economic Statement.*

Queensland Treasury, 2009a, *State Budget 2009-10: Budget Speech 2009-10,* budget paper no. 1.

Queensland Treasury, 2009b, *State Budget 2009-10: Budget Strategy and Outlook,* budget paper no. 2.

Queensland Treasury, 2010, *State Budget 2010:11 Budget Strategy and Outlook*, budget paper no. 2.

Queensland Treasury, 2011a, *State Budget 2011-12: Capital Statement*, budget paper no. 3.

Queensland Treasury, 2011b, *Carbon Price Impacts for Queensland*.

Queensland Treasury, 2012a, *Incoming Government Brief: Fiscal Reform Blueprint*, tabled in Queensland Parliament on 21 May 2015.

Queensland Treasury, 2012b, *State Budget 2012-13: Budget Speech*.

Queensland Treasury, 2012c, *State Budget 2012-13: Budget Strategy and Outlook*, budget paper no. 2.

Queensland Treasury, 2013, *State Budget 2013-14: Budget Strategy and Outlook*, budget paper no. 2.

Queensland Treasury, 2014a, *Mid Year Fiscal and Economic Review*.

Queensland Treasury, 2014b, *Queensland Treasury Response to Commonwealth Grants Commission 2015 Methodology Review*.

Queensland Treasury, 2015a, *2015 Review of State Finances*.

Queensland Treasury, 2015b, *Queensland Budget 2015-16: Budget Strategy and Outlook 2015-16*, budget paper no. 2.

Queensland Treasury, 2015c, *Queensland Budget 2015-16: Budget Speech 2015-16*, budget paper no. 1.

Queensland Treasury, 2016, *Queensland Budget 2016-17: Budget Strategy and Outlook*, budget paper no. 2.

Queensland Treasury, 2017a, *Mid Year Fiscal and Economic Review 2017-18*.

Queensland Treasury, 2017a, *Queensland Budget 2017-18: Budget Strategy and Outlook*, budget paper no. 2.

Queensland Treasury, 2017b, *Queensland Budget 2017-18: Jobs for Queensland*.

Queensland Treasury, 2017c, *Mid Year Fiscal and Economic Review 2017-18*,

Queensland Treasury, 2017d, *Queensland Budget 2017-18 Service Delivery Statements: Department of Tourism, Major Events, Small Business and the Commonwealth Games*.

Quiggin, J., 2009a, *Economists statement on Queensland asset sales*, 24 November 2009, published on johnquiggin.com blog.

Quiggin, J., 2009b, *Statement on Asset Sales*, 8 December 2009, published on johnquiggin.com blog.

Quiggin, J., 2012, *The Queensland Commission of Audit Interim Report—June 2012: A Critical Review*.

Quiggin, J., 2013, "The Queensland Commission of Audit Final Report: A Critical

Review", *RSMG Working Paper Series*, no. P13_1.

Quiggin, J., 2015, *Strong Choices or weak evasions: How the effective sale of public assets will weaken Queensland's fiscal position*.

RBA, 1997, "Privatisation in Australia", *RBA Bulletin*, pp. 7-16.

Remeikis, A., 2014a, "Solar users the champagne and latte sipping set: Tim Nicholls", *Brisbane Times*, 6 June 2014, available via www.brisbanetimes.com.au.

Remeikis, A., 2014b, "Asset sales divide economists—but they are united in saying 'Strong Choices' is flawed", *Brisbane Times*, 28 April 2014, available via www.brisbanetimes.com.au.

Remeikis, A., 2014c, "New Queensland Rail boss Helen Gluer resigned two months ago for personal reasons", *Brisbane Times*, 10 January 2014, available via www.brisbanetimes.com.au.

Riley, D., 1993, "Goss the destroyer", *Green Left Weekly*, 4 August 1993.

Rochester, S., 2014, "Foreword", in Holliman, J., 2014, *Sir Leo Hielscher: Queensland Made*, UQ Press.

Rodrigues, M., 2009, "Queensland Election 2009", *Parliamentary Library Research Papers 2008-09*, no. 34.

Ryan, C., 1993, "Financial and budgetary management", in Stevens, B. and Wanna, J. (eds.), *The Goss government : promise and performance of Labor in Queensland*, Macmillan Education.

Sammut, J., 2016, "Silicon Valleys for Health", in *Politically-Feasible Health Reform: Whatever Will it Take?*, Centre for Independent Studies.

Sheldon, J., 1996, *Budget Position and Outlook for 1996-97*, 2 April 1996.

Sheldon, J., 1997, *Ministerial Statement: Queensland's Long Term Budgetary Outlook*, 20 March 1997.

Skene, K., 2017, "'Rustbucket' perception dogs Tugun Desalination Plant a decade after its conception", *Gold Coast Bulletin*, 27 April 2017.

Smith, W., 2017, *Unemployment Policy in Australia: A Brief History*, Per Capita.

Somerville, D., Blanch, S., and Camp, J., 2004, *Summary Report of the Independent Panel for Electricity Distribution and Service Delivery for the 21st Century*, Queensland Government Department of Natural Resources, Mines and Energy.

Stanford, J.D., 1987, "The long-term effect of federation on the Queensland economy", *Working Papers in Australian Studies*, working paper no. 37, Sir Robert Menzies Centre for Australian Studies, Institute of Commonwealth Studies, University of London.

Strachan, P., 2017, *Queensland Rail train crewing practices commission of inquiry: Final Report*.

Sydney Morning Herald, 2007, "The making of Kevin Rudd", *Sydney Morning Herald*, 21 February 2007.

Tanzi, V., 2016, *Pleasant Dreams or Nightmares in Public Debt Scenarios?*, Centre for Economic Studies.

Taylor, J., 2014, "Three new Queensland hospitals cost $2.2 billion more than promised, auditor-general says", *ABC News*, 21 October 2014, available via www.abc.net.au.

Templeton, A., 2016a, "LNP accuses Palaszczuk Government of breaking promise over asset sales", *Courier-Mail*, 12 October 2016, available via www.couriermail.com.au.

Templeton, A., 2016b, "Infrastructure spending plummeting in Queensland", *Courier-Mail*, 23 September 2016, available via www.couriermail.com.au.

Tin, J., 2016, "Queensland public service: New pay deal and special $1300 bonus", *Courier-Mail*, 29 April 2016, available via www.couriermail.com.au.

Todd, M., 2005, "Court edict kills inquiry into Patel", *Sydney Morning Herald*, 3 September 2005, available via www.smh.com.au.

Treasury, 2014, *Response to Professor Tony Makin's Minerals Council of Australia Monograph—'Australia's Competitiveness: Reversing the Slide'.*

Walker, B. and Walker, B., 2012, *Review of the Costello Report: Crude analysis. Not 'independent'. Not an 'audit'*, report prepared for the Queensland Council of Unions.

Walker, J., 1995, *Goss: a political biography*, UQ Press.

Wanna, J., 2003, "Wayne Keith Goss: The rise and fall of a meticulous controller", in Murphy, D., Joyce, R., Cribb, M. and Wear, R. (eds), *The Premiers of Queensland*, University of Queensland Press, pp. 357-386.

Wardill, S. and Tin, J., 2015, "Debt reduction plan to gut the Budget—ALP's $1.3B black hole", *Courier-Mail*, 17 January 2015, available via www.couriermail.com.au.

Wardill, S., 2015a, "Queensland election 2015: Electricity prices to fall under privatisation, says audit", *Courier-Mail*, 21 January 2015, available via www.couriermail.com.au.

Wardill, S., 2015b, "Labor pulling a 'two-card' trick with its much anticipated economic plan", *Courier-Mail*, 16 January 2015, available via www.couriermail.com.au.

Wardill, S., 2015b, "Today's problems in Queensland bigger tomorrow after Budget, say economists", *The Courier-Mail*, 17 July 2015, available via www.couriermail.com.au.

Wardill, S., 2016a, "Privatisation of Queensland's assets: Why voters and some economists seem to be against it", *Courier-Mail*, 24 September 2016, available via www.couriermail.com.au.

Wardill, S., 2016b, "Federal Budget exposes Queensland's flimsy accounts", *Courier-Mail*, 7 May 2016, available via www.couriermail.com.au.

Wardill, S., 2017, "Public service wages threaten bottom line", Courier-Mail, 26 April 2017, , available via www.couriermail.com.au.

Wear, R., 2003, "Robert Edward Borbidge; In the Shadow of Bjelke-Petersen", in Murphy, D., Joyce, R., Cribb, M. and Wear, R. (eds), *The Premiers of Queensland*, UQ Press, pp. 387-389.

Williams, C., Hurley, J. and Morris, B., 1999, "An economic model of interstate migration", *Economic Analysis and Policy*, Special Edition May 1999, pp. 93-112.

Wiltshire, K., 2004, in Australasian Study of Parliament Group (Queensland Chapter), *Parliament and Public Servants—Separate or United in 21st Century Westminster Practice?*, Queensland Parliament.

Wiltshire, K., 2016, "Take the politics out of policy", *Courier-Mail*, 2 November 2016, available via www.couriermail.com.au.

Wolf, M., 2018, "Nationalising utilities is the wrong answer to a real question", *Financial Times*, 12 January 2018, available via www.ft.com.

Wood, T., 2012, *Putting the customer back in front: How to make electricity cheaper*, Grattan Institute.

Young, D., 2010, "Vertical integration delivers the goods", *The Australian*, 15 June 2010, available via www.theaustralian.com.au.

Index

307